WHISTLE WHILE YOU WORK

Viv Billingham Parkes

Cover photographs: Mike Notman, Studio North, Carlisle

Line drawings: G W Billingham

Photographs: Brenda Herdman, Ian Hossack, Douglas Low, Frank Moyes, Philip Parker, Arnold Wilson

Published by Atlantic Publishing, Holebottom Farm, Hebden, Skipton, North Yorkshire, BD23 5DL

ISBN: 0 906899 93 1

First published 1998

Design and layout: Trevor Ridley
Printed by The Amadeus Press Ltd, Huddersfield, West Yorkshire

British Cataloguing in Publication Data
A catalogue record for this book is available from the British Library

CONTENTS

FOREWORD   5

INTRODUCTION   6

1   EARLY MEMORIES   8
2   ERNEST CRISP – a country character   13
3   ARRIVAL AT SWINDON   17
4   LITTLE GEOFF   20
5   GARRY, A HILL DOG   26
6   THE SCOTTISH NATIONAL 1982   31
7   THE MATING GAME   36
8   FIRST INTRODUCTION TO SHEEP   43
9   SHEEP DOG TRAINERS, MAKERS OR BREAKERS?   47
10   BASIC TRAINING   54
11   ON JUDGING TRIALS   61
12   NURSERY TRIALS   64
13   THE FLOCK   68
14   SPRING IS IN THE AIR   82
15   MAD MARCH   91
16   APRIL 1st   98
17   RURAL LADIES AND LAMBING TIME   100
18   THE AMERICAN EXPERIENCE   107
19   PREPARING FOR THE TRIAL   115
20   SHEEP DOG FANATICS   120
21   LIFE AFTER BOWMONT   125
22   FROM SHEPHERDESS TO BUSINESSWOMAN   129
23   OUR FIRST VISITORS   132
24   OMEGA   139

In memory of Calom, a gentle man

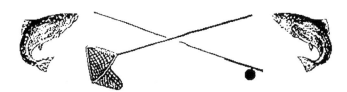

Foreword
by
Phil Drabble

The real thing is not like that. Having to turn out on winter nights, with twenty degrees of finger numbing frost, to rescue sheep entombed in snowdrifts is less romantic in the flesh. Finding a ewe, "cast" helpless on her back before the crows peck out her eyes imparts a sense of nerve wracking urgency. And, in spite of all man's efforts If a sheep makes up her mind to die, she dies! is an uncomfortable truth that puts reality in perspective.

This is a real book, by a real shepherdess who can hold her head up high in company with the most skilful shepherds in the land.

The first time I met Viv Billingham, the author, was at a television sheep dog trial *One Man and His Dog* – and she proved that a woman and her dog were as good as anyone there. Although she is as attractive as the most glamorous Dresden china shepherdess, she is as tough as whipcord and made the perfect other half of the partnership with her husband Geoff.

Her book describes their life together and, although not much like the daydreams of romantics, it bristles with vitality and the deep satisfaction of the real life in wild places, where there are no soft options.

It is the story of a real family, extremely funny in patches and yet never ducking the hardships that make the life worthwhile.

Winter in the wilds is so hard that Viv's geraniums shrivel by the sink and the Busy Lizzie wilts, even in the airing cupboard! But their family life is always fun and always fulfilling.

A woman can't be as good a shepherd without the world finding out about it, and she is invited to judge sheep dog trials in the depth of the New World, which she calls her American Experience. My guess is that it was at least as memorable and exciting an experience for the Americans!

Whistle While You Work is a stimulating book because it is packed with a highly personal account of how a most attractive family cope with life that can't have changed much since biblical times. They enjoy every minute of it – and take delight in sharing it with her readers.

Phil Drabble

In these times of great change and insecurity it is common to look back on 'the good old days' with nostalgia and long for the simple life.

The solitude of wild hills and the intimacy of traditional farming life are light years away from the ruthless competition of city offices and factories. Or so the armchair theorists think when they view it through their rose tinted specs!

Introduction

One could stay long enough watching the hide-and-seek of cloud shadows on the hills that for me, at least, are like turning the pages of its story. Joy and sorrow chase each other through the years, and the only things that remain constant are the hills and the plaintive ripple of water.

George Burnett

IT'S happening again, a quenchless desire to put pen to paper. Descriptive sentences are forever forming inside my head, as my four footed companions, Holly, Jed, Jess, Jan, young Garry, and I explore windswept woodland trails through lonely hills.

I have been far too long away from my writing! My hectic summers leave few spare moments for the gathering of thoughts. Now thankfully, in the peaceful lull of winter the pace of life has slackened to a mere trickle and I can begin the enjoyable task of conversing on paper, the stimulus provided by the ever changing beauty of the surrounding countryside.

These days my bedroom acts as an office. I lie in my large comfortable Edwardian bed propped up by pillows, swaddled in a rose patterned quilt. Holly, the resident OAP collie, snores gently beside me on a reindeer rug given years ago as a gift from friends in Norway.

In the field outside my window the other dogs occasionally grumble in their kennels while the sheep bleat forlornly, longing for an early breakfast. Here I feel at ease, after what seems like having travelled a long distance in a remarkably short space of time. However, I can't help but wonder what lies around the next corner.

I was born after the Second World War and christened Vivien Maybelle Parkes. My place of birth was near Billingham in the north east of England. My mother's maiden name is Woolley. All of this information is written on my birth certificate. My destiny, had I but known it, would appear to be hinted at in this very document.

My late father Arthur William Weldon Parkes was descended from the Macleans, sheep farmers on the Isle of Mull. My mother Mabel's family originated in Wales. Her grandfather worked on Lord Delamere's estate.

There are those who may consider a woman presumptuous in putting pen to paper on the hallowed subject of sheepdog training as there are many men more qualified to do so. May I say in my defence that I do not consider myself an expert, or a literary genius. I have read or acquired most of the books written about sheepdogs and find the methods of training in them somewhat mechanical. There is so much left unsaid regarding adapting to the individuality of each dog and working with its instinct. Years ago there were very few handlers who were willing to disclose their methods of training. I disclose mine in the genuine hope that 'Man's Best Friend' will be the main benefactor. It is said that 'There is a man for the dog and a dog for

INTRODUCTION

the man'. Only on very rare occasions do we meet a trainer capable of adapting to the whims and ways of any dog, in my opinion a true handler in every sense of the word. Strangely, the most successful partnerships are often due to similarities in temperament and values between dog and man. Some collies are impatient and ill-tempered by nature, however, an impressionable young dog will rapidly become so in the wrong hands.

The following pages are written for people with a love of animals and the countryside, especially the hills, and for those starting from scratch who are keen to breed and train Border collies for sheep work.

My dogs have taught me much more than I could ever teach them. They are bred to do the job whereas I am not. Because animals are creatures of habit it is important to create circumstances whereby they can perform their tasks correctly. Bad habits caused through instinct are difficult to cure and must be eradicated gradually in a kind way without the dog realising – a dog's life expectancy compared to ours is relatively short and therefore should be sweet. Patience, kindness and common-sense cannot be over-emphasised in the creation of a trustworthy and useful partner.

Viv Billingham Parkes
Hammerlands, Moffat
January 1998

GW Billingham with Bett, Jan II and Moss at Swindon, Bowmont Water. Acknowledgement is given to GW Billingham whose sympathy, understanding and handling of Border collies, in the author's opinion, knows no equal.

1
Early Memories

When I was about four years old, I accompanied my mother and younger sister to a sheepdog trial, my very first! It was held in a field on the outskirts of Norton, not far from the 'duck pond' where we regularly picnicked on warm summer days. I remember vividly my first sighting of a real shepherd and his dog and can still recall how enraptured I felt by the entire proceedings. For me it was definitely a case of 'once seen never forgotten'; I was well and truly smitten.

From that day on, my ambition was to be a shepherdess. (I was so impatient to grow up, and desperate to learn how to train a sheepdog.) As well as yearning to become a shepherdess,

I confess to further ambitions, all in some way closely connected. One ambition was quite small and therefore not too difficult to achieve, the other, for a girl, I considered would be quite an achievement, if I could master the art.

Believe it or not my smallest ambition was to pick up and cuddle a live lamb. Although I had seen plenty skipping and playing together along the banks and hedges near my home, I had never actually touched one, never felt its soft woolliness against my cheek, and I was very anxious to do just that. One Sunday afternoon, whilst out for a walk, my big chance finally arrived for, under a shady hawthorn, sleeping among the last of the spring daffodils, lay a large woolly lamb.

Inch by inch I crept up quietly and, with bated breath, I carefully picked it up. My disenchantment will never be forgotten. Lambs, like everything else, are not what they seem. This one, instead of being soft and cuddly to the touch, had a harsh, coarse coat. It writhed, bleated in fear and proceeded to pee all down my best frilly blue gingham dress. I dropped the disappointing creature in disgust and ran home.

One would think the lamb episode would have taught me a lesson; but no, on I went undaunted until a suitable time arrived for me to proceed with my second and most important ambition which was to be able to whistle loudly through my fingers just like the shepherds at the sheepdog trial.

By then, we were living in 'Little England Beyond Wales' or Pembroke Dock in south Wales, as it is defined on the map! School was a three-mile walk over Barrack Hill which gave me an aerial view of the peaceful setting of Milford Haven. Often I would pause to watch the breathtakingly beautiful sight of a white Sunderland flying boat skimming across the calm water until finally it effortlessly ascended against the picturesque backcloth of the blue Prescelly mountains. It was from these same mountains that the famous blue stone pillars of Stonehenge in Wiltshire were hewn.

It was high on Barrack Hill I practised my whistling, all alone except for the somewhat surprised sheep. It went on and on for weeks, me blowing through my fingers until I was dizzy and, on arriving at school, being sent in disgrace to the headmaster's office for being late. One damp and misty morning, it finally happened. I actually managed the tiniest of whistles - I was so surprised I could hardly believe my ears. Within days, my attempts grew louder and shriller. I could imitate the birds, whistle tunes, use two fingers or four and even manage a 'baritone' through a space between my thumbs. At long last I could whistle!

Many years on, despite jibes about a 'whistling maid and a crowing hen', I am still whistling. Apart from being necessary, to work a dog over a great distance, I found it was an extremely useful way to attract the attention of a certain shepherd and small boy when dinner was served. If they failed to appear, a dog or two would always arrive instead!

All through childhood one of my most treasured possessions was a copy of Black Bob, the Dandy comic wonder dog. This book is about the exciting adventures of a working Border collie. Although it is frayed at the edges, I still have it today, tucked safely away in a drawer.

Nowadays, during the summer months, I often pass through the lovely Border town of Selkirk, the car overflowing with collies, looking more like Noah's Ark, en route for the many sheepdog trials in the area. I am reminded that, for me as a child, this was where the action was. Black Bob and his master, the shepherd, Andrew Glenn, put Selkirk well and truly on the map for me and if I could afford it a statue in their honour would not come amiss, for the interest of the tourists.

First employment

A friend of my aunt was responsible for finding me my first job on a farm. The fact that it was, to quote, 'in a wild and lonely spot', did little to dampen my enthusiasm. Letters of introduction were exchanged and subsequently it was arranged that I would be given a one month's trial.

I – and a few practical belongings – were to be collected at a nearby town. Filled with excitement and determined to be punctual, I hurried to the rendezvous with my mother. 'He' was already waiting - a dapper, wiry man wearing spectacles. His hair was auburn and crinkly and his complexion was ruddy and lined through squinting at the sun. Being a Yorkshire man, most of his sentences were punctuated with 'nay' and 'naw-but' and his speech was slow, his words well thought out.

The introductions over, I said my goodbyes, climbed into his little maroon and cream van and, with a wave to my mother, sped off into the unknown. After a journey through breath-taking countryside, we finally drove up a steep and bumpy lane which caused the little van to vibrate so much I thought it surely must shake to pieces. Suddenly we were met by an awe-inspiring sight for here, built of mellow stone, set snugly into the hillside, was an old farmhouse over-looking a green and peaceful valley. Towering in the background were the Yorkshire moors, dark, mysterious and inviting.

The family - his wife and two small sons - came out to greet us. One boy was shy, the other grinned from ear to ear. They were as different in looks as chalk and cheese - Colin was quiet, sturdy and fair, a gentle boy with his mother's eyes whilst Lennie, chubby and red-cheeked, had round, bright 'forget-me-not' eyes.

Within the hour, after a scrumptious meal, I had settled in and unpacked my few belongings. At bedtime, the boys showed me to a room next to theirs which had a lovely view of the moors and, within moments of sinking into the billowing feather mattress, I was sound asleep. The following morning, I awoke to the sound of clanking pails and crowing cockerels. My life on the farm had begun.

There were several collies there. I soon befriended Moss, an elderly dog with more character in his face than any dog I've met since. Moss honoured me with his limping arthritic presence as I explored the surrounding moors for, until our meeting, he had been a one-man dog. Perhaps he thought I needed a chaperone.

As the glorious April days passed by, one by one the local bachelors put in an appearance at the farm but it was Dick, a roadman-cum-shepherd and his ebony bitch, auld Lass, who became my special friends. More than twice my age, Dick showed me great kindness and respect, patiently teaching me about country life and the ways of sheep.

At the end of the month my employer asked if I would stay on and, in lieu of wages, presented me with a pair of boys' stout leather boots to wear on the hill. Although my badly blistered feet bled in protest at their starched presence, I refused to take them off, firmly believing that without them I could not call myself a true shepherd in every sense of the word.

One day it was suggested I should have my own sheep dog and so, after a trip to pick a pup, Kim came into my life. She was bare-skinned, black, white and tan and I doted on her. Little did I realise at the time that our relationship would be short-lived.

One balmy summer's eve, high on the open moor, auld Lass pointed out a sick ewe, a Swaledale of good breeding, her udder blue and painfully swollen with mastitis. I elected to stay beside her whilst Dick, with Lass at his heels, hurried home to fetch a tractor and transport box. When the sun went down, it became cold and dark and I snuggled up to the ewe for warmth.

After what seemed an age, I became aware of a bright orange glow in the night sky. Curious, I scrambled through rough heather on to high ground to gain a clearer view. I will never forget the sight that met me for, stretching as far as the eye could see, the moor was a burning inferno. Acrid smoke choked my nostrils as the flames leapt skyward, dancing and flickering higher and higher. We'd had a particularly hot dry summer that year. All country people dread moor and forest fires which can occur so easily through the carelessness of the unwary and on that August evening, the conflagration before me was like the end of the world. For a while I stood there mesmerised, bathed in firelight, until I was brought to my senses by the roar of a tractor engine, throttle wide open, wheels churning as it raced to our rescue... and not before time.

Two weeks after this, a severe and prolonged attack of jaundice ended my memorable stay at the cosy little farmhouse in the lovely undulating Yorkshire moorlands and I went home to recuperate and plan my next adventure.

Going west

After a period of convalescence which lasted several weeks, I decided to see life further afield and placed an advertisement in a popular farming magazine. Within a fortnight, protected by a thick layer of puppy fat and brimming with enthusiasm, I sallied forth once again, this time by train to west Wales sadly minus my devoted bitch Kim, whom I was requested to leave at home. I had been told: 'We already keep two working dogs - quite enough for a small farm'. My good friend Dick therefore offered Kim a home, promising to send her on should my new employer change his mind.

After a long, slow journey south, then west, I arrived at the railway station in darkness. It was pouring with rain and the platform cold and empty. Fortunately, the buffet was still open so I went inside to warm myself and drink a steaming mug of tea. I emerged later to find an elderly, stooped gentleman with long white hair anxiously looking about him. On seeing me, suitcase in hand, he came over and introduced himself in an extremely cultured tone enquiring about my journey as we proceeded to the station car park where he had left his wife. I was greeted in a warm, friendly way by this gracious lady.

After securing my suitcase, we climbed into the car and drove off into the wet night. The lady and I huddled closely together, our knees covered by a thick blanket. Out of the darkness, my future employer remarked: 'I do hope you like cats'. Having been educated by my mother to the contrary after two stray kittens she had taken pity on soiled her bedspread, I mumbled: 'Er, not really'. However, since then, I must admit that I have come to admire most felines, as a swarm of cats on my own door step was later to confirm.

We started a long climb in low gear up a bumpy lane. (Was my life to be filled with bumpy lanes, I asked myself?) Finally, we slithered to a halt. 'Well, here we are, dear, home at last!' exclaimed the lady of the house. I leapt out, landing on soft, muddy ground and was more than a little surprised at the incredible sight before me - a bright oil lamp had been placed in welcome beside what could only be described as a broken and battered back door, completely devoid of paint. Milling around our ankles, mewing, pressing, pushing and purring, were a delighted throng of scruffy cats. What on earth have I come to, I wondered, as they tickled my bare legs with their wet fur. 'There must have been a million of every shape and size!' The words of the song flashed through my mind, and I giggled somewhat hysterically.

I was taken inside and given a hot drink. Afterwards a candle was placed in my hand and I was shown to my room. It was dark, damp and dismal. I slept fitfully. The following morning at breakfast I was introduced to the only other member of staff, Elizabeth, whom I was to replace just as soon as she had shown me the ropes.

Translated from Welsh into English, the name of the farm was 'Hill of Birds'. To me, even to this day, it will remain 'Hill of Pussies' for they really were everywhere - in the milk jug, in the sink, in the custard and often, much to my horror, squatting in corners. On these occasions, I would say in a loud voice: 'What is pussy doing?' but it was all to no avail and so I would return to chasing cat hairs with a spoon as they whizzed around my tea cup, pretending to be oblivious to what was taking place around me.

Two of the 'dear creatures' particularly attracted my attention. One was called Mouser. He was yellow and closely resembled a mangy ferret, both in looks and scent. He was also battle-scarred with non-existent ears and wore a permanent snarl on the left side of his face. At meal times he would glare balefully in my direction through amber slits, every now and then pointing at my plate with a 'club' foot. The other was fluffy Tortie, an extremely beautiful specimen. As her name implied, she was tortoiseshell with a flowing, silky coat and luminous green eyes. Tortie bred a mischievous tail-less ginger kitten whom I christened China as he looked very ornamental perched on the window ledge.

One day at lunch I tentatively asked the master of the house if China could be my very own pet. Without a word, he rose from the table and left the room. He plucked my favourite from the window ledge and disappeared with him in the direction of the cow byre. I never saw China again.

It was always the author's ambition as a youngster to pick up and cuddle a live lamb

Elizabeth, who shared my life at the 'Hill of Pussies' was quite a character with a great sense of fun. We made our own amusement - we had to. Our main source of excitement was provided on washday when, doubled up with mirth, we would peg our frilly knickers on the line, either side of our strait-laced master's long, woolly underpants.

At meal times we were regularly reminded by him that he disliked greedy girls, with the result that we ate little. Every Friday both he and his wife had an 'away-day'. The moment they departed, we sprang into action and baked furiously, hiding the goodies under beds, in suitcases and anywhere else that came to mind. During the rest of the week, if we felt peckish, we would creep quietly into each other's rooms to partake of midnight feats. I'm positive it must have been the crumbs which brought about our downfall for, in no time at all, I was deemed able to cope and my friend went off to pastures new.

For a long while after she had gone I felt extremely lonely. At Christmas I was at my lowest ebb. In order to cheer myself

up I decided that, after milking on Christmas Eve, I would open the gifts I had been saving. So on the stroke of 10 o'clock, by the light of a flickering candle, there I sat, on a damp steaming bed surrounded by a mountain of gift paper, sipping sherry from a cracked cup without a handle and stuffing myself with dates and marzipan. From that day onward I stopped feeling sorry for myself determined that I would try to see the funnier side of life, whenever possible.

The farmhouse was large, gloomy and extremely eerie. With only a candle which constantly threatened to blow out, bath nights were a real nightmare. I can still feel hot wax dripping on to unsuspecting fingers as I made my way up the dark and draughty stairway to the bathroom. The cause of my fear was a huge bat, a terrifying creature which often frequented the place. He would hide high up in the rafters, lurking in the shadows until I stepped, naked and trembling, into the water. Then, just like Count Dracula, he would swoop swiftly and silently in my direction. The only thing I could do was submerge quickly and only surface for air when I felt my lungs bursting. The first time he put in an appearance, I let out a shriek loud enough to waken the dead. It didn't even wake the living!

As time passed by I got used to George, as I called him, and his peculiar anti-social antics. I realised that he was just inquisitive, and discovered that if I blew out the candle he would leave me alone. Perhaps he was lonely.

It was at the turn of the year that the accident happened. Each evening, before milking, I would sit at the kitchen table priming the two oil lamps, one for each end of the cow byre. On this particular evening the mantle of the first lamp began to glow and so I removed the butterfly clip which, when soaked in methylated spirits and ignited, was used to light the lamp. I blew on it as usual but failed to notice that it was still alight as I popped it back into the jar. There was a loud bang and a flash as it burst into flames. I leapt backwards stepping on poor Mouser who let out a terrified meow and raced for safety. Suddenly the green serge tablecloth burst into flames. Quickly, and much to my admiration, the lady of the house took hold of it by the corner and trailed it out of the kitchen, down the tiled passage and out of the back door.

Panicking cats fled in all directions and not one, after the fright they received, dared venture back over the doorstep, much preferring the safety of the outside window ledge where they sat wearing disgruntled expressions and badly singed whiskers.

Within the space of a week, and hopefully not due to shock, the old gentleman fell ill and took to his bed. The doctor was called and brucellosis diagnosed. I was thrown in at the deep end overnight. The whole responsibility of the farm, its cows, calves and Llanwenog (Welsh blackface) sheep became my responsibility and remained so for the following long and arduous six months.

I had to work as I had never done before - up each morning at 5 o'clock - just in case the Lister engines failed and I was forced to milk by hand - then wash the machines before taking the milk by tractor to the end of the lane where it was collected by a lorry. All of this was completed before breakfast at 9 o'clock. Oh, was I ravenous by then! On top of these tasks, there were calves to feed, sheep to look after and hay to cut, truss and bring home for the cows. At night, there was the same milking procedure as the morning then, after mucking out the byre, my final chore was to refill the hods with coke, a job I dreaded. With only the oil lamps to help me I had to define which was coke and which was pussy poo ...

To crown everything, the hydram responsible for our water supply decided to go on the blink. It took two weeks for the spare part to arrive. Two weeks of wet back-breaking work as I toiled time and time again up a steep and slippery incline, carrying two three-gallon pails of clean water. Weeks turned into months. The poor old gentleman, gravely ill, tossed, turned and sweated indoors whilst I sweated out of doors.

Thankfully every cloud has a silver lining and it was during this time that I struck up a marvellous friendship with the two farm collies - Bob, a small hairy fellow with large pleading eyes, and Ben, his bounding black offspring.

Bob worked for me from the word go, except when it poured with rain. On such occasions he would walk out on tiptoe then beat a hasty retreat back to his bed. Ben, though yet untrained, was full of enthusiasm. Secretly, I relished the thought of training him myself. Dare I? Yes, of course I dare.

At the end of three months Ben was extremely competent and was working like a dream, a natural born sheepdog. Gradually the old gentleman gained strength. The day I was dreading finally arrived. I was told very politely that it would no longer be necessary for me to exercise his dogs. The hardest part was yet to come. Bob and Ben, by now used to accompanying me everywhere, flatly refused to follow their master. I was told to discourage them by sending them away. I had no other choice and as long as I live will never forget the hurt expressions on their faces.

Perhaps, lurking in the back of my mind, was the faint hope I might be allowed a dog of my own and on one occasion, I tentatively broached the subject, but it was to no avail. Finally, after a great deal of thought and with the hope that somewhere there was a kinder farmer who would allow me to keep a dog of my own, to the old gentleman's surprise, I handed in my notice.

2
Ernest Crisp
– a country character

Because we are impressed by our human mentors, unintentionally we adopt certain sayings and mannerisms that remain with us until the end of our days. Ernest Crisp represented such a character to me. In the early sixties, he was my third employer and the first to allow me to own as many dogs as I wanted. Originally, I went to his bleak, north of England farm as a lamber, but ended up remaining for twelve enlightening years employed as his shepherdess-cum 'Jill of all trades'. Shortly after I arrived Ernie gave me Kim II, a rough coated black and fawn tearaway. 'Mind ye'll nivver git her to stop,' he warned in his broad Northumbrian dialect and I 'nivver did', until she was dog tired!

One morning Kim ran away to get married. Unfortunately she got mated by her Sire Rob, who resided on a neighbouring farm. Rob's claim to fame was that he spent his spare moments biting people, first having knocked them off their bicycles as they peddled through the farmyard to work in a local quarry. His busier times were mostly spent submerged in the water trough avoiding what he had been bred for - namely sheep work.

A bonny dog pup came of Kim and Rob's union. He also tended to bite people but compensated by being a great worker. I called him Shep and he was my first trial dog. On his first outing he somehow managed to pen the sheep in the secretary's tent, which didn't go down too well with the other occupants. Unfortunately, poor Shep, due to his close breeding, had an unusual affliction. He was cross-eyed and I often wondered how many sheep he actually saw. In those days I travelled to the trials by bus with my crook and Shep stowed safely under the seat. Shep didn't care for this mode of transport and as a result was in a great state of nerves by the time we reached our destination. Not surprisingly we never won a prize, but we certainly had lots of fun.

In all the years I worked for Ernie I only witnessed him lose his temper on one occasion and that was when Shep bit him on the ankle. It wouldn't have mattered according to Ernie, had it not been for the fact that the dog bit him on his own doorstep!

Although neither Ernie nor his wife, Sadie, were sheep dog trial enthusiasts, they began to accompany me, giving me every encouragement possible and as the years passed, I grew to admire and respect Ernie, mainly for his honesty and integrity, but most of all for his dry humour. I found his oft-repeated jokes and comical quotes hilariously funny. To him a crane fly was a 'spinning Jenny', a plover was a 'pea-sweep', a wood pigeon was a 'cushit' and the plaintive curlew was described as a 'warp'.

Because Ernie was one of the old school, work always came first. He was a firm believer that you only got out of both life and land that which you were prepared to put in. He stood 6ft 1in in his size twelve tacketty shepherd's boots, with their turned up toes. 'All the better for rocking uphill,' he would say with a smile as he adjusted his weather worn cap to an even jauntier angle.

He was lean and wiry with a slight stoop, apple-red cheeks

The author with Kim, her second collie

of horror as I proceeded gingerly up the field, wooden lathes pinging off the canvas because Ernie had forgotten to instruct me how to tighten it up.

In the winter months I endured long, wearisome hours forking sheaves of corn to the feeder on top of the threshing machine from Ernie's beautifully thatched stacks. How I detested the dust, noise and the scurrying rats, ever threatening to escape up my trouser leg until Ernie showed me how to tie binder twine - below the knee!

Regardless of what strain of oats we drilled in the fertile soil, like Topsy they just 'growed and growed'. One summer a wild Galloway bullock leapt over the fence into forty acres of six foot high oats and went AWOL for two days, finally emerging extremely thirsty but unscathed.

'Fattening beasts' were well into their third year before the word 'mart' was mentioned and once there if the price wasn't right, back home they came for another three months of feeding. The hoggs (yearling sheep) were folded on 'turnip breaks'. In the late afternoon I was instructed to 'Dog them oot', so that they could 'lie dry' on clean ground and be fed corn at both ends of the day. We spent many a day 'shifting the sheep nets', often in weather so cold that my fingers became numb and fumbling so that when 4 o'clock came I was glad of the chance to rush away and corn the ever hungry sheep. Then with darkness rapidly descending and the stars suspended clear cut in a deepening winter sky I would race home, my dogs dancing around my heels, to do the evening milking and feed the calves before settling in for the night to play a game or two of cards, beside a roaring fire.

In fine spring weather it came as no surprise to find Ernie sowing grass seeds throughout the night. He used an old fashioned 'fiddle' hung from his neck on a canvas strap and would stride up and down, left leg and right arm moving in unison, like a ghostly musician, with only the moonlight to guide him on his march to the headland. I can still see him quite clearly, resting on one knee while his dear wife filled the empty seed bag. At 7.30 am prompt she would be relieved of field duty to milk her two house cows, June and Mary Ann, before preparing breakfast. Ernie's main regret in life was that he hadn't bought the farm (he was a tenant) 'and the next one to it! Land was dirt cheap after the war' he would say.

Ernie's complexion was flawless. Each evening he would remove his collarless striped 'wark shart' and stand with braces

and deep set blue eyes and he worked his three hundred acres in the old fashioned manner in which he himself had been raised.

When I first appeared, as a very inexperienced youngster, one of my first jobs that autumn was to learn how to cut corn and service a rattling ancient binder. I can still recall my feeling dangling at the kitchen sink while he washed himself all over with household soap (the green kind). Although a stickler for cleanliness he didn't care much for his appearance, except on a Sunday when he smartened himself up to perform his duties as sidesman at St Mary's Church. During the rest of the week he walked about in any old thing. Many's the occasion visiting reps would enquire of him 'Where's the boss?' Often he would say 'Over there', giving me a wink and pointing in my direction with a grubby finger.

At lambing time he presented me with a bottle of gin that someone had given him for Christmas. 'Fer the weakly lambs, warm it in your mouth and spit it intae theirs'. I tried, but by the end of the day, there was very little left and I felt decidedly queasy. It was a bitterly cold day but I was warm and glowing both inside and out. Ernie took one whiff of my breath then plied me with peppermints 'Just in case Sadie finds oot'. Needless to say that was the first and the last bottle I received 'for the lambing'.

In addition to being a sidesman, Ernie cut the cemetery grass with a scythe and provided produce for the harvest festival. As the time approached we would busy ourselves scrubbing potatoes and turnips but it was the preparation of the corn which I enjoyed most. I would watch Ernie and think: This is how I'll remember him in years to come - sitting in the corner on a bag of binder twine, gnarled hands putting together neat bundles of corn, strong fingers running through each bundle stripping the straw from the stalks, tying the bundles top and bottom before cutting them to the correct length with an old pair of rusty sheep shears.

It was Ernie who taught me to hand shear sheep. 'The outbye method' he called it. First you clipped away down the right hand side, starting at the back of the sheep's neck carefully keeping her 'lugs' out of the way with your other hand. After clipping the right-hand side, you would step over your fleece, at the same time hoisting the often protesting sheep up on to her rump before proceeding down the left hand side. Ernie could clip with either hand. I could only clip with my right. Consequently his sheep always looked better than mine. After a couple of seasons, fool that I was, I began shearing more sheep in a day than Ernie. When he finally noticed he downed shears with a clatter muttering, 'When the pupil gets better than the teacher, it's time to quit' and quit he did. I was left to do the lot from then on.

Most winter weekends found us sawing logs. We used a crosscut saw. I asked why he didn't use a chain saw. With a smile he explained that by using the former we got two warmings for the price of one.

In Ernie's latter years his eyesight began to deteriorate. After a deal of persuasion he paid a visit to an eye specialist who told him that if he went on smoking his pipe his sight would 'worsen'. Even after this warning Ernie continued the habit. He explained that it was extremely difficult to give up what had become his 'only pleasure'. He would smoke where his wife couldn't see, but owing to the strong aroma of tobacco on his clothes she began to have an inkling and asked if I would keep an eye open and report back. Unintentionally, I would discover him in the most unlikely places and rather like a mischievous school boy his eyes would twinkle as he attempted to waft away the smoke and hide the offending pipe. Blind or not, I couldn't bring myself to tell tales but by being regularly caught out he smoked less with the result that his sight gradually improved.

Ernie had been born on Hallowe'en. His father Robert caught rabbits for a living. He had married Ernie's mother when she was over thirty. She was at that time in service, employed as a cook, and 'workin' in a big hoose'. She bore him six children in quick succession. The first born, Robert, was

Ernie and Sadie Crisp with the author's son, Geoff

killed in action during the First World War. Then came Samuel, William, Ernest and Mary in that order. Sadly another daughter died in infancy after swallowing a half penny piece.

Ernie's first childhood memory was a painful one - being inquisitive he shoved his forefinger between the rollers of the mangle as his mother wrung out the clothes. The finger was never quite the same again.

When he was a boy Ernie heartily disliked school, or 'skee-ool' as he pronounced it. This was probably due to the fact that the master heartily disliked Ernie who nicknamed him 'the German spy', because of his accent rather than his origin! One afternoon things finally came to a head and Ernie, a big lad for his age, thumped the angry master on the end of his nose, then, deciding that he'd had enough 'skee-ooling' he went hill lambing instead.

Ernie would relate these stories over and over again on wet afternoons as we sat cross-legged on the dusty floor of the granary, mending corn bags. Occasionally he would pause for breath, pushing back his 'pee-sweep's tail', a long piece of grey hair cultivated especially to cover up the bald patch on the top of his head. Following this he would grin impishly showing his few remaining tobacco-stained teeth before continuing on with some other yarn or ditty, his favourite being

'I'm gonna marry a shepherd laddie,
Aww, you canna' marry a shepherd laddie,
Far too many doggies.
There's only Tip and Tam and Toosie,
Dick and Nan and Susie,
You wouldna' call them many doggies?'

Ernie's wife Sadie was a farmer's daughter. He'd courted her on his motor bike. She'd worn long black stockings, short skirts and a shapeless hat. One dark night he invited her down the garden to take a look at his ferret. She liked it (the ferret) so Ernie proposed. They lived happily though childless, but as Ernie pointed out, 'We've nane tae please us and nane to vex us either.'

One day Ernie's sister Mary invited us over for tea. She had bought a new carpet and recently had central heating installed. Although the weather was warm the heating was full on. All the windows were opened wide to let out the heat, or let in the

cool, we couldn't decide. Ernie surmised that we had been invited so that she could show off. The table was covered by a lovely lace cloth and laden with scrumptious food, for Mary, like her mother before her, had been a cook. We sat down to feast. Suddenly, from out of nowhere there appeared a large tabby cat. It leapt up on to Ernie's lap and promptly dug in its claws. Now Ernie hated cats so his reaction was severe to say the least. 'Get off, you brute,' he yelled, attempting to knock the startled cat to the floor. Filled with alarm it stuck its long sharp claws into the lace tablecloth with the disastrous result that both it, the cloth and everything on it landed in a sticky, messy, broken heap on the new carpet.

It was a long, long while before we were invited back again.

We were threshing corn when poor Ernie came through the granary floor. I followed him in and was just about to carry my burden up the staircase when much to my surprise a long thin leg with a tacketty boot on the end of it appeared dangling comically through the ceiling. He had been carrying a twelve stone bag of barley when it happened so it must have been quite painful. Anyway we lifted him out and, apart from walking a bit strangely, he didn't show any ill-effects. That evening over supper I asked if it had hurt. 'Na,' he grunted. 'Then why,' I enquired in all innocence, 'were you walking funny?' There followed an embarrassed pause before he replied 'There's five pounds in the Bank of England for anyone who can mind their own business.'

Sadly, in 1978, at harvest time, Ernie passed away after a brief illness. He had recently retired from farming to a stone built cottage on the edge of the village where he was born and after all his years of hard work I considered that he deserved much more than his allotted 'three score years and ten', but it was not to be and so I lost my dearest friend.

Shortly before he died I visited him in hospital. Sat at his bedside he could see my sadness and grasped my small hand in his large workworn one, squeezing it tightly, comforting me. When it was time to leave no words were spoken other than a whispered 'goodbye'. We both realised that it would be the last. I paused in the doorway for a final look at the man who had moulded me so caringly in his ways. He had a faraway look in his eyes, no doubt dreaming of times gone by.

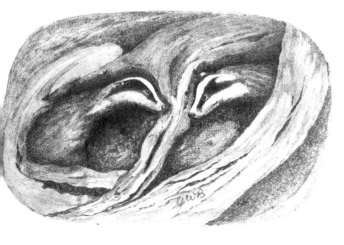

3
Arrival at Swindon

Geoff Billingham and I met at a sheepdog trial, and in all honesty I must confess to being attracted to his lovely bitch Meg long before her master caught my eye. I suppose one would call it 'love at second sight' with Geoff and me, for it was some years before we were married.

Geoff (or GWB as he signs his sketches) achieved his boyhood ambition in 1973 when we came to live in the Scottish Borders 'Sheepdog Country', he described it, with our young son Geoffrey William ('Geoff Junior'), then a babe in arms. It was on a bright October day when we unloaded our possessions and animals on Cheviot soil and made Swindon House on the Duke of Roxburghe's estate our home.

We arrived with mixed feelings, having been warned that tradition played a vital part in the running of things in this remote beautiful area. Therefore who you knew could prove more important than what you knew.

I remember on that glorious autumnal day, the valley's scenic beauty warmed and welcomed us after our one hundred mile journey, and we immediately felt at home surrounded by its bracken strewn, sheep dotted, sheltering slopes.

We drove into the yard and up to the back door, our somewhat battered ancient estate car overflowing with panting curious collies, my grandmother's delicate and greatly cherished china laid carefully at my feet. Little Geoff had chuckled and chortled throughout the long journey securely strapped in his car seat, whilst two disgruntled cats Jemima and her daughter Silver meowed plaintively from a cardboard box securely tied with string.

On sighting the house, Pip, our somewhat tatty off-white, miniature poodle, leapt back and forth over the seats, perhaps remembering our previous visit, (when we came to see what the job entailed) eagerly looking forward to exploring the surrounding countryside.

Dear little Pip, how my heart warms at the thought of the ragged cantankerous bundle we discovered many moons ago living among the ewes at Wiserly Farm, in a remote corner of county Durham.

This previous farmhouse home was set snugly within the shelter of wild, untamed hedgerows that during the summer months swarmed with sweet-scented honeysuckle and ever hungry twittering fledglings – the last place one would expect to find an off-white, tatty, miniature poodle living rough!

Throughout the cold winter months the little dog slept underneath the stars, curled in a tight round ball in an effort to keep himself warm. Living wild, he had become completely unapproachable. The only way we could gain his confidence was to put out a bowl of food beside the garden gate before we went to bed. We had no idea from where he had originated until a neighbour mentioned that some months ago he had seen a car draw up at the roadside from which a small white bundle had been flung. By the time he arrived at the scene there was no sign of anyone.

As winter turned into spring the little dog failed to come for his food. Sadly, we surmised that he had died. However, come Easter time he again put in an appearance. We were in the village doing our weekly shopping when my husband spotted him trailing along the pavement with head bowed, in an emaciated state.

'Quick, run and catch him!' urged my husband, reaching over to open the car door. I jumped out in pursuit of the pitiful bundle and gathered him up in my arms. To my horror he immediately showed his appreciation by sinking his sharp yellow teeth deep into my arm.

'Hang on, don't let go of him,' ordered my partner from the driver's seat. With gritted teeth I returned to the car with the ferocious little beast's fangs still firmly embedded in my flesh and dumped him unceremoniously on the back seat. After a brief examination of my by now rapidly swelling arm, we drove home with our ungrateful passenger grinning fiercely at us, uttering the most insulting doggie swear words.

Back home, I went indoors to disinfect my arm, leaving my husband to extract our 'guest'. At least ten minutes went by and they had still not put in an appearance so I went back outside in time to witness a furious poodle being hauled out of the car with a long shanked shepherd's crook.

After an anxious, painful week during which I became firmly convinced he'd given me rabies, Pip, as we decided to call him, began to settle in - and in our heart of hearts we accepted him after all his suffering, as a permanent fixture. That is until one morning the telephone rang. The call was from a middle aged couple. Their much loved pet had expired and they had heard through the grapevine that we'd acquired a stray. They were prepared to take Pip and provide him with a caring home. He was even welcome to sleep on their bed!

I did my best to explain that he was no ordinary dog. Apart from a split personality, his breath was absolutely putrid, and as for sleeping in their bedroom it was a must, because if left to his own devices he would pee on everything except the ceiling and wail like a banshee. The couple were not to be put off.

'All he needs is love,' they assured me, and they had plenty to give. The following day he went off jauntily to his new abode and I could almost have sworn that he gave me a wink as he swaggered by. I couldn't be certain because his wicked little coal black eyes were barely visible beneath a tangled topknot.

The following morning I was woken by a frantic phone call. On the other end was the 'adoptive father', who I am positive was down on his knees. 'Please take him back,' he pleaded. 'He bit the wife when she tried to groom him, he bit me when

I tried to bath him and now he's gone and bitten the paper boy!'

My mind boggled. I had to suppress a smile as all kinds of visions flashed before my eyes.

One hour later the prodigal was returned to the fold and delirious with delight, began to show off by exploring every room in the house upright on his hind legs, as though he was the man of the house. In front of the television he paused to admire his reflection in the screen. Butter wouldn't have melted in his mouth.

That same evening the dreaded Pip reverted as I knew he would, from the kindly Dr Jeckyll to the shocking Mr Hyde! Unfortunately it was my husband who bore the brunt of his animosity. We were drinking our cocoa when he slipped unobtrusively out of the room. After settling the fire, we climbed the stairs to bed. I was first between the sheets, leaving my husband to turn out the light. Suddenly all hell broke loose, as a snarling demon shot from beneath the bed and sunk needle sharp teeth into his 'new' master's ankle. The sight that met my eyes when I switched on the light - Pip hanging on like grim death to my husband's pyjama leg - left me chortling for days. From that night onwards, my 'other half' became adept at the long jump, until he had the idea of moving the bed nearer the light switch.

The next task was to get the little dog looking like a poodle. After a glance through Yellow Pages, an appointment at a dog beauty parlour was duly arranged. When the day finally dawned Pip was full of the joys of spring, especially when he espied his brand new lead which spelt out 'Walkies' to him. He leapt gaily into the car automatically raising a hind leg to steady himself, making it obvious he had clocked up a fair mileage before landing on our doorstep.

In town he was completely in his element. His first reaction was to drink in his surroundings, after which he sped off with me in hot pursuit on the end of his new lead to the nearest high-rise concrete lamp post, where he proceeded to hop hurriedly round it first one way, then the other with hind legs pointing skyward, purely for the delight of performing an act that had obviously once been to him an everyday occurrence.

Our appointment at the beauty parlour was for 2 o'clock. We arrived precisely on the dot. I do not believe I have ever seen anyone's expression change quite so swiftly as the poodle trimmer's did. 'Good Lord! What on earth have we here?' she exclaimed, in a voice so incredulous that I wondered if we had come to the wrong place.

'This is the dog beauty parlour?' I enquired hesitantly.

'Well, yes,' was the reply, 'but I'm afraid we are fully booked up today.'

'But we made an appointment for 2 o'clock,' I pointed out.

'Well dear,' she said after a pause, 'there is no way I am going to tackle that, it's completely out of the question.'

Suddenly, the 'That' in question unexpectedly came to life, barking, leaping high into the air and fiercely wagging his apology for a tail as though greatly relieved to have wriggled out of his hair cut.

'How on earth could you have allowed him to get into such a dreadful state?' asked the trimmer in critical tones. I was forced to explain that he was an abandoned waif and stray that nobody wanted and that I would be more than happy to trim him myself, but I had only ever shorn sheep and didn't have the foggiest idea where to begin on a poodle. 'Why didn't you explain all of this in the first place?' she admonished, giving us a beaming smile and taking the lead from my grasp. Then in one fell swoop she leaned forward and scooped the disappointed Pip up into her arms holding him tightly against her ample bosom. Startled, he made to amputate her right ear but she had seen it all before. Quick as a flash she reached into her overall pocket and whipped out a large handkerchief, securely tying it around his nose. Then, turning her attention to me, 'Off you pop dear, and do your shopping, come back in an hour and I'll guarantee you won't recognise him,' she smiled.

Two hours later the laborious task still wasn't finished. The professional mopped her brow for the umpteenth time. 'Won't be long now, dear,' she gasped. 'My, hasn't he got a lot of coat?' I nodded, glancing at the growing pile of dirty wool below the bench. Then all of a sudden, there stood one of the most handsome poodle dogs I had ever come across.

The trimmer refused to take a penny for her services, even though I pleaded with her. She argued that firstly, it was because Pip was a stray, secondly I could not be held responsible for his condition. Thirdly, she thought I deserved a medal for adopting such an obnoxious creature, and finally, in view of his obvious advanced age she did not expect him to survive much longer, but if, by some remote twist of fate, he did, she would gladly pay me to take him somewhere else for his next hair cut!

One month later the doctor told me I was pregnant. Unfortunately in the early stages I became ill and was confined to bed. My husband had his work cut out caring for pregnant females of another species so during the long days that I was housebound my entertainment came mainly from two sources. One, the radio and two, Pip, who proved to be my salvation because from early morning until late into the evening he provided an amazing floor show, howling along with pop stars, waltzing to Strauss and gaily leaping on and off the bed to Tchaikovsky's Dance of the Sugar Plum Fairy. Come lunch time he would take a well deserved break, flopping down exhausted on to the carpet, his saucer-like eyes riveted to my plate awaiting his reward. Perhaps he had been a circus dog?

Most weekends found us on the road to one trial or another. It was when I was competing at Kelso that the unexpected happened. I was standing at the post with my dog Garry, when from behind, the judge Jock Richardson of International Trials winner Wiston Cap fame enquired in a surprised tone, 'Running brace today, are we?' I glanced round and to my amusement found Pip standing at the ready, gazing up at me enquiringly. Jock, to my horror, lifted up the offending dog and dropped him through the car window on to the seat. I never plucked up the courage to tell him how near he was to losing his whistling fingers!

4
Little Geoff

I continued competing in trials until my condition became obvious and fortunately by that time it was the end of the season anyway.

My sister Jenifer who lived in Hong Kong, gave me a luxurious scarlet cape with an ocelot lining which she had worn when living in a much cooler climate during her first pregnancy. Although I pitied the poor ocelot the cape kept me lovely and warm throughout the long winter months.

With the colder weather upon us Pip too had to be considered so I made him a little jacket in the same bright red colour as my cape, but without the ocelot lining.

Pip was highly delighted with his new garment and when we went shopping he strutted on in front swaggering gaily past all the other dogs we met.

When December arrived we certainly looked the part, Pip with his long white beard and me with my rapidly expanding waistline. When in mid December I hit the 11 st mark after being a mere 7 st 8 lbs I began to believe that I would have a 'ginormous' baby but to my great embarrassment it was not to be, for when in January the happy event finally occurred my long awaited bundle weighed in at a mere 5 lbs. So ladies be warned, lay off the porridge swimming in cream, smothered in syrup, and no slipping away to the Chinese restaurant, or you too could end up like I did - BIG and FAT!

To get to the nearest village involved a two mile drive down an exceedingly bumpy lane, and if that wasn't difficult enough we also had to cross over a railway line. Granted it was only a single track, but if your car just happened to be prone to stalling, and ours was, you could find yourself in a sticky situation.

One of my worst experiences happened in mid December a month before Geoff was born when Pip and I were off on a Christmas shopping expedition. I only just managed to squeeze myself behind the steering wheel, and with a wave to GWB who was moving off in the direction of the sky-line with a large flock of ewes, started up the engine and away we went. Sure enough, just as soon as we reached the railway line the engine cut out, leaving us stranded in the middle of the track. My immediate reaction was to glance at my wrist watch - to my horror I realised there would be a train along at any moment. Panic stricken, out of the car I shot. (It is surprising how quickly you can move when you have to.) Pip fortunately followed hot on my heels and for once I remembered to place the gear lever in neutral.

I leaned my full eleven stone against the car's rear bumper, and heaved and pushed, and pushed and heaved, momentarily wondering if giving birth bore any comparison.

Suddenly from far off in the distance I heard the faint toot of a train. Fear gripped me, making my frantic attempts more urgent and helping me discover a super strength I never knew I had. To my surprise the car began to move. Slowly at first, then gathering speed. Overjoyed, I wiped the perspiration from my brow, carefully observing its steady progress as it rolled gently over the line and out of sight down the bank on the other side.

Down the bank? Oh my goodness, I had't contemplated that at all. I had heard of 'the runaway train', but this was ridiculous. I set off after the rapidly disappearing car as fast as my condition would allow with Pip dancing gaily at my heels.

Fortunately the road evened out a little further along and I was able to catch up with the car. Miraculously it started at the first turn of the key.

How Little Geoff didn't arrive a month prematurely after my ordeal, I'll never know.

Once Christmas was over, an urgent nesting instinct that I had previously admired in wild creatures began to stir within me and I began to surround myself with all the usual baby paraphernalia one requires, arranging and re-arranging it from morning until night, driving my mate potty with my efforts until finally I was satisfied and settled down to wait for January, the final and longest month of all to pass.

Happy Birthday

It was the morning of Tuesday, January 22nd, 1973. I awoke at 6 am and knew instinctively that the great day had finally arrived. Little Geoff was on his way at last.

'Where's your suitcase? Hurry up and get ready, have you forgotten anything?' Pip whined with excitement as GWB got into an awful flap. How could I tell him that I felt fine, had been organised for weeks and that all that I really wanted was an enormous plate of creamy porridge washed down with a cup of tea. This was the most exciting day of my life, and I wanted to relish every moment.

The car started first time. We'd had it serviced the previous week in readiness for the occasion.

The journey to the hospital took approximately three quarters of an hour. We arrived at around 7.30 am and were shown into a small annexe. GWB left almost immediately. The heifers were calving and had to be watched, also the puppies and kittens would be wanting their breakfast. I can't say that I was sorry to see him leave, for unlike some ladies I strongly believe that giving birth is woman's work. Does the ram linger around the ewe at such times?

I was handed a short starched white garment to wear that was supposed to tie at the back had there been anything to tie it with, but even if there had been I couldn't have reached.

The hospital was extremely short staffed so instead of entering the room the nurse on duty peered through a porthole set in the door, making me feel more like a goldfish than an expectant mother. Halfway through the morning in glided sister, as though she was on wheels. After checking to see how far along I was she left, warning me not to get out of bed, to lie still, not to crumple the sheets and to keep very very quiet because the person in the next room to me was extremely ill!

I found out later that everyone who was in labour was given precisely the same instructions to keep them from bothering overworked nurses.

Round about lunch time the door flew open and in rushed an 'expert' followed by half a dozen fresh faced students. 'You may think this is a silly question Mrs Billingham,' he said, 'but what makes you believe that you are actually in labour?'

A prolonged and painful contraction prevented me from telling him.

Five minutes later I was unceremoniously dumped on to a trolley and hurriedly whisked down to the delivery room past a row of anxious fathers-to-be. As we flew on by them I couldn't

The Christening party

Father and son

bantam weight infant. However, over the last couple of decades I have both witnessed and assisted at births too numerous to mention. Granted, they were mostly lambs and calves, but the procedure is basically the same. I have noticed in most cases that it is the state of mind of the mother-to-be at the time of giving birth that influences whether or not she has an easy time or a difficult one. Providing the birth is progressing normally, a confident mum who knows what to expect is often more relaxed than one who has no idea what is going to happen to her. I wouldn't dream of pretending that the birth of my baby was completely free from pain. Contractions, especially when they are coming fast and furious can only be compared with being run over by a steam roller. Not that I have ever been run over by one, mind you, but surprisingly I found the actual birth to be as easy as pie - well, almost.

There is truly nothing to compare with the feeling of elation one experiences when confronted with the sight of one's first born. I was only allowed a quick peep at mine before he was whisked hurriedly away wrapped in a towel to be placed in an incubator. 'Just for a little while' the kindly midwife did her best to reassure me. Then I was alone, left in the delightful warmth of the delivery room to rest, whilst everyone ate lunch. Little did they realise that I too was extremely hungry, so much so that I could easily have eaten a horse, and I had never been so thirsty in all my life as I was on Little Geoff's birthday.

Meanwhile ... back at the ranch a newly calved heifer in my husband's care had just been given a pail of water, with the chill taken off, and she didn't even say thank you.

I had to be grateful for small mercies, at last I had my long awaited bundle of joy and what more could anyone possibly want? Even if he was a bit on the skinny side at least he was healthy and he'd soon fill out.

The time I spent in the maternity ward was without a doubt one of the best holidays I'd had. It was like being in a girls' boarding school except that we were pampered, fussed over and fed on the best. Our doting husbands, relatives and friends showering us with gifts. What a shock most of us were in for when finally we went home with our tiny puckered faced infants warmly cocooned in their new woolly shawls.

The teenage mum in the next bed but one presented Little Geoff with a soft bristled hair brush as a going home present. She had brought it in with her so that she could brush her baby's hair when it was born. How dreadfully disappointed the

help but smile as I envisaged the 'eye-full' that they would undoubtedly have got had I been facing in the opposite direction, for I had not been able to pluck up enough courage to request a more modest delivery gown.

Giving birth should surely be one of the most natural things on earth - that and dying! It is perhaps easy for me to make such a sweeping statement having only ever produced one poor girl was when the baby arrived, for she hadn't a single hair on her head.

The Home Coming

Oh what a joy it was to be back! Even though hospital had been such marvellous fun there is no place quite like home, no bed quite as comfortable as one's own.

As we drove up the bumpy lane and into the muddy yard with the new babe fast asleep in my arms, he stirred, yawned and stretched contentedly as only a young creature can and I felt an overwhelming feeling of protectiveness towards him. On hearing our approach the dogs set up a tumultuous welcome. Cats and kittens of all shapes, sizes, colours and creeds lined up on the garden wall to pay their respects to the new baby and as we stepped inside the door Pip slunk guiltily out of the arm-chair then, realising that I was home, went delirious with delight leaping high into the air barking excitedly, reminding baby Geoff that it was time for his lunch.

Afterwards I changed him for the first time in his new home and he settled down contentedly for an afternoon nap.

All went well until bath time! GWB stoked up the fire whilst I carried in the towels and washing-up bowl, for as yet we hadn't invested in a baby bath.

I set them down on the rug in front of the fire, hastily checking the water temperature with my hand. I was instantly reprimanded by my husband. 'Not like that,' he said in horri-fied tones professionally rolling up his shirt sleeve and expertly dipping his elbow into the washing up bowl. 'Now what do we do?' I asked, cradling the naked babe on my lap. 'You're sup-posed to be the mother' came back the exasperated reply. We stared anxiously at one another then suddenly burst out laugh-ing. For we who had dipped sheep in their thousands had never once bathed a real live baby before, and humans were entirely different, or so we thought!

'There's only one thing for it,' GWB stirred into action. 'You take his arms, and I'll take his legs and we'll dunk him up and down in the water.' So we did, and that is how Little Geoff got his first real dip, correction bath, in front of the living room fire.

All of that first night I never got a wink of sleep because I had no idea at all how resilient is the average infant. So there I sat on that chill winter's evening in my dressing gown, huddled

on the end of the bed poking and prodding our brand new son in order to satisfy myself that he was still breathing. I shudder to think what the poor little mite thought now that he was in the outside world.

In the weeks that followed I quickly established a routine, and everything ran smoothly, helped by the fact that Geoff was such a good, long suffering and cheerful little chap.

There was a marvellous health visitor in the area, and she called round regularly in the early days giving much valued and extremely useful advice. I have heard some mothers resent this intrusion, I could not have been more grateful.

Pip accepted the presence of the new baby right from the start but it was many months before we trusted them alone together.

We purchased a cat net at the same time as we purchased a baby bath and with the warm spring weather quickly upon us baby Billingham spent most of his time in the garden beneath the shade of an old apple tree with the result that he developed a dappled sun tan.

I was greatly surprised one afternoon sitting out in the gar-den when a large ferocious dog appeared from nowhere and ran in the direction of the pram. Before I could even rise to my feet Pip shot out from underneath a bush where he had been sleeping, and barking loudly proceeded to run backwards and forwards between the dog and the pram, like a collie herding sheep. The big dog, taken by surprise, stopped dead in his tracks, Pip flew in his direction snapping at his nose, chasing him away from 'his baby', out of 'his garden' and off 'his prop-erty!' If I hadn't seen what took place with my own eyes, I never would have believed it.

With the lambing and the calving well out of the way we decided that it was high time that Little Geoff was Christened, so I duly wrote away to our local vicar asking how to go about it.

It was one of those dreadful days that we all experience when nothing goes right. The kettle boiled dry, the milk boiled all over the cooker, the cat ate the lunch, the baby wouldn't stop crying and to crown it all, Pip kept up a constant and annoying yapping on the doorstep in all probability admonish-ing the cat for stealing the lunch.

Finally I could stand it no longer, something snapped and in utter exasperation I called out to him 'shut up or go away, you horrible little B.....!' There was a deathly hush and I breathed a sigh of relief. It was short lived, for much to my great embarrassment and horror a loud genteel voice rang out down the hallway, 'It's only the vicar Mrs Billingham, come about the Christening. I do hope I haven't chosen an inopportune moment?' To this day I still live in hope he didn't hear me.

The Christening

We arose at the crack of dawn, to a cloudless sky, and the morning air warm and still. GWB immediately set off to 'look' the stock, his dogs frisking at his heels, whilst I went into the garden, the wet grass tickling my bare legs, to cut armfuls of dewy roses and arrange them throughout the house before waking Little Geoff.

When I slipped upstairs, he was already awakened and lying, gurgling happily in his cot, playing with his toes. I bathed, fed and changed him before wheeling him out into the garden in his pram.

His Christening gown had not as yet arrived and I hastily crossed my fingers hoping against hope that it would come with the morning post.

Later, when GWB and I had breakfasted, I set to and made scores of cucumber sandwiches arranging them carefully on trestle tables in the hall, borrowed especially for the occasion.

Then out of the tins came the butterfly cakes, apple pies, cheese scones and jam tarts! I gazed on them fondly - such a pity that they had to be eaten after all my efforts, I thought, covering them over with a large table cloth.

Little Geoff, bless him, obligingly slept on and on in the sun as I did a quick flip round with a duster and a hurried tour with the vacuum cleaner.

I had bathed the protesting Pip the night before, and had meant to give him a once over with the sheep shears. His coat had grown in so quickly, but there just wasn't time.

As I passed by I picked him up and gave him a quick hug telling him that this was to be his first important social occasion and therefore he must be on his very best behaviour. In return he gave a grumpy growl and made a half hearted attempt to snap off the end of my nose. Just then the post lady chose to arrive, bringing with her a beautiful crocheted shawl that she had made as a gift for Little Geoff, a huge pile of congratulatory cards and the anxiously awaited Christening gown wrapped in reams of creamy white tissue, carefully folded in a cardboard box.

The Christening was to be at 1.30 and at 1 o'clock sharp we were ready and waiting for transport, dressed in our best bibs and tuckers. In Little Geoff's case I mean this literally, for around his neck hung an enormous bib, to prevent him dribbling down the front of his Christening gown.

I had purchased a wide brimmed, flower decked, pink frilly hat especially for the occasion and much to the amusement of our friends I wore it throughout the day, simply because I couldn't imagine when I would ever get the opportunity to wear it again.

Richard, a friend and local publican, insisted that the Christening be done in style and very kindly chauffeured us to and from the church in his immaculate, gleaming red vintage car.

The village church was filled with the perfume of summer flowers. Brilliant shafts of sunlight spiralled in through the stained glass windows, making this the most perfect of baptisms. In the pews sat smiling relatives and friends from all walks of life. Unfortunately when the service began we were minus a godfather, namely Albert, our friendly neighbourhood mechanic, whose car broke down on the way to church.

Fortunately we were able to find a willing substitute in my uncle Reg without too much ado. Albert appeared breathless, a short while later, apologising profusely for not arriving at the church in time.

After the ceremony my aunt, uncle, the two Geoffs and I piled into the car with Richard and his wife Jean and did a couple of laps of honour around the village with the baby held aloft for gaily waving friends to see, then afterwards sped home for the celebrations to continue.

Once tea was over we wet the baby's head, yet again, then it was fun and games outside on the lawn. Games like tug of war and charades - in fancy dress to make the guessing easier.

Our good friend Albert had a secret ambition to become a shepherd, so with Pip as his sheep dog, a funny hat on his head and the aid of some sheep's wool pulled from the hedge, the transformation was quickly achieved. Try as hard as they might, no-one could guess his occupation and eventually they gave in. When Albert said that he was a shepherd the men folk said it wasn't fair because he didn't look the part to which Albert admitted that perhaps he'd got the century wrong. So they put him in a wool sheet and hung him in the apple tree until he got it right.

It was without a doubt the most unorthodox Christening that I had ever attended but oh, how much we enjoyed it.

The Flitting

From his earliest childhood days it had been my husband's main ambition to become a hill shepherd. As a boy he spent many happy hours out on the heathlands of southern England in the company of an elderly shepherd, watching while he worked his dogs and tended his large flock. Come evening the sheep were driven back to the farm by the old man's dogs and fastened within the fold until the following morning.

GWB's first job was that of a keeper's lad but his heart was in shepherding. He came to the north of England when he was nineteen years old and became foreman shepherd on a large farm, eventually taking over as manager when his employer became ill.

Twenty years on, the farm was sold and it was then that he finally realised his lifelong ambition of becoming a hill shepherd.

Eventually we came to live and work in the rugged hills that separate the English and the Scots. It is in and around this wild area that the Border collie first originated in the capable hands of some of the greatest sheep dog handlers of all time.

Fortunately I shared my husband's ideals and strangely the word 'Cheviot' had always held a magical ring even though I had no idea what it meant. I never dreamed for one moment that one day I would be living in full view of the mountain itself.

When we first told our friends that we were moving to Scotland they shook their heads and smiled. 'Hadn't you better learn the language first?' they suggested.

As we drove up the winding valley road for the very first time, three months before we actually came to live there I thought it was the most beautiful and peaceful place that I had ever seen, and immediately felt at home.

My first impression of the house was that it looked cold and bleak standing on its own, and I immediately christened it 'Bleak House'. However, when I saw the inside I was pleasantly surprised by its character and the mellowness of the natural wood that abounded throughout.

In the months that followed I was kept busy arranging and

'Old Shep' with Pip

rearranging the furniture, decorating and making curtains until finally we could call the new house a home. By that time Little Geoff, had passed his first birthday and his character had begun to form. He would sit happily playing in his low chair. (I was always afraid he would fall out of a high one.) Every so often he would call out Pip's name in a baby staccato, endearingly holding out a soggy ginger snap. How sweet, I thought ... until one day I realised to my horror that perhaps I had bred a monster. For I discovered that when the little dog came scurrying for his treat, the sticky offering was snatched smartly away and replaced by a large table-spoon that was used to rap him smartly on the head. I deduced that perhaps this was baby logic on how to get even for the many times Pip had stolen his lunch and piddled on his pram!

When Geoff began walking he conquered Pip once and for all. I was hanging out the washing when I heard a dreadful commotion coming from the house. I rushed indoors and there in the corner of the kitchen was a furious Pip, imprisoned by a well padded bottom, protected by a thick nappy. At long last the all conquering hero was finally beaten. His fierce nips were ignored and met with gales of laughter. He couldn't understand it, lost face and from that day onwards, never attempted to bite anyone again.

5
Garry, a Hill Dog

evening whilst out for a walk she decided that the time was ripe and slipped quietly round a flock of ewes and lambs, bringing them expertly to her master's feet as though she had done so all her life. From that day onwards Meg never looked back in her career both as a working dog and top trial competitor.

Her method was beautiful to watch. Incredibly smooth with a quiet though authoritative approach, she followed her charges at the correct speed and distance and could adapt to all types of sheep. Her outrun was careful, drifting in steadily to the point of balance in order to weigh up the sheep and lift them accordingly, without any commands from the time she left her master until she returned to him.

Meg excelled at the pen. She would look awkward sheep straight in the eye, all the while firmly backing them inside with quiet power. During a trialling career spanning several years she won and was placed in trials too numerous to mention.

When the International was held at Chester, Meg gained fifth place after an almost flawless run. Normally when she came off the field she would lie quietly at the edge of the course studying the efforts of her rivals, occasionally wandering over to the refreshment marquee in the hope that someone had dropped a sandwich. We never kept her chained as it wasn't necessary and the only occasion this gave us cause for concern was at the Chester trial. After competing, she completely disappeared. We searched high and low and just when we were beginning to fear the worst she was discovered curled up fast asleep beneath our car! There were hundreds of vehicles in the designated parking area which was some distance from the course. We had only owned this particular vehicle for two days and Meg had only travelled in it once - and that was to the Chester International.

Unfortunately, Meg was not a prolific breeder, producing only three small litters in her lifetime. Unless she approved of her would-be mate she would have nothing to do with him. The few puppies she bred proved both intelligent and sensitive. Her final litter produced Trim and Jed who went on to do great things for my husband, being placed in Brace and Singles at trials throughout the country. They won the Doubles class at the Scottish National and represented Scotland at International level on three occasions. They were second at the Bala International. In 1980 and in 1981 they became Champion of Champions at The Royal Welsh Show. Also in '81 aged ten and a half years they walked away (in Jed's case ran away) with the

Old Meg was an extremely competent collie with an unmistakable intelligence in her pale-coloured luminous eyes. Bred by Bob Short out of Gay and sired by Tom Watson's Jeff - a brother to R. Fraser's famous Mindrum Cap, Meg was incredibly faithful and devoted to her master. She came into my husband's hands as part-exchange at the age of five months and quickly grew into a medium-sized, prettily marked, black and white bitch with semi-erect ears and a soft dense coat.

During the first eight months of her life Meg showed no interest whatsoever in the sheep she had been bred to herd, preferring to spend her time eyeing the cat. However, one

BBC Trophy in the Brace Class on the programme *One Man and His Dog*.

My sheep dog Garry, came into the world on a bright May morning within sight of the mist-shrouded Cheviots, three weeks after his mother, Jed, had completed a busy lambing stint on the steep hill ground of the Swindon and Whitelaw. He was the smallest dog in a litter of five, sired by another Jed, known locally as 'The Sourhope Dog', not due to his disposition but because of his address.

This particular Jed was a thick set, curly-coated dog with a white head, whose power, lining-up ability of sheep and quiet method of handling them, had greatly impressed my husband as he watched him work a flock of blackfaces on his home-ground, from the east side of the Whitelaw.

The silverware - trophies won by Viv and Geoff's dogs

Jed's sire, the half white-headed Cap, had been even more noted in years gone by, with a pedigree that contained the blood lines of J M Wilson's famous 'war years' dog Cap, 3036, and a great deal of Bob Fraser's powerful Mindrum strain.

Garry eventually developed into a medium-sized dog with a luxurious curly coat. He had a neat head with a wide brow and a pronounced stop. In profile, his skull was noticeably long and flat. His markings appeared hand-painted and he had a white blaze that extended between his ears to a wide white collar. Garry's most pleasant features were his eyes. They were a sparkling orange-brown in colour, full of expression and burning with enthusiasm out of an honest face.

He had an endearing habit of gazing up at me for long periods, desperately trying to comprehend every word as well as every thought. From a very early age there was a noticeable quality about Garry. It was obvious in his stance, the proud way he held his head and his calm attitude to life that he inherited from his sire and his maternal grandmother Meg. Unlike other young dogs, he never attempted to cross his course when

sent for sheep, and he could see and scent them across great distances. When putting in a tight turn on difficult sheep his tail never left his hocks. Garry was a great dog not because of me, but in spite of me.

I chose him on the day that he was born - mainly because his markings bore a strong resemblance to those of Black Bob, my childhood hero.

There were three other dog pups in the litter, and a bitch with quite a lot of white on her, but it had to be Garry.

When Garry was a puppy he rarely joined in the fun and games with his sister and brothers, choosing to solemnly survey their antics. He was a real old-fashioned type and for such a tender age was exceptionally faithful, refusing to follow anyone but me. This he did so closely that he was constantly under my feet. As he grew older, and gained more confidence, he gradually increased the distance between us. However, when he got

Jed's litter left to right: Duke, Tweed, Ben, Garry and Lark

too far ahead he would sit and wait, glancing every now and then in my direction, as if to say, 'Do hurry up!'

Most families of puppies are boisterous, but there was something different about this litter. They appeared serious-minded, more like old dogs, and they did everything in unison. When the puppies were ten weeks old they followed me across a shallow part of the burn, in single file. I wanted to observe their reactions to a quiet flock of ewes on the other side.

The moment the puppies sighted the sheep, down went their heads and tails, and quivering with anticipation they began to drive – all in a row, like soldiers on parade. The sight of these tiny, fluffy creatures fully in command of a flock of full grown ewes, held me absolutely spellbound.

The first hint I got that Garry lived to please, was when he slipped away quietly one morning, while I was feeding the poultry. I failed to notice his disappearance and set off over the fields, crossing the burn to where Flick my shepherding horse, was stabled. When I got there I was more than surprised to find Garry sitting on a trailer, patiently awaiting my arrival. I had lifted him on to the trailer the previous day to keep him out of the horse's way. Garry was then only five months old and to have anticipated my actions the following day, was no mean feat.

Garry was naturally clean in the house, and never attempted to steal food, so he was allowed indoors. One lunch time during my meal, I felt a gentle tug on my sleeve. The tug that followed was so forceful that some of the food fell to the floor, where Garry took full advantage of the extra tit-bits! Since that day Garry would pull on my sleeve with varying degrees of strength, until he had my undivided attention.

It was obvious at an early age Garry had inherited his parents' power, and their determination. When sheep were moving he proved over-enthusiastic, pushing them at too great a speed. Once he was trained, a harsh whisper was all that was needed to convince him to 'Take time' and if I gave him a command that he considered unnecessary, he would hesitate, and I knew not to repeat my mistake.

As he gained in experience he became capable of working for long periods without any supervision. However, at the end of every trials season, it took a while to replace the initiative he lost through constant direction.

Working on really rough terrain, Garry was obviously in his element, enjoying the space and freedom. It was wonderfully peaceful to watch him gather and drive. He would drift effortlessly across the hill face until every family of sheep was joined and brought to me.

By the age of eight months he would gather any distance. He had exceptional eyesight and could spot sheep long before I did. If they were out of sight, he used his nose.

During his first winter, when around eight months old, unknown to me he slipped away, up the steep hill behind our house, collecting a large flock of Cheviot ewes and hoggs on his travels. The sheep had been lying in the shelter of a deep hollow out on the tops a couple of miles from home. Garry picked them up and brought them down to our yard in a line, as straight as any arrow – and this was in complete darkness. The ground had a light covering of snow and I was able to follow the sheep's tracks.

Because of his extreme sensitivity, his first trial was a terrifying affair. I deliberately let him run free so that he wouldn't feel trapped when suddenly he ran off into the crowd. He was later found seated happily in the back of the car. People, trees, even shadows made him nervous, affecting his performance. During our early excursions, he was so afraid of the men who let out the sheep that he would cut in, and rush down the field with his sheep, refusing to stop until they were through, or past the Fetch gates.

Towards the end of his first trials season, he began to settle down and enjoy himself. Often he would walk out to the post and stand in readiness while I was chatting to friends and if he lost me in the crowd, he would go first of all to the liquid refreshment tent.

We competed in our first Scottish National trial at Earlston in 1978, when Garry was two years and three months old. Apart from a couple of long outruns away from home, I gave him no special training. My main hope on the day was for 'heavy' sheep, and even heavier rainfall, to deter spectators.

We were drawn to run on the Saturday. (Known as the 'posh day' because everybody comes!) Thursday and Friday dawned blustery and sunny, and the sheep were 'light'. I didn't sleep a wink on Friday night. On Saturday we rose at dawn and I gave Garry a long hill gather before breakfast.

When we arrived at Earlston I couldn't believe my luck. I found well-herded, 'heavy' ewes and rain that was heavy enough to dampen the spectators' enthusiasm.

My knees wobbled like jelly as I awaited my turn. Garry had a look down the field, calmly summed things up, then stretched out at my feet in a deep slumber. At last it was our turn, and by this time the rain was descending in torrents. As we walked to the post I shakily asked the course director if it was too late to change my mind. He said it was, as he abandoned me in what seemed like the loneliest place on earth.

My dog glanced up at me with calm eyes. I asked him 'Can you see the sheep?' The slight forward movement of his ears told me that he had. With a quiet, slow whistle I set him off on a right-hand outrun. He cast out wide from my foot, but on seeing the men at the other end, came in flat in order to get between them and his sheep. The startled half-breds bolted to their left, making me realise too late, that I should have halted Garry fractionally short. The lift was awry, to say the least, and the sheep bolted down the course nearly missing the Fetch gates.

When they reached me I made another mistake. Instead of turning them wide round about me to calm them, I flanked Garry too tightly, causing the sheep to come in front of me. They were brought back by a dog that was becoming more anxious by the minute.

Fortunately, the sheep began to run out of steam. After a reasonable down-drive they made the gates and Garry managed a tight turn into the cross-drive. For me this was the most perfect part of his run - probably because he was able to accomplish it without any directions from me! He tucked himself in behind his charges and with head down and shoulders high marched them to and through the last gates. Once in the shed-

ding ring it took several precious minutes before a suitable gap could be made, allowing Garry to shed off two sheep without collars.

Then off to the pen where I stood well back, holding the end of the rope. Luck was surely with us, as all but one, a plain-headed ewe wearing a red collar, walked inside. The ewe made a dash for freedom but Garry was much too quick for her, and managed to turn her in with the others. At the single shed, the same plain-headed ewe momentarily paused to glance over her shoulder. The chance was not to be missed. Garry flew in,

The Scottish National - Viv and Garry

Garry (right) with grandaughter Nell on a duck drive

the country, the first contest being held in 1898 'on a day of howling gales and torrential rain'.

The Thursday and Friday trials were the qualifying heats for the 'Double Outrun', taking place on the Saturday. Garry gained the highest points for Friday and was presented with the Lonsdale Cup. This provided him with the opportunity to compete in Saturday's 'Double Lift', with the chance of winning a valuable silver teapot. On Saturday, Garry led the field until the last three competitors ousted him into fourth place with near perfect runs and it was Harold Loates and Jill, who deservedly gained first place.

Subsequently, Garry became much sought after as a sire. Unfortunately he decided he preferred work to play and would run beside a bitch all day long, ignoring her overtures. Eventually, I came to the conclusion that as a stud, Garry was a failure. Surprisingly, he eventually fell for a pretty little tri-colour called Nell - Leadburn Nell, to give her her full title.

Nell successfully reared five litters of intelligent, classy, well-marked puppies sired by Garry. On seeing the family all together a handler whose bitch had been ignored was heard to complain ''Them two think they're married!'

I kept a service pup from each litter and was well pleased with my choice. Usually a loner, Garry went through a complete change of character whenever new offspring appeared on the scene. It was as though a dormant instinct to protect (which appears in some wolves, known as 'uncles', because they stay home and mind the children), took over.

Normally walking on in front, so as not to become involved in the boisterous ear-nipping and tail-tugging games of his older sons, he would hang close, keeping a watchful, protective eye on the puppy - who was totally unappreciative of his efforts. If Garry considered his puppy in any way threatened by the 'Big Boys', he would immediately intervene, tipping the offender on to his back, and fixing him with a fierce glare while growling a warning in his ear.

causing her to stop dead in her tracks. She turned and was easily worn.

The two judges shouted 'That'll do'. The spectators clapped and cheered. I bent low to pat Garry and hide my embarrassment.

Our first National was over. I left the field elated with a score of $182\frac{1}{2}$ points. Not enough to get into the team on that occasion, but a good score nevertheless.

Three weeks later Garry won two trials in one weekend. At Chatton Sandyfords high out on the heather where a blustery wind blows continuously off the North Sea and at Holystone, where he was presented with the most prestigious trophy on the Northumbrian circuit, the Coquet Shield, which dates back over seventy years. Inscribed round the perimeter are the winners' names, many of them famous handlers from the past. I was honoured to place my name among them, in the last remaining space.

In September of 1981, we travelled to the famous Longshaw three day event, reputed to be one of the oldest in

6

The Scottish National 1982

The 1982 Scottish National Sheep Dog Trial held at Strathaven, Lanarkshire will go down as one of the best. It was certainly ideal from both the competitors' and the spectators' point of view. Held on a gradual slope, clearly visible to all, the course was well situated with even the smallest detail taken into consideration by the local committee.

I set off for 'Straven' with little thought of making the Scottish team. Garry had always given his best at previous Nationals but this was, after all, our fifth try. I even put on a dress, something I hadn't even contemplated before. This particular garment was flowery and flowing. Also, much to my embarrassment, it was prone to blowing upwards in the slightest breeze.

Our turn arrived and we walked out to the post. The sheep, if anything, were slightly more stubborn, and rather more suited to Garry's determined tactics. I stepped up on to the stand, provided for the not so tall, thinking that big people had an unfair advantage at most trials. They were all arms and legs at the pen and could look right into the drive gates.

Our sheep were already out, and my heart sank as one of them walked off from the others. Garry was already away right handed on the four hundred yard outrun. Without any commands from me he gently gathered up the offender and drove her back to her pals. Apart from minor deviations, we managed to hit all our gates - a pleasant surprise.

I heaved a sigh of relief as the sheep came towards me and I stepped down into the shedding ring. The next part proved to be somewhat difficult to say the least. My billowing skirts scared the life out of those suspicious blackface sheep. Every time I made to advance, they retreated to the far side of the ring. Finally, in sheer desperation, (time was running out) I barged Garry into a tiny gap and fortunately the rough tactics paid off. We then went to the pen where surprise, surprise, the sheep gave no opposition at all. When it came to the single we employed the same tactics as before. Thankfully they worked and we were home and dry.

Our score from judges Andrew Ferguson and Willie McMillan, was 185 points, the second highest on the day, placing us in twelfth place on the Scottish Team.

I was living in a dream. On reaching home I suddenly realised that I had achieved one of my main ambitions in life. I climbed with my devoted dog beside me, to the highest point of the Whitelaw, from where I could look down on to the loveliest view imaginable and, after a careful glance around to see that no one was about, shrieked 'Yippee!' at the top of my voice, startling a family of crows as the echo reverberated around the neighbouring hills. Garry looked up at me in astonishment as I collapsed laughing on top of him. He licked my nose, and I gave him a great big hug of gratitude.

The atmosphere and the excitement of my first opportunity to compete in an International will remain with me always. The venue was in undulating parkland surrounding a fairy-tale castle, home of His Grace, the Duke of Athol.

Garry ran in the Qualifying on the Thursday. True to

character, he never put a paw wrong. Unfortunately the sheep were poised for flight and far too light for a dog with his presence. Although I failed to get him through to the final day, the experience was well worth the effort and we didn't come away empty handed. Being the only lady competitor I received a large bottle of perfume from the French contingency, and my proudest possession today, a gold enamelled badge depicting the legendary Jock Richardson's famous Wiston Cap, given to each team member.

One Man and His Dog

The letter from the BBC arrived in April, 1982. It was an invitation from the producer, Ian Smith, to compete in the *One Man and His Dog* televised sheep dog trial held at Fairlie on the west coast of Scotland.

We were filmed at home on a tempestuous summer's day, I having been discovered by my visitors, furiously scrubbing the kitchen floor in my best clothes. During the 'shooting' I was caught in a torrential downpour until one of the crew was sent to rescue me. I was bundled unceremoniously into a vehicle already brimming over with people and equipment whilst poor Garry remained on the hillside guarding a flock of impatient Cheviots.

Presently the sunshine returned and a soggy Garry was rubbed dry with a couple of grubby handkerchiefs discovered in somebody's raincoat pocket. I dragged my fingers through my dishevelled hair and with the aid of a warm breeze repairs were soon complete. The filming was quickly accomplished, my favourite sequence being Garry retrieving a lame duck from the river, although soaking wet, he was so engrossed in the task that he forgot to shake himself until reaching home.

So here we were at the crack of dawn, on Monday, September 13th, heading in the direction of Fairlie; in the back of the car was our son Geoff, aged eight, sleeping soundly, using Garry as his pillow.

On arrival we were greeted by our friend Alastair Cutter who was running Midge in the competition, and Alastair's wife Sandra. Together we walked the course, which at first sight filled me with trepidation but, after exploring it, it began to grow on me and I felt excited by the challenge. The venue on this occasion was a rock-strewn slope with a deep ditch running across the centre. A shady forest flanked it to the right, giving shelter from the blustery wind, the most difficult aspect being a row of leafy trees and thorns which hid part of the course.

The day of the trial dawned, thankfully dry. After breakfast we made our way to the location where along with judges Mervyn Williams and Thomson McKnight, we were briefed by Eric Halsall on what to expect. The draw was made to see who would go first. Women's intuition told me it would be me, and I was right. And so, after lunch, I sallied forth, microphone tucked carefully out of sight. I waited as instructed at the edge of the course with Garry calmly gazing up at me, watching for his cue. At last it came in the form of a wave from the stage manager.

I sent Garry left handed, just in case the seven blackface sheep decided to bolt downhill. He ran out well against a breathtaking background of sparkling sea and the Islands of Cumbrae silhouetted against the mist shrouded peaks of Arran. He arrived quickly behind his sheep and they 'lifted' perfectly staying on 'line' until the Fetch Gates, where they bent off slightly before coming through.

Then down into the dip and over a narrow stream. Because I couldn't see them at this stage, I dare not encourage Garry in case he startled them. Anxiously, I awaited their reappearance, standing on tip-toe and sighing with relief as they came back into view. The Drive was to the left, down a steep incline. I was allowed to walk part of the way, halting on a large rock.

After this, the dog was on his own, driving his charges through a gap in the trees. Once I saw that Garry and his sheep were through, I was allowed to make my way back to the shedding ring. Suddenly, I froze in my tracks, as I witnessed the sheep calmly walking on the wrong side of a white marker post that was difficult to see because of the trees. I groaned inwardly. There was nothing I could do now other than try for a good finish. The last gates were safely negotiated, the red collared gimmer cleanly shed off and then to the pen where the sheep obligingly walked into the mouth but stood leaning heavily against the gate. I moved Garry fractionally and for a moment my heart was in my mouth as the last sheep attempted a dart for freedom. Quickly the dog barred her way, and the seven sheep walked into the pen.

I called Garry to me and waited for the signal that would tell us the cameras had ceased to roll.

The Scottish heat was won by John Templeton. Garry and

The *Blue Peter* studio

I were second and Alastair and Midge, a good third.

In the interview that followed Phil Drabble said 'You must feel very proud of your dog'. I wish I had told him that Garry sensed an important occasion and could always be relied on to do his best.

I have heard it said that dogs do not think. Most dogs have remarkable memories. I heard of one who recognised her master after an absence of several years. Surely, in order to remember, a dog must be able to think.

Among all living creatures there are the incredibly wise and the incredibly foolish. I placed Garry firmly in the former category. When sent to a distant hill to gather sheep spread over a wide area, he would run steadily around the perimeter, occasionally glancing inwards to establish where each 'cut' or family group were located so that if he should lose sight of them due to the irregularity of the terrain he would remember their whereabouts. If he did miss any he would leave the ones already in his charge above a plantation or in a deep hollow to prevent their escape whilst he retrieved the others.

The occasion I felt most proud of Garry's reasoning ability was when I was running him and his son, Laddie, in the Brace at the 1983 Scottish National at Bonchester. We had a good course, managing to get through all the hurdles. Foolishly, I penned first with Laddie, who was the more inexperienced of the two dogs. While we were busy with the penning Garry was dutifully watching over his charges who were grazing further up the field.

Penning proved difficult, due to an awkward sheep, but eventually the task was completed. In my haste, I foolishly left Laddie on guard too far inside the mouth of the pen. The moment I turned my back the sheep bolted either side of him to freedom. It was not unlike a cavalry charge as they made to run up the field and join up with Garry's. Speedily, the ever watchful dog summed up the situation and, without being commanded, he swung in front of his charges and drove them expertly in the opposite direction.

Unfortunately on that occasion we ran out of time but I was extremely proud of Garry regardless. Later that same day the President of the New Zealand Sheep Dog Association came to me, and said that he was amazed by Garry's reasoning ability. He was the only person, other than myself, to notice that Garry acted on his own initiative.

Garry definitely had the ability to fathom, reason and ... think. A favourite memory for me that will always hold pride of place happened when Gail Dapogny, an American friend, was staying with us. We were standing below the house admiring the view. I put Garry away to gather the Swindon hill, the summit of which was some two miles distant. When covering a large area he would often be seen crouching motionless, allowing the sheep to do the running. Eventually the whole hill was gathered together and Garry proceeded steadily, keeping a nice distance so that the sheep automatically moved before him, with only his strength of 'eye' holding them to him, as though attached by a piece of elastic! At the bottom of the hill there were two large fields to pass through. This meant Garry cross-driving his sheep several hundred yards and negotiating two gateways. The gate into the first field was standing open and the flock of five hundred Cheviot ewes passed through without any problems. The hurdle into the second field had been fastened with string. Garry patiently flanked back and forth trying to no avail to drive his charges through. Remembering another gap halfway up the fence in the opposite direction, I was tempted to whistle him into the corner.

However, before my fingers reached my mouth he swung in on his own initiative, determinedly driving the flock up the steep incline until the gap was reached. All of this small drama took place on the far side of Bowmont Water, at least half a mile away. I remember feeling very humble, an emotion experienced on many occasions since.

No words were spoken. Finally I glanced across at my companion and noticed that there were tears of admiration in her eyes.

I know that Garry also possessed a sense of humour. We were competing at Heighington in the north east of England. I was talking to friends while Garry rested his head on his paws, one eye closed, the other on me. Unexpectedly, a difficult Swale ewe ran off the course, refusing to rejoin her companions. She took a flying leap at the fence close to where Garry was relaxing, and hit the top strand of wire, falling over backwards, where she lay with all four feet pointing comically skywards. Garry never so much as stirred, instead, his eyes sought mine. I was some thirty yards from him. When he found me his tail slowly thumped the ground as he glanced alternately from the unfortunate sheep to where I was standing.

I was invited along with Garry, his son Laddie and some ducks to travel to London to appear on the childrens' TV programme *Blue Peter*. We set off by train at 5 am with three ducks safely incarcerated in a large yellow plastic box, tightly fastened with string. Shortly before we reached London, a city gent complete with briefcase and bowler, entered the carriage. He chatted politely for a few minutes, eyeing the box from which scratching noises could be heard. Finally curiosity got the better of him and he asked what was inside. I couldn't resist the temptation and replied that I was an erotic dancer and that the box contained a large python.

Conversation ceased and he hurriedly moved away. After one or two suspicious glances in our direction he got out his newspaper. When it came time for us to alight, he looked across and said in a rather puzzled tone, 'Don't you mean an exotic dancer?' I decided to tell him the truth, at which he roared with laughter, picked up the box and carried it along the platform for me. There was more fun to come. After I arrived at my destination one of the ducks laid an egg which, when the box was opened, rolled from one side of the studio to the other.

Garry worked beautifully on the set, whilst Laddie, affected by the heat from the lights and the slippery floor, was quite a handful.

After penning the ducks, Garry, much to the amusement of everyone, tried to round up the programme's pet tortoise as well.

Where sheep were concerned, Garry was a kind, gentle dog. When he was a youngster he never opened his mouth to one. Once he got a lambing under his belt and had been bumped by an irate ewe he began to square up his aggressors with a quick nip of retaliation after first of all clicking his teeth as a warning.

He never lost his love for trials competition, but he was a perfectionist and considered his time far too valuable to mess about with unmanageable sheep. When he saw me in my 'tidy clothes' he would sit waiting beside the garage door. He was always in the car first and would hold his paw high in welcome until the other dogs jumped on board.

In July 1989, along with his son Laddie, and my bitch Holly we were presented to Her Majesty the Queen and His Royal Highness the Duke of Edinburgh at Broughton, during their visit to Tweedale. Her Majesty, looking at Laddie and my bitch Holly, enquired if there was any difference between the rough coated and the smooth.

To my delight dear old Garry received a Royal pat on the head and from that day, was dubbed 'Sir Garry' by one and all.

The paternal Garry

7
The Mating Game

concerned.

Because most bitches become mothers, they tend to mature mentally at an earlier age than dogs. They are quicker to start work and are more devoted to their owners, although some dogs are also extremely faithful. I have found that males prefer female owners and vice versa.

For 'hard graft', I prefer a masculine or 'doggie type' of bitch to a feminine one. If you own a useful, well bred female you have a good chance to start your own breeding line. She should be registered with the International Sheep Dog Society and eye-tested by a qualified veterinarian.

When searching for a mate for your bitch it is advisable to look for one that has the working and physical attributes that she lacks. Personally I study pedigrees and observe a 'would-be-mate' on the trial field, in all kinds of conditions, working with all kinds of sheep. For me, consistency is what counts.

On average, a bitch comes into season every six months. There are, however, some that only 'come in' once a year and others, thankfully rare, that are in season every four months. Some appear never to be in season, or so slightly that they can go undetected.

Sometimes a change of environment is all that is needed to induce a bitch to come 'full on'. The older the bitch, usually the less fertile she becomes and the more likelihood of deformities in the offspring.

At the onset of heat the bitch becomes more friendly and usually she has recently cast her coat. Some bitches will take the dog at any time during their heat and produce puppies. Generally, a bitch's fertility is at its peak towards the latter part of her heat. Preferably, she should be mated more than once to be sure that she becomes pregnant.

Bitches vary as to the length of time their heat will last. Usually when the bitch will stand for the dog with her tail to one side she is ready to be mated. Often heat will go off a bitch when she has been successfully lined.

Mating isn't always as straightforward as it would seem. A nervous bitch that may be inclined to attack her would-be mate should be held. A friendly bitch should be allowed to run free but once mating is accomplished, should be held.

Bitches carry their puppies for approximately nine weeks. I have known them to pup a large litter earlier and a small litter, five days late - regarding the latter, I was beginning to chew my fingernails!

Male collies vary enormously in regard to sexual drive and prowess. Some exhaust themselves mentally, howling throughout the night, and vanish into thin air the moment you release them after merely the suspicion of a whiff of a bitch in heat in the area. If you have a hill to gather this type is next to useless. In my experience, the best of collies, just like the best of people, give their responsibilities priority. (Well, most of the time!).

Many a good sheep dog is ruined by allowing too many bitches to come to him. Mating in abundance is bound to be energy sapping and can definitely cause a dog to go 'off the boil', as far as giving a polished performance on a trial field is

During the pregnancy it is important that the bitch receives a balanced diet. Halfway through gestation she should be wormed. Spring time is the best time for puppies to be born. If the weather is cold an infra-red lamp should be installed in the place of whelping, at the correct height so as not to cause discomfort to the new mother and her offspring. Sometimes a 'first time mother' or an older bitch may have difficulty delivering a large puppy. Most shepherdesses are skilled in midwifery, but if in any doubt a veterinary surgeon should be consulted.

At the onset of labour a bitch will begin to scratch a nest. Preferably 'the nesting area', should be in a quiet, draught-free area known to the mother-to-be. As a base I use strong, clean sacking tacked to a wooden board. Puppies can become buried if straw is used.

It is important that the 'nest' be spacious enough for the bitch to turn round in but not so large that the puppy can crawl away from its mother's warmth and perish from the cold.

During whelping bitches need privacy. Constant disturbance and intervention by an anxious owner will only prolong the birth. I usually allow twelve hours without intervention and just an occasional peek.

After whelping I give the bitch a drop of warm milk before leaving her in peace. Water must be on offer but in a safe place in case the puppies fall into it and drown.

If the puppies are constantly whimpering and look empty consult a veterinarian regarding topping them up with a milk substitute. Thankfully I have never been faced with this problem.

It is wise to keep young children and the farm cats away from the new mother. I have seen normally docile bitches leap out of their kennels and attack a child, believing it a danger to their offspring.

A new mum's puppies should not be handled immediately after birth as I have known bitches to eat their puppies because of the scent of human hands.

Two-day-old puppies require the insides of their hind legs examined for dew claws. Should they have them they can easily be removed with the aid of a small pair of sharp scissors and a helper. Dew claws can be a hazard later as they can tear in heather or bracken when the dog is gathering sheep.

Most puppies begin to open their eyes at around the twelfth day. They should be wormed for round worms at three and five weeks of age and again at twelve and fourteen weeks. Bought in puppies suspected of being 'worm ridden' must be relieved of them very gradually, using a small dosage of worm killer otherwise internal blockage can result.

At around two weeks of age puppies can be introduced to a little warm milk by gently dipping their noses and forepaws into it. From milk they will quickly progress to mince and gravy and/or puppy meal given in three feeds per day. By six weeks of age they can be weaned off the bitch gradually, and ready to go to their new homes by eight weeks.

Always tell the prospective owner what the puppy has been fed on, that it has been wormed and that it will require vaccination

Fetch my slippers!

against disease.

Any puppy in the litter failing to react to noise or refusing to awaken when you clap your hands is probably deaf. This is a genetic problem that occurs in mainly white coloured puppies.

It is important to provide ample feeding dishes, well spaced, and to supervise puppies at meal times, otherwise a timid puppy may get into the habit of not eating. A small amount of bullying must be allowed in order that the weaker members of the litter be goaded to retaliate and in so doing become stronger members of the pack.

Unfortunately, there is truth in the saying 'Dog eat dog'. For that reason mature dogs should be fed on their own, and the more submissive types in total privacy.

In play, puppies cultivate many of the balanced movements that they require to work sheep efficiently when they become adults. They benefit greatly from being exercised on rough hill ground to ensure that they become well co-ordinated and sure-footed.

A number of years ago I acquired a stud service pup (a puppy in lieu of a stud fee) who at the age of four months had never been outside his kennel. There was an incredible difference between him and my home bred eight-week old puppies when we went out walking. The newcomer had to be lifted over clumps of heather and large rocks and on one occasion I had to rescue him out of the burn where he had taken a flying leap. At the time I found the incident amusing - on reflection I find it rather sad.

When puppies are allowed freedom from an early age (providing they are inoculated) it saves an awful lot of time later on. However, a large puppy is never quite as nifty on its feet as its smaller contemporaries and it takes longer to pull itself together.

The human voice plays a very important role in the early part of a puppy's life. The tone of the voice is associated with praise and punishment, the latter never exceeding a mild shake, which is reserved for extreme naughtiness e.g. poultry worrying, chasing puss and chewing valuables.

Origin

We are given to understand that the domestic dog can be divided into four main groups, each of these descended from individual wolf ancestry. Over the centuries, these groups have been interbred with the idea of improving existing strains or, in some cases, have come about by accident. Those of us with a keen eye will be able to attribute the various present day breeds back to their origin.

People of a stone-age culture are thought to have been the first to domesticate wolves. At a much later period both Vikings and Romans brought their guarding, herding dogs with them when they invaded Britain.

Bearded and shaggy-coated dogs are said to be of mixed ancestry, derived from mastiff and other northern types, developed in the Russian Steppes by shepherds. The narrower skull of our present day collie is attributed by some to an infusion of sight hound blood.

'Faithful, constant, resolute, steadfast and true'. All these qualities pertain to loyalty, the mastiff's celebrated virtue. If coupled with sensitivity and determination, I value loyalty above most other sheep dog traits.

I believe a sensitive collie to be more receptive. However, too large a dosage of sensitivity is undesirable, as is an animal considered by its owner to be 'too clever'. The latter is frequently guilty of anticipating commands even before they are given. This can prove annoying, especially on a trial course where obstacles must be negotiated.

Training a sheep dog can be compared with driving a high powered car. One must know instinctively when to accelerate and when to apply the brakes. The misguided believe that the finely tuned trial dog is merely a step away from the 'green young pup' at home in the kennel. There are phases, almost too numerous for me to divulge, in between - and no short cuts.

Above all virtues, my collies have taught me patience, for without it no progress is made and most important, the trainer must be prepared to adapt to the individuality of each dog, being, in the immortal words of James Gardner (a well-revered 19th Century sheep dog trainer) 'Careful not to blunt the genius of the pupil by over direction'.

At all costs, emotions must be held in check; any hint of irritation must be banished from the voice and replaced with encouragement. Young dogs should always be asked rather than told. After a period of months, should all else fail, displeasure can be communicated by voice tone and body movement.

Young collies readily respond to sound before they understand the spoken word. An immediate reaction can be expected if the dog has been addressed and handled in a quiet manner from puppyhood.

Puppies must be spoken to constantly, using a persuasive, reassuring tone. They should not be chastised for grabbing wool when they are trying to prevent sheep from escaping. An adult dog that refuses to catch a sheep and hold it is next to useless to a hill shepherd at lambing time.

The importance of working a youngster close at hand over a period of many months cannot be over-emphasised. Developing the correct habits ensures that the dog will eventu-

Holly and her puppies

ally work in the same manner at a distance.

I have come to believe that the most beneficial relationships develop between humans and dogs of a similar disposition. It is more probable that a boisterous dog will reach its full potential in the hands of an extrovert. Among working breeds it is those with co-operative natures that are of most benefit, a willing disposition being a much valued attribute.

We must never underestimate the perception of our forebears, to whom necessity was very much the mother of invention. I feel great admiration for their intuitive examples which are still valid today. For example, the Border collie is a result of countless generations of careful breeding; method, initiative, loyalty, even coat texture, (the short-haired variety are better for hill work as they do not ice up in wintertime) and colouring - (the black moves sheep and the white pacifies), were carefully evolved in this herding athlete.

The past centuries have produced a wide variety of herding dogs, bred to suit the conditions in which they were required to work.

The shepherd's mastiff was originally bred to ward off dangerous predators – both animal and human - and at a later date to guard precious kale-yards. A 'heavy, steady type' was used in-bye for folding flocks on root crops, while agile, lighter-framed beasts, with a natural cast, were preferred in hilly and mountainous regions to gather 'The wild Forrest sheep': the latter possibly carrying the blood of noblemen's soft-mouthed setters and black pointers' blood in their veins. The black pointer with its dash of greyhound to make it 'less slow and ponderous' was extremely popular in the 17th and 18th centuries.

North of the Scottish/English border, the collie has long been dubbed 'The shepherd's right arm'. 'Collie' means 'useful' in the common Gaelic known as Q Celtic. In the Situations Vacant column of *The Scottish Farmer* magazine the phrase 'must have a useful dog', is still in evidence.

CHOICE & REARING OF PUPPIES

Puppies treated with firmness, patience and kindness, grow into adulthood with an inbuilt confidence, whereas those who are rarely spoken to, handled or taken for walks, are often reluctant to leave their handler's side when training commences, because they lack the necessary confidence to do so.

Dog puppies are sometimes slower to mature than bitch

puppies, however they are more consistent when they become adults. Coming into season and producing puppies can play havoc with a bitch's temperament.

Especially, I would advocate bitches for beginners. Adult males can be quarrelsome towards one another and rather chauvinistic if they find you lacking!

Two puppies are as easy to rear as one - dogs are a pack animal and so it is therefore unnatural for a puppy to grow up alone. Like children, they need to play, quarrel and generally let off steam, in order to develop into well-balanced adults.

When purchasing puppies it is advisable to choose a dog and a bitch from un-related litters, my preference being a smooth-coated bitch and a rough-coated dog, because I have always had the best results from mating these two types. If they turn out to be exceptional workers with intelligence and quality you can begin your own breeding line.

I prefer puppies from hill parents that can work at a distance without constantly being told what to do. I would purchase from a shepherd or farmer who has had the same line or family of dogs for a number of years. Obviously, he has found them to be sound and capable.

Dogs with determination and sensitivity are usually strong with sheep yet easy to handle. Make sure that the puppies are eligible for registration with the International Sheep Dog Society and their parents are clear of Progressive Retinal Atrophy and collie eye.

Choose puppies that are well fed, clean and nicely marked. Very white puppies should be avoided as sheep tend to challenge them in a working situation.

Personally, I would not choose an excitable, grossly over-friendly puppy. If living in the wild it would welcome a predator and probably not survive for very long. I prefer a calm-natured puppy that weighs up situations.

These days, because I usually breed my own puppies and spend time with them, I tend to allow puppies to choose me! As a result I end up with 'characters' who are constantly under-foot and usually have a cheeky expression.

As well as checking a puppy's hind legs for dew claws, check the mouth is correct and that it is not under shot. The top and bottom teeth should meet. Many are fractionally short in the lower jaw - if it is only a fraction I would not worry unduly. Black pigment on lips and nose looks better than pink and is said to be a sign of good breeding (possibly originating from the nobleman's black pointers!). Piebald noses often turn darker, pink lips do not. Some shepherds swear by a black roof to the mouth. I have been unable to substantiate this but prefer black to pink.

Plenty of space between the ears is often a sign of intelligence. A large bump of knowledge towards the back of the skull, not noticeable in a small puppy, is often found on the head of a brainy dog.

A tail reaching to the hocks is preferable as too much can go wrong with an excessively long one. I would not keep a puppy with a wall eye(s) (blue eye) caused by a lack of pigment. Often a dog will close the offending eye(s) in bright sunlight.

If possible, puppies should be purchased in the spring or early summer in order that they get some sun on their backs before the onset of winter.

When collecting puppies they feel more secure packed with straw in a dark well-ventilated box than rattling about in the back of a car. Always enquire about their diet as a puppy's stomach is easily upset. They travel much better on an empty stomach, and on arrival should be given a drop of warm milk and clean water until their digestion settles.

The puppy or puppies' bed should be inside a small shed. It should be warm, dry, free from draughts with plenty of light, preferably from a window high up or in the roof. Puppies develop the habit of barking when they can see movement outside. When contained in the recommended manner they look forward to seeing you and wish to please. There must be no chinks or cracks in the kennel door as, believe it or not, puppies can and do develop a squint.

Young dogs chained to a kennel, constantly leaning to see what is going on can develop a bent foreleg or legs. All of these must be taken into consideration for the rearing of perfect physical specimens. How to produce specimens as psychologically perfect as their genetics will allow, comes later!

Puppies should be quarantined until your veterinary surgeon can inject them against Parvo virus, Distemper, Leptospirosis, viral Hepatitis and kennel cough. This is normally given at three months of age in two separate injections with a fortnight's interval.

It is important that puppies are kept free from lice, mites and ticks, all of which can cause discomfort and anaemia. The kennels and the puppies should be regularly dusted with louse powder, with careful attention given to the base of the ears.

Mites take refuge in dogs, ears and cause infection. Gentle scratching of the ears and shaking of the head warrants examination.

Puppies are prone to stomach upsets. Attacks of diarrhoea can be caused by enteritis, parvo virus, a change of diet and/or worms. Never hesitate in seeking advice from your vet. To delay allows the puppy to dehydrate which can be fatal.

So...you have your pup(s)! They have been named with short traditional names that carry to them on a windy day, they are clear of vermin, wormed, and injected against disease. They are warmly housed, lively and hopefully raring to go!

Regarding their food, puppies should be fed a balanced diet - as much as they will clean up, at least twice a day. My dogs each have their own dish. Clean water is also available and a half a pint of milk is fed until the puppies go on to one meal a day (fed last thing) when they are six months old.

At three to four months of age the puppies are taken out for exercise morning and evening, accompanied by the older dogs, who invariably bring them down to size and save me teaching them manners.

During these excursions I watch the puppies closely, studying their temperaments and characters. I also teach them their names and to come quickly when they hear a soft repetitive whistle. I accomplish this by calling and/or whistling whilst moving away from them. This encourages them to come quickly. I like them to return speedily and lavish them with praise when they comply. The reason being that much later when I teach them to 'shed' (cut individual sheep from the flock) they need to respond immediately or they may lose the required sheep. If the puppies show a reluctance to return, I hide from them. Deliberately losing them usually causes enough panic to do the trick.

Very occasionally on these walks, I give the adult dogs a 'stop whistle' of one short note. The attending youngsters seeing their elders 'freeze', invariably follow suit. This is termed 'Backing' by the gundog fraternity. It is a natural reaction inherited from wild ancestors so as not to disturb prey.

The majority of youngsters go through an annoying phase of not wanting to go into their kennels. Like human children they believe bedtime to be a bore. If you walk on past the kennel most puppies will come to you if you speak kindly to them and go down on your knees to a less threatening height.

When they become wise to this ruse, slip a string on your pup(s) at a different location before you reach home. Never chase a puppy or scold him as you will frighten him and cause problems later on. Should this kind of naughtiness re-emerge when the pup is over a year old, put him on a chain and insist that he goes in and out of his kennel several times with you giving the appropriate command. The same lesson applies if he refuses to get inside a vehicle. Always give plenty of praise when he complies.

Never leave puppies, or adult dogs, tied to a fence. It takes a very short duration for any animal to strangle. Dogs can easily become entangled with one another. They may leap a fence and be left hanging on the other side. I speak from experience.

When I first began shepherding I owned a young dog named Fleet. When not working Fleet was kept on a long chain inside a building. Behind him, high up in the wall was a small window with a narrow ledge. The window had been boarded up for a number of years to prevent draughts and had been forgotten. Young Fleet was a beautiful bare skinned, prick eared dog for whom I cared deeply. One day I set off with an older dog to gather some sheep. Fleet, disappointed at being left behind, somehow managed to leap up on to the narrow ledge where he removed one of the boards, and in trying to jump down the other side hung himself. Poor Fleet died not through lack of care but because of my lack of thought.

The Importance of not 'Spoiling' a Pup

It is well to remember right at the start that a working sheep dog puppy is neither a baby, a toy or a status symbol. It is a dignified animal evolved with care over a long period of time by working shepherds.

Very young puppies need gentle and careful handling so that human hands hold no fear for them.

Because I run a sheep dog visitor centre my puppies are handled and spoken to by the public from a very early age. It gives them confidence, especially when we compete in sheep dog trials - but it doesn't help me win more!

As I have mentioned previously, collies were never bred for their temperaments. Living miles from anywhere it wasn't necessary. Sensitive dogs were found to be more receptive. Unfortunately this type tend to bite people because of fear rather than through aggression.

The most sensitive of the breed tend to be the most intelligent. The disadvantage here is that when taken to trials, they are afraid of the public and their surroundings. Years ago, my two cleverest collies avoided running into the shadows of trees when first taken away from home.

I am often asked whether a sheep dog can be a house dog and a trial dog at the same time. This is where one must judge the individual - once they are 'fully fledged'. When they are trained and you have sussed out their characters there will be some that you can pet and some that you can't.

Dogs are like children. If you spoil a child for no reason the child will become resentful when asked to do something it doesn't wish to do. If you are constantly petting a working dog – and it's the humans who require this constant reassurance that goes with touch – how is a dog going to know when it has done well?

It is better to praise and caress with your voice and save a 'clap' along the ribs for those special occasions. I have known great dogs that merely tolerated patting. They were being condescending to their masters and not the other way round.

Jim Wilson of Mayshiel, one of Scotland's top sheep dog trainers and handlers – and a gentleman to boot (I know that he would want it written in that order) once made the announcement, 'If things is right ye dinna need ter clap (pat) yer dug'.

When Jim uttered this statement, taking it literally I thought him to be a hard man. Many years on I realise EXACTLY what he was trying to get over.

Puppy Points

Always take your crook with you when walking your pup(s). This essential part of shepherding equipment must never be regarded by them as a threat, rather as an extension of yourself, designed to assist you walk uphill, catch and pen sheep and most important to lean on when you talk to friends!

In your puppies' company, endeavour to move calmly and deliberately. Hopefully, then your puppies will react likewise.

Never throw objects for your pups to retrieve or allow them to work ducks or poultry for long periods. This behaviour will become obsessive, and is to be avoided. When entering an area where there are sheep, always give them a wide berth, encouraging your pups by your movements to 'hug the

dyke back'.

Exaggerated movements on your part are necessary as your movements are body language to an intuitive puppy.

The working instinct is the hunting instinct with the killer instinct greatly modified. Because eventually you will take the pups to hunt sheep, they will come to accept you as pack leader. A canine pack leader conveys when and where to hunt by sound intonation and body movement.

Right from the start it is important that you have the correct attitude. There are pack leaders who rule with a dominant attitude and there are pack leaders who rule by example. My bitch Holly is pack leader to eight dogs. She is intelligent, patient, firm and extremely gentle.

The dominant trainer will end up with a mechanical dog that does everything it is told when it is told. On a hill, this type of animal is next to useless.

Initiative must be developed to the extreme in a young dog, so that hopefully one day it will be capable of working two miles out on a hill, in mist or blizzard for hours on end without commands, and never be afraid to contradict the handler. After all, it is bred to do the job. You are not!

As soon as a rapport develops between you and your pup(s) you must map out the grounding and preparation firmly in your mind. Above all, your puppy will teach you patience and self control. You will also learn to adapt to the individual to obtain the best results. Without this attitude, little will be achieved.

Finally, it is important not to force human values on to your pup(s). It is better to become one of them rather than the other way around. They must be encouraged first and foremost to be dogs. When out for exercise, ninety per cent of the time they should be ignored.

This is their 'prime time'. The pup(s) attention should be on their surroundings and what's up ahead - NOT on you! When I used to 'look the hill' with my dogs Garry and Laddie, I hardly laid eyes on them. They would be ranging ahead, looking the hill on my behalf, flushing out sheep with problems and delving into hollows where ewes might be 'coupit' (on their backs).

One very misty morning Garry amazed me by gently shepherding a blind ewe in my direction from a different 'heft' (part of the hill).

8
First Introduction to Sheep

When I am out for a walk with a puppy I like it occasionally to look me straight in the eye, questioning me as to what we are about to do next. You can see everything going through a dog's mind by studying its expressions.

I take my puppies to sheep for the first time when they are around four months old. We are accompanied by an older, experienced dog who acts purely as a nanny, ensuring the puppy is never hurt or frightened by the sheep. The nanny is also used to keep the sheep away from fences and out of corners - difficult tasks for a youngster to accomplish on its own. (Should an experienced dog be unavailable the puppy must be carried or led along in those situations).

Later, if the puppy fails to head its 'charges' naturally, the nanny may be used to drive them off in the opposite direction, thus encouraging the puppy's instinct to head to be aroused.

Over the next few months the puppy is taken at least once every couple of weeks to visit the sheep in a securely fenced area. On arrival the first few minutes are usually spent 'having fun', which allows both puppy and sheep to rid themselves of their exuberance.

When the puppy initially sees sheep – which, incidentally, should number at least a dozen to twenty well-behaved, easily-dogged matrons – the following reactions are perfectly normal and acceptable.

● The puppy chases the sheep and splits them.
● The puppy barks and attempts to run home.
● The puppy gets between you and the sheep and sets in to drive them in the opposite direction.
● The puppy, showing great 'eye and style' runs round the sheep and brings them to you – a rarity!
● The puppy makes a dive at the nearest ewe and disappears over the horizon hanging on to its underwear with great tenacity.

The latter behaviour at this early age should not be taken too seriously. It is usually caused by over excitement and the puppy's need to prevent the sheep's escape. After a while, being dragged at speed over rough ground doesn't have the same appeal. The compulsive 'gripper' who accompanies the deed with growls while endeavouring to shake his poor victim like a terrier with a rat, is better kept away from the sheep until old enough to stand a reprimand.

It is imperative that the pup be allowed to 'do its own thing'. I usually sit back and smile at its antics. Interference at this stage will cramp its style – particularly if the pup is of a sensitive nature. It is important to ensure that this type does not get hurt or frightened by the sheep or it may not attempt to work again. Once a pup has got over its excitement you will begin to see something of its true character emerge, accompanied by some stylish little moves.

As the puppy grows older, working regularly with free moving sheep on rough, undulating ground encourages it to give the sheep room so as to be in better control and to cast naturally on the outrun. Rarely during these excursions do I interfere with the puppy's method of working, choosing to

allow the ground and the sheep to teach it the rudiments. A puppy, naturally, is often reluctant to leave sheep when it is time to go home! If you have two puppies, it is advisable after the initial visit, to take only one. Like children, one is much easier to manage.

When a pup refuses to leave the sheep, arrange for them to run into a corner of the field. Place yourself between the pup and the sheep and encourage the pup to come to you (on bended knee if necessary). If it complies, praise it lavishly and release it, otherwise it will make sure that you don't catch it next time. Repeat the exercise three or four times praising the youngster each time it comes to you. Alternatively, should you be unable to catch the puppy, attach it to a light cord or clothes line - still allowing its return to the sheep - but making

Introduction to sheep

it much easier to get hold of.

When finally removing the puppy tell it: 'That'll do'.

You could say that at the start I train pups by not training them – apart from teaching them their names and encouraging them to come quickly on hearing a soft repetitive whistle. Getting the pup to return to you at speed will be useful when it's older and you want it to dash in and stop a galloping ewe when shedding (cutting out individual sheep from the flock).

Later on, the 'come here' whistle will have many uses. For instance it can be used when cross driving sheep to get a young dog to come quickly in your direction (before he knows his left and right commands). It can also be useful to pull a dog inclined to flank too tightly, off the corners of the flock when driving sheep away from you, and on the fetch when sheep are running helter-skelter it can be used to encourage the dog tightly down the side of the flock and in front, should it be the only means to prevent their escape.

The pup must only be trained with the sheep. Training away from them and disciplining a puppy at an early age will only cause confusion resulting in resentment, souring what would otherwise have been a partnership. Teaching a puppy its commands while it is working sheep at around a year old - when it can see the reason as well as the results - keeps the relationship sweet, ensuring that the commands are learnt in half the time.

Occasionally, you will come across a pup that is a natural from the word go. When working, it makes all the right moves as well as being highly intuitive and in tune with you. This type is considered a great responsibility by the seasoned trainer who is anxious not to spoil their protégé.

By giving a youngster freedom to develop at its own pace, by the time it reaches one year old, you can see in which areas it needs assistance and in which it shines. It is foolish to expect any young dog to behave consistently. We all experience 'off-days'. Dogs are no exception. Their 'off-days' are best spent in seclusion. After a couple of days away from work you will be pleasantly surprised how refreshed and anxious to please the pupil has become.

Once a dog is old enough for serious training it is vital that it enjoys its lessons. These must not be prolonged to the extent that it grows tired and bored by them. Working in different areas on different types of sheep helps stimulate a young dog. When the dog is several months old, once it has accepted me as pack leader and is heading the sheep and holding them to me, I take a few sheep 'walkabout'.

The dog comes to accept its handler as pack leader because he or she takes the dog to hunt the sheep. The working instinct is, after

all, the hunting instinct exaggerated through breeding, with, in the case of the collie, the killing instinct carefully modified. I have found, when breeding Border collies, the best results are achieved by continually crossing the rough and smooth coated varieties. The long coated dog tends to be steadier. Possibly it inherits the gentle disposition and soft mouth of setters. Continually mating smooth coated dogs because of greyhound ancestry which possibly came into the breed via the nobleman's black pointers, produces a dog that is more inclined to grip. Often, because they are built for speed, they tend to act before they think - however, when it comes to wider outruns and shedding, on average they are much better than their longer haired brothers.

Once the pup and I are on a 'walkabout' I deliberately encounter all of the hazards it is likely to meet as an adult, obstacles such as rough hill ground, forestry, streams and gateways. When we first go 'walkabout' I say little or nothing to inhibit the puppy. I allow it to counteract every movement that the sheep make in a natural fashion as well as encouraging it to develop initiative and confidence in its own abilities - after all, it may be required one day to work out of sight, without commands, in all kinds of conditions.

On some occasions the young dog may appear disinterested in the sheep. If this occurs it is advisable to give it a break

Long and the short of it

for a few days. When resuming work the company of another dog will often guarantee that keenness returns.

Always make allowances for youth and inexperience - Rome wasn't built in a day – but we do know it was built! More serious faults are better corrected gradually. Generally, if the handler is in the correct place in regard to the sheep, the right movement will be achieved from the dog. Dogs are creatures of habit. It is up to the trainer to form acceptable habits while at the same time realising that there are occasions when the dog must be allowed to make mistakes in order to recognise that there is a right and wrong way of doing things - the correct way being easier for the dog.

If the handler plays on a fault, endeavouring to cure it by repetitive practice the fault will be ingrained even further. It must be remembered that, when nothing is going to plan, 'what is easy to achieve, is of little value'.

Should, by chance, you and your puppy have a major misunderstanding, leading to the pupil being taken home and banished to bed do remember to make your peace before darkness sets in. Facing a long lonely night is a daunting prospect to a young dog in disgrace.

If you are considerate, quiet and consistent on all occasions, a bond of trust will develop that will only be broken by your being constantly unreasonable.

On sighting cattle, some pups will go haring after them, barking their heads off. Do be on the watch - it is so easy for a limb to be broken or an eye put out. Sometimes contact with cattle is unavoidable. If it does happen, try speaking quietly. Coax the pup away. Roaring and shouting can encourage a dog to attack. The same remedy applies when dog fights occur.

Regarding collies, I have found nine times out of ten, if you do the opposite to your inclination, you will be right! Quiet handling of dogs or any kind of animal is nearly always more effective. The trained dog will learn to crane its ears to hear quietly spoken commands. It is important to practically whisper to dogs so that when it is necessary to scold them the raised voice will come as a shock and probably be the only punishment that they require. When handlers continually raise their voices their commands eventually fall on deaf ears. A strong, impetuous dog especially needs quiet handling. If 'killed with work' in rough steep ground, it will be glad to stop when asked

to do so.

A compulsive 'gripper' should be given every chance to change his ways by first of all using a non-drastic method – however, being an inherent trait, this can be difficult and the culprit may be better working cattle.

Usually you can see when a dog is going to get hold. I growl at the dog and chase it back just before the misdemeanour. Alternatively, you can attach a light rope to the collar. Take the rope down the centre of the dog's back, under its belly and through above the hips so that it tightens in front of the hind legs when the dog pulls i.e. when surging forward to grip a sheep. This 'rope trick' can also be used on older dogs that flatly refuse to stop when asked.

Some misinformed people believe that it is a bold dog that likes to bite livestock, whereas gripping is usually a sign of cowardice, which occurs because the dog is afraid. Never be too hard on a puppy for pulling wool or you could end up with a dog that refuses to catch a sheep for you at lambing time. Mild gripping has its place, for instance, when an awkward sheep faces up to a dog. I would prefer a dog that resorts to gripping after it has tried all other means.

Like humans, dogs vary enormously in their make-up. That difference must be taken into consideration and allowances made accordingly. Sensitive, easily handled collies must be given free rein in order to build confidence.

Training this type must advance much more slowly and help should be given in difficult situations. Training when too immature will make a 'soft' dog less inclined to use initiative. The less initiative a dog shows, the longer it must be allowed to do as it pleases. Ideally it should be taken to work and be allowed to run with an older experienced dog that is afraid of nothing. In the case of the 'easy' dog, let 'least said soonest mended' be the rule. To a certain extent this also applies to the determined or 'hard' dog. Exercise too rigid discipline with this type and it will become neurotic and have the equivalent of a nervous breakdown. It is important that it be allowed to learn by its mistakes and gain confidence in its own ability.

With certain dogs there are a hundred little steps in between every big step – with others there are a thousand. I look on a dog's mistakes as an opportunity to show it how the job should be done and, in doing so, win its co-operation.

9

Sheep Dog Trainers, Makers or Breakers?

There are trainers who 'make' dogs and those, sadly in the majority, who break dogs in a military fashion, never giving a thought to their feelings or individuality; either because the handler is impatient for results, or because he or she lacks imagination.

Sensitive, artistic people recognise that there is an art in training and handling a sheep dog. Because they wish to make or create something beautiful they can sometimes lose all sense of reality, amusing spectators by unintentionally performing a kind of primitive ballet with whistling as an accompaniment. In their minds these imaginative shepherds are in some far off magic land with only the hill, the sheep and a dog that is creating poetry in motion before their very eyes.

The category into which one comes depends largely on individual make-up and upbringing.

'Making a dog' is a lengthy process which can take up to four years or, as a respected Scottish handler put it, 'A dog is at its best when it has a year's experience under each leg'. Trainers must be prepared to create circumstances where a dog can do what is required in a natural happy fashion. More effort is needed but the end result makes it all worthwhile. Instead of owning a slave you will be the friend and partner of a calm and capable sheep dog.

There are those who would argue that today's Border collie is better than it has ever been. It is certainly more suited to present day conditions. With the days of the drover fast receding into the mists of time, his dog has been replaced by motorised transport while the shepherd is being partially substituted by portable pens and men who excel mainly as motor bike jockeys.

As the trial field increasingly becomes the shop window of the world, in my opinion, initiative is being replaced by subservience. I believe that work must come first, with trial qualities looked on as a bonus.

The Plain Worker

Today's average trialling conditions – which consist of wild sheep, worked over a flat, medium-sized course have resulted in a 'plain' dog being favoured by many sheep dog handlers. Obviously the less 'eye' a dog possesses, the easier it will be to flank about. Plainness in itself can be acceptable if partnered by brains and quiet power. A dog with a plain method, if well handled, can look classy. Badly handled, it is boring to watch. The less this type of dog sees sheep, and the fewer sheep it sees, the more 'eye' it will gather.

A plain dog sometimes alters with age - by the time it comes to its best, at around four to five years old, it will probably have developed the required amount of 'eye' to look good. Very plain dogs tend to have a high head carriage. This represents a 'stalemate' when working awkward or heavy sheep. A dog that works with a low head carriage does not represent a challenge by meeting the sheep's gaze, because its eye level is often below the sheep's brisket.

A 'plain' dog lacking in power, is not a good combination.

Unfortunately there are a number of dogs being bred of this type, from easily handled, wide running trial dogs.

The 'plain' dog that lacks power can win and be placed in trials but, under rigorous conditions – e.g. on a large hill course, in bad weather or with heavy awkward sheep, both dog and handler will have a difficult time beating the clock.

The Weak Dog

Working a weak dog gives you plenty of opportunity to eavesdrop on your critics. They will not show you any sympathy. When competing, it is necessary to over-command a weak dog, to keep things moving. At home, the dog will benefit from working alongside other dogs to give it confidence and should, when possible, be given few or no commands in order to develop its initiative.

It is pot luck regarding how much 'eye' a dog will possess as it matures. A dog with a very strong 'eye' that lies staring at sheep as though mesmerised by them will benefit from a nudge with your toe should it repeatedly ignore your command to 'Walk up'. A dog over-endowed with 'eye' should improve and 'free up' if worked regularly in the sheep pens and flanked around large numbers of sheep. A shortage of work will ensure that it gathers more 'eye' and becomes even stickier to move.

A particularly pushy, determined dog is best kept away from the sheep for a couple of days prior to a trial. The 'eye' it will gather due to this enforced rest should steady it up sufficiently for you to get a controlled 'lift' which hopefully will help to keep things settled throughout the rest of the run. The advantage of running a powerful dog is that you are so busy keeping on top of it that you tend to forget any nervousness you may feel.

Feeding a dog quantities of meat will affect its temperament and attitude, in that it develops more 'oomph' and can become excitable and even ill-tempered due to the high protein intake. This will not occur as long as the dog is given plenty of work.

Due to its above average intelligence a Border collie unlike some herding breeds can be taught every aspect of herding e.g. gathering, flanking, driving and singling out individual sheep. Most collies are gifted in one or more of these skills and need to be taught the others. The reason for this being that, in the wild, when out on a hunt for food, each animal would carry out the task to which it was most suited. Few 'predators' have the stamina necessary to accomplish driving, flanking, singling

and 'the kill', except in a cool climate and/or where food is plentiful and the pursuers are in excellent physical condition.

Occasionally a dog will not even give sheep a thought until it is two years old. Thankfully these dogs are in the minority and strangely, due to a magical transformation that literally takes place overnight, they often become the best dog the person has ever owned.

By the age of twelve months a young dog should respect and know its owner fairly well. When called or whistled it should respond quickly. It should have a good idea what 'stand' means and should leave sheep willingly when asked to do so. The one-in-a-million ideal dog, possesses a willing nature, a natural, pear-shaped outrun, natural balance (more about that later), will flank freely off either hand, does not over-flank will walk right up to a sheep's face without any sign of fear, is good-tempered and not inclined to grip unless greatly provoked and last but not least, works with a tight, perfectly set-on tail. 'If the tail's right the head's right,' means that an erratic tail denotes an erratic brain!

Should one dog of this calibre cross your path during your lifetime count yourself extremely fortunate and do everything in your power to be worthy of such a generous gift.

The average dog either lacks power or has too much. The ideal is a quiet power – sometimes called 'method'. Unfortunately this is a rare quality. It is important not to confuse weakness, which is a genuine fear of sheep, with 'too much eye'. In time, with plenty of work and encouragement 'too much eye', will leave a dog. A very weak dog is afraid to look sheep in the face and is always ready to move them with its teeth. Weakness comes in varying degrees. Allowing a weak dog to grip will boost its confidence, but it is a cruel method to resort to. This type of dog is better working cattle.

When a dog with power, presence, or determination appears on the scene, sheep automatically move away from it. Power is immediately obvious, but like weakness, there are varying degrees of it in different dogs.

Quiet power is recognised as an authority over sheep that does not frighten or upset them.

Choice of commands when working your dog(s)

Before serious training commences you will need to decide on a different set of commands – both words and whistles, for

Sheepdog trainers – makers or breakers?

each dog. The equivalent whistled commands must be as different as possible and also different for each dog, so that working together they will not become confused. Once chosen, the commands must be adhered to. When you have your dogs fully trained it will be possible to hold conversations with them, using whistled instructions that vary in tone, speed and length, when they are at a distance, either out on the hill or in fields.

When working a dog at hand, remember to use quietly spoken words. Sheep emit a shrill whistle down their noses as a warning. At a trial, handlers who whistle when turning sheep around the post, and at the pen and shed can cause fear in the sheep making these tasks more difficult to accomplish correctly.

FLANKING commands: Dog number one: For his or her left I say 'Bye'. For his or her right I say 'Out'. Dog number two: For his or her left I say 'Come' and for right I say 'Way'.

Both of my 'Brace' dogs are on the same stop whistle. However, a shrill blast means 'I would like you to stop immediately!' and a softer whistle simply means, 'Go into first gear'.

When teaching 'Look back for more sheep' it is better to have a different whistle for each dog or you can end up with a rapidly dispersing flock and no dogs to hold them. Both dogs can be asked to 'Walk up', but each dog should be given a different whistle command for this procedure.

Working Two Dogs together – The Brace

There is nothing to equal the beauty of two mature collies working in close harmony, either within the confines of a trial field or preferably on a distant bracken-strewn hillside. Both they and their charges appear to flow effortlessly along as though on an incoming tide, one dog counteracting the gentle pressure of the other, until at last the tumbling, cascading mass arrives at your feet, eyes questioning, ears twitching and nostrils quivering.

After a couple of lambings it is a simple task to acquire the habit of using two sets of commands.

Established handlers of single dogs warned me that running brace is the quickest and surest way to ruin a dog. Of course it depends on the dog – but there is no doubt that some faults do occur.

I faced several problems, the first being that instead of allowing the dogs to reach the twelve o'clock position when sent to gather the sheep, it was necessary to stop each one frac-

tionally short, and in so doing, develop the points deductible habit of 'stopping short', when running singly. In defence, the majority of brace handlers say that they encouraged their dogs to cross once they got behind the sheep. Other reasons against, varied from making the dogs sour, because it was necessary to over command them, to removing most of their initiative, so that they became mechanical in their method of working. I certainly worry about the effect brace running has on my dogs but unfortunately I need to do it for my living.

I believe that dogs from the same pack or family work more happily together. A bonus was that my determined dog became easier to handle due to his partner pushing sheep on to him. During the winter when my dogs are rested from demonstration work I tend regularly to send them both off the same hand so that they race each other to the twelve o'clock position.

At home I do not insist that the dogs keep to their 'sides' as is expected in competition. By allowing them to keep crossing each other's paths, they avoid becoming one-sided, or lacking in initiative. The worst fault that has developed is that my dogs have become 'clappy' – they keep stopping and lying down when once they 'flowed' and kept on their feet.

By the time a young dog is a year old, providing that it has been bred and reared correctly, all manner of 'nice moves' have been developed.

At this stage, when taking a few sheep 'walkabout', it is relatively easy to create situations whereby voice and whistle commands can be fitted to what the dog is actually doing.

When using this approach the dog can see the reason and the benefit, ensuring that the commands are learned over a period of three to six months, depending on the dog's learning capacity. Training is all the better being accomplished gradually, without the dog realising it is being taught.

If a young dog is inclined to work tightly around the sheep, I introduce a little command most Scottish shepherds use when penning and shedding at sheep dog trials. 'KEEP' is a gentle word that most collies like, and readily respond to.

The effect can be accomplished, gradually, when on 'walkabouts', by positioning oneself between sheep and dog - and with the crook encouraging the dog to make a wider movement.

The crook must only be used in a threatening manner as a last resort after months of gently persuading the dog to 'give room' by your being in the right place at the right time.

Timing is of the essence regarding obtaining the correct moves from a dog - especially when competing at a trial. If your timing and positioning is incorrect during training sessions, a dog will lose confidence in both you and itself, leading to fast erratic work and general disobedience.

The Outrun and Lift

The year old dog needs to be worked in a well fenced area of around ten acres on free moving sheep with a good flocking instinct – south country Cheviot hoggs being the best that I have worked with.

On entering the field, a young dog should be asked to stand before being primed with the words 'See sheep'. If he breaks away, he should be brought back and the exercise repeated until he learns not to. The sheep should number around a dozen and should be held by an experienced dog at a distance of around fifty yards.

Should the young dog be inclined to stop short of its sheep it is advisable to arrange that they are moving away - thus encouraging the dog's instinct to head them.

A young dog which is reluctant to leave your side can be encouraged to do so by being allowed to follow an older dog that is a good outrunner. Sending a dog up a slope, will often encourage it to run wider – however, at this stage if the dog is inclined to gather straight, don't worry! It is not important how a young dog gets to the sheep. We are only interested in developing the habit of 'hunting' and 'fetching' to the pack leader.

For the present, the Outrun, Lift and Fetch must be accomplished by the dog only, with an occasional command thrown in, but not necessarily obeyed! The dog must be encouraged to pick up sheep at the point of balance, i.e. at the sheep's heads because this is the 'heavy side' or direction in which the sheep will break. If they come away straight, the dog has lifted them correctly. Once the habit of heading and bringing sheep to you is established you have climbed the first rung of the ladder and you can begin to lengthen the distance you send the dog.

Should you try to open him out on his gather as he is leaving your foot during early training, there is every likelihood that he will come in tight, flat, or stop well short of the sheep. To prevent the latter you will need to send him on short gathers 'shushing' him on and calling 'Get back' until he reaches the point of balance. By using the command 'Keep' and/or positioning yourself between the dog and sheep, wider outruns will eventually be accomplished, should the dog not have 'opened out' using the methods described.

Do not endeavour to cure faults overnight. If you are patient they usually disappear. Otherwise, you will need to create situations whereby it is simple for the dog to perform the task correctly. Regularly keeping a young dog that is inclined to work tight, back off the sheep close at hand, will ensure that it will give them room when working at a distance.

Some dogs make no attempt to head sheep but are happy to drive them away. Sometimes it helps to allow the sheep to bolt through a gate. If this ruse fails, ask the dog to 'stand' while you walk to the other side of the sheep. Move backwards encouraging the dog to fetch the sheep. If the dog makes to slip around the flock in your direction block it with your crook and insist that it obeys the command to 'get back'.

Then, by stopping the dog and moving ahead of the sheep, he should realise that for the time being his place is at the other side of them.

It is rarely too difficult to teach a dog the 'walk up' command. If there is a problem, place the sheep in a corner and both you and the dog approach them from a distance.

Should the dog be in too much of a hurry when fetching the sheep, eventually you will need to teach him to come on at a slower pace. Position yourself between dog and sheep. Stop the dog by going towards him, allow thinking time, then, leaning in his direction, slowly repeat the words 'Take time', emphasising the movement you require by the use of your hands. Move back when the dog complies – forwards and repeat. Should the dog come on too fast, chase him back and begin again if necessary.

Dogs with 'power' and a natural ability to fetch sheep in a straight line, often require to be taught to gather correctly and give sheep room. A free flanking dog, not over endowed with 'eye', often has a natural cast and is usually more proficient at penning and shedding. However, a dog inclined to work on to his sheep is more practical for hill work. You may not get the perfect pear-shaped outrun required at trials, but you will be able to place the dog exactly where you require it and leave it to get on with the job.

On a big trial course when the wind and distance make

your commands inaudible, the powerful, or strong dog, providing he has been allowed to do so, will be able to line the sheep up on his own.

Should a young dog show reluctance to line sheep up to you, set him off on an outrun then high-tail it to the other side of the field. You will be surprised how quickly he will learn to keep one eye on your whereabouts and the other on his charges.

A particularly wide-running dog should be set off slightly in front of you – a tight runner well behind – or when young, from your opposite side and behind you.

Some dogs will travel great distances to retrieve sheep whilst others show a reluctance. If, when you have sent the latter on an outrun, he makes to cut in, stop him, allow thinking time, get his attention, then by leaning your body and moving a few steps in the appropriate direction, convey that you wish him to re-cast wider. Follow up with a slow flanking whistle. You may need to stop the dog and repeat the procedure - keep calm! Should he continue to come in, call him back to your foot, ask him quietly what he thinks he's playing at (these conversations work wonders!) then set him off again. With some dogs once or twice is enough to make them understand, with others it can take weeks or even months.

The ideal situation is a large flock which is spread out. When gathered regularly it helps the dog get into the habit of gathering correctly. Eventually, when a young dog knows his flank whistles he can be taught that a short sharp whistle means you require a fast tight flank. 'Urgent' commands appear to be easily translated, possibly because in the wild, the urgent sound of an animal in distress would have the effect of bringing predators to the scene very quickly.

A fully experienced dog eventually will 'open out' or 'tighten up' on sheep, when only hearing half of a whistled instruction.

Once the young dog is casting out nicely from your foot, encourage him to get to the 12 o'clock position on the sheep as quickly as possible. Numerous short gathers, from both ends of the field, with you 'shushing' him on. Following him a few yards and telling him to 'get back' will be beneficial in getting him to the correct 'lifting position' quickly.

Sheep must regularly be gathered off both hands or you will have a dog that will only gather one way. It is very tempt-ing to allow a dog to run on the side he prefers and is best at, but inadvisable.

The Lift:

An older steady dog, can be allowed to 'lift' the sheep without being stopped. It looks much smoother and upsets sheep less.

Young, keen dogs learn by first of all being asked to stop, then after a few seconds have elapsed they should be encouraged to 'lift' with a slowly spoken 'Take time', followed by a slow 'walk up' whistle.

The Fetch

Young dogs must regularly be allowed to fetch sheep on their own without commands. This will teach them to find their 'distance'. By 'distance' we mean the position that the dog must take, in order to move the sheep authoritatively without upsetting them. The exception is the dog that weaves back and forth; he must be worked on fewer sheep and kept well back until he learns to follow straight.

A youngster with excessive 'eye' sometimes becomes so engrossed with a sheep literally 'on the end of his nose', that he disregards the others. I use this as an opportunity to teach the dog what 'look back' means. Mistakes often provide golden opportunities.

Some dogs are born with a natural 'distance' whilst others need to find theirs. The remainder will continue to chase sheep until they are taught to 'take time' – probably one of the most important commands. It is unfair to expect a youngster continually to go slowly. He must on occasions be allowed to run riot in order to differentiate. It is on such an occasion that you can take him completely by surprise. Bend double and run quietly up the field and through the centre of the flock chasing the dog back off them, while at the same time asking in gruff tones just what he thinks he is up to.

The look of surprise on the dog's face when you appear unexpectedly out of the blue will make it difficult for you not to laugh. I usually do, with the result that the dog thinks that it's all a game.

A dog that continually 'claps' or lies down when working, is not as desirable as a dog which keeps on its feet. The 'upstanding' style upsets sheep less, and is more pleasing to the human eye. Some collies are inclined naturally to work on their feet. Others have to be taught. From an early age the former, when asked to stop, tends to do so in a sitting position, gradually developing the habit of working on 'all fours'.

When serious training begins, if the dog will stop when asked, there is no necessity to make him lie down. Ideally he should be allowed to choose his own position. The dog that lies down constantly will require teaching to work on his feet.

At a sheep dog trial there are only two occasions when it is necessary for a dog to lie down – these are at the pen and prior to shedding, and only then if the sheep are of a flighty disposition. To encourage bold sheep into a pen the dog has more effect standing on his feet while looking them squarely in the eye and walking them in backwards if necessary!

Providing a collie is not over endowed with 'eye', it is a relatively simple task to teach him to work on his feet. The more 'eye' the dog possesses, the more inclined he will be to flatten to the ground and the more time and patience it will require to get him out of the habit.

A relaxing and rewarding method of teaching a youngster to stand is to spend any spare moments grooming him. At first, embarrassed by the attention, he will either roll on to his back or cower in a submissive posture, creating a golden opportunity to lift him up and at the same time tell him to 'Get on your feet' and 'Stand'. Most dogs quickly learn to enjoy being groomed and rise to the occasion!

A dog that repeatedly flops to the ground when working, must be approached quickly and in an encouraging voice asked to 'walk up' to the sheep. The moment he rises he must be asked to 'stand'. The lesson should be repeated until the dog realises that he is required to halt in a standing position. When this is accomplished, he must be greatly praised.

It will also be helpful in getting the dog to understand, if occasionally you walk quietly over to him and lift him on to his feet. Once he learns the command 'On your feet', all that will be required to keep him there will be a stop whistle, quickly followed by the verbal command 'Feet'.

10
Basic Training

The basic do's and dont's when training a youngster are as follows:

Do not interfere with a young dog's 'Outrun' until the habit of bringing sheep is firmly established.

Do allow the dog, whenever possible, to 'Lift' and 'Fetch' the sheep without commands.

Do teach him to 'Take Time', rather than repeatedly stopping and starting him.

Don't send a young dog for sheep that are out of sight or too far away. Longer gathers must be achieved by you and the dog positioning the sheep, so that he knows where they are.

Do gather a large flock of spread sheep regularly to prevent the habit of 'stopping short' developing.

Do set the dog up correctly. Before sending him to gather, ask him to stand beside you. Enquire 'Can you see sheep?' Should he look in the wrong direction, or at sheep in the next field, tell him 'No' in a firm voice. A sound young dog should see sheep immediately. However, some, due to excitement, low intelligence or anxiety, do not.

Do lend a hand should a young dog encounter difficulty in moving awkward sheep.

Flanking

It is insulting a young dog's intelligence if initially he is expected to circle a stationary flock, first one way then the other. It is relatively simple for the trainer to move the sheep clockwise and anti-clockwise so that the dog's instinct to 'head' them is aroused. He will then have it in his mind that 'free flanking' is done for a reason, and you will be able to fit in the appropriate whistles and voice commands with what he is doing.

There is nothing to equal a flock of wild south country Cheviot hoggs, racing down a steep brae, to encourage a young dog to flank in a happy manner – if he doesn't, he will certainly lose his sheep! Unfortunately, not all of us enjoy such ideal conditions and thus must resort to other available means, creating situations which give the dog an opportunity to respond in a natural fashion rather than a mechanical one.

Should you insist a young dog repeatedly runs around a stationary flock for the purpose of learning his 'sides' and 'freeing him up', more serious problems may be created. For instance, the dog will have no idea where the point of balance is, and this may cause him not only to 'stop short' but to stop anywhere. He may also 'over flank' when running to turn sheep.

Only on rare occasions, and with a very hard and determined 'Line Dog' have I found it necessary to spend time circling stationary sheep.

The easiest method I know of introducing the 'green' young dog to the art of shedding, driving and flanking, is to go walkabout with a few sheep, as though out hunting. (In Scotland, shepherds still call sheep dog trials 'Dug Hunts', and speak of 'Hunting their dugs oot').

To accomplish this, sheep must first of all be shed from the flock and driven to the nearest gate. At first these feats must be accomplished more by the skill of the trainer than that of his dog who must be positioned and told to 'stand' on the opposite side of the flock. The trainer must then calmly cut off half a dozen sheep. With this achieved and a large space made between the two lots of sheep, the trainer must encourage the dog to come to him – on bended knee if necessary, and much praise be given when this occurs. Then, both trainer and dog should attempt to drive the shed sheep to the nearest gate.

A 'Line Dog', because he follows straight, should not find this task unduly difficult, as this type is a natural driver without much teaching. Should the shed sheep attempt to break back to the others in a determined manner, the trainer must quickly move on ahead of the sheep and out of the dog's way, leaving him (with words of encouragement) to fetch them – his instinct to fetch usually being far stronger than his driving instinct. The trainer should always remember to encourage and 'lay the dog on', with his voice when sheep are being difficult, especially on rough ground.

If by chance the shed sheep do manage to get back to the others, so much the better. This will convince the dog to try harder next time. Once you manage to get the sheep through the gate it is of no consequence where you take them. Uphill, down dale, over burns, across bridges - the world is your oyster.

Whilst they are fresh, your sheep will repeatedly endeavour to break away. Your dog's instinct will tell him to head them giving you the opportunity to fit in both whistled and spoken flanking commands.

Going 'walkabout' benefits the dogs in more ways than one. Dogs which gather equally well off either hand are few and far between. Most, like us humans, have a preference, and to make life more complicated they can and do, alternate between favouring left and right.

Usually, the dog flanks happily and at the correct distance from the sheep on the side he prefers. Eventually he must be persuaded to flank both ways correctly. Should you become impatient and insist that he flanks correctly on the side he dislikes, there is every possibility he will become sour on that flank permanently. The dog that flanks freely off both hands, obviously does not present any problems, but will still benefit by occasionally being taken by surprise and asked to flank off the heavy side of the flock and in the opposite direction.

It is inevitable that at some stage in training, and often unintentionally, you are going to offend your dog. (Some are more sensitive than the trainer may have realised). If a dog 'takes the huff' it should be kept right away from the sheep and the location for a few days – or as long as it takes for the incident to dim.

Should the dog be extremely offended, try a different location, say very little so that he can perform the task on his own. For example, should the dog refuse to flank in a certain direction the trainer should position a few sheep alongside a fence, and ask the dog to 'stand', allowing the sheep to 'break' down the fence. The dog will be unable to resist the urge to head them. The exercise must be repeated around the perimeter of the field, after which he will have lost any reluctance for the flank in question. Should the dog flank tightly he should not be interfered with as this can be corrected later. To help the dog stay 'sweet', try alternating from word to whistle when giving a command he has become offended by.

On the next walkabout, if he is flanking tightly, walk quietly in between him and the sheep and gently push him off the 'corners' with your stick, and at the same time ask him to 'KEEP'.

Usually, the dog will happily give 'room' when the sheep are tired and steady. Occasionally, when the sheep are wild and fresh, call the dog to your foot allowing them to surge ahead. Because the dog thinks he is going to lose them he will set off straight, hot on their heels. Stop him, allow thinking time, then set him off with a slow opening out whistle as discussed previously. Repeat until he gets the message. Undulating ground helps perfect this exercise more easily.

When the sheep are flagging it is possible for the dog to hold them to your heels. You can assist in keeping them there by moving your stick from side to side. Holding the sheep thus, helps replace the 'Balance' the dog has lost, owing to the repeated flanking he has done to retrieve the sheep. Certain aspects of training remove qualities which you also wish to improve, therefore means must be devised whereby they are restored. Most of what I have written applies to the 'Line Dog'. You may own a free flanking dog, with enough power, which is amenable and quickly learns its 'sides'. It is possible to train this type within the space of three months. Others may take a year or even longer if polishing for trial competition. Weaker types lacking in courage, learn their sides quite quickly as they are generally more than delighted to flank in a free perfect

Shedding - and driving

with a good penner it teaches you where to position other dogs to encourage the sheep to go inside.

For the purpose of teaching a dog its sides, sheep must be allowed to frequently break around the pen. When you provide a pen for the purpose of teaching a young dog the art of penning, it is necessary to use sheep that have been penned already so that the dog does not become despondent at having a difficult time persuading the sheep to go in. A young dog will often attempt to hold the sheep to the trainer. To show him where you require them, it is beneficial if you stand outside, and at the back of the pen.

Previously penned sheep will soon teach the dog what is expected. As soon as they go inside, the dog must be encouraged into the mouth for a few seconds and be rewarded with plenty of praise. The gate must then be closed and if training with trials in mind, the dog should be flanked wide behind the pen where he must stay until the sheep have been released, and allowed to settle in readiness for the shed.

Balance

'Natural Balance', as well as being an asset, is a rare and much to be admired quality in a trial dog.

A dog fortunate enough to be bred with 'Balance' doesn't upset his sheep, and can hold them with little or no flanking, preferring to use his shoulders to block the sheep's escape. 'Balance' is an essential feature, especially at the pen and shed; a dog without any, must be 'balanced up'.

Encouraging the dog to hold four sheep up against a wall or fence is one method. The dog must be asked to come up to the sheep until they split and break in opposite directions. After repeating these performances, hopefully the dog will learn to be in the right place at the right time —thus holding the sheep together. Following this type of session, the dog must be sent to bring the sheep OFF the fence a few times, otherwise he may get out of the habit of performing this more important task.

A less harmful method to put 'balance' into a dog is to shed three sheep from the main flock and 'drive' them away to a suitable distance. The dog must then be positioned with his back to the larger number of sheep. The trainer can then gently attempt to push the three sheep past the dog, who should be encouraged to counteract their movements. If the dog applies

fashion, as it supplies them with an opportunity to leave the 'heavy side' of the sheep.

Once your young dog is gathering reasonably well, course crossing, should it occur, must be discouraged. When it happens, call the dog back and ask him gruffly what he's playing at. If he is half way to the sheep when the cross is attempted, stop him, scold him, then re-direct with a slow, opening out flank whistle.

To date, I have only owned two dogs that NEVER attempted to cross. A dog that I took in for training was very hard to cure of this habit. He was used to sheep leaving the post before he arrived there, and coming full gallop towards his handler. The poor dog had got into the habit of crossing because in his mind he was 'heading' to prevent their escape.

Another method to help a dog learn his sides and the 'keep' command, is to erect a pen. Some dogs are natural penners of sheep, instinctively balancing them in a calm manner - knowing where to be at the right time. Once you have worked

At the pen

too much pressure, the sheep will attempt to run by the train-er's outstretched arms. As this occurs the dog must be quietly admonished so that he eases back.

After practising this on several occasions the trainer should end up working with a beautifully balanced dog.

Shedding and Driving

Some dogs are born shedders requiring little or no encourage-ment. To the hill shepherd and in the lambing field a 'good shedder' is worth its weight in gold.

'Shedding' is a natural instinct waiting to be aroused, that can be soured by impatience and the trainer expecting too much too soon. A dog will become reluctant if it picks up irri-tation in the trainer's voice, if it is unsure what is expected and if overfaced by too few difficult sheep.

Providing that you have done your ground work correctly, by regularly encouraging the dog to come quickly to you from an early age, it will not be difficult to get him to come to you through a large gap, in the middle of a quiet flock.

The first step is to flank the dog to the opposite side of the gathered sheep, ask him to 'stand' and allow half of the flock to move well away. When there is a sufficiently wide gap, turn sideways looking at the remaining sheep. Put out your hand and point to the sheep, (I always place my crook in my other hand before I start, so that it is not a threat to the sheep, causing them to bunch together). Encourage the dog to come towards you by moving away. Most dogs show no hesitation, while others look bewildered.

Instinct may tell the dog to flank around the perimeter of the whole flock and put them back together. You must persuade the dog – on bended knee if necessary, that he must come directly to you. With gentle perseverance eventually you will convince him, and he will comply – probably wearing a sheepish expression!

Be lavish with your praise, before helping to drive the shed sheep well away from the others, this being an easy method of teaching a young dog to 'drive' as well as to 'shed'.

Using this method of teaching, the 'Line Dog' will become a proficient 'Driver' literally overnight. The flanking type usually endeavours to head the sheep and put them back together at every opportunity. To counteract this action, move quickly ahead of the shed sheep. This will encourage the dog to fetch them after you until they are safely away from the remaining sheep.

When the habit of coming through the flock is formed, in the following months you can gradually narrow the gap, and shed fewer sheep, until the dog realises what you are trying to achieve, i.e. to cut out certain individuals from the flock.

It is important to shed regularly from both ends of the flock – a one way shedder can use up valuable minutes when competing in a trial. Always shed with the dog's back to the

sun. Convey excitement to the dog by the tone of your voice when you ask him to 'come in'. I usually say 'Here, this', when more than one sheep is required, and 'This one', when he is very experienced and I require a single. Again, remember to turn sideways and look at the sheep you require.

When the dog has come in on his sheep, encourage him to take charge. Then, not only will he be confident in what he is doing, he will also enjoy doing it.

At the onset of teaching a dog to shed, take the shed sheep walkabout. When the dog gains confidence and begins to show initiative, allow him to push on ahead, with you gradually falling back, thus encouraging him to drive the sheep as far as possible on his own, and where possible, through gaps and gates, over bridges and up steep hillsides, until he is completely in charge.

A useful exercise to get a dog to go to the exact 'Point of Balance' as well as 'putting it on its mettle', is to cut out a few sheep and, with the dog, drive them a suitable distance from the remainder. When accomplished, ask the dog to 'stand', allowing the sheep to bolt back in the direction of the others. Before they reach their destination (you will need to get your timing right) send the dog to stop them. Call 'Here, this', to get him to come in and praise him when he is successful. This is a beneficial exercise which most dogs, providing they are fresh, thoroughly enjoy.

At some trials running on four sheep, you are told that 'It's a split', meaning it is permissible to take any two sheep. At other trials it is the 'Last two' sheep that run by you. Towards the end of summer, the newly weaned and hopefully more sensible ewes come on the scene, and then it is the last single sheep that is required. No wonder some of the dogs are confused!

The 'Look back' for more sheep, command

Once a dog will shed and drive sheep away with enthusiasm, it is time to teach the 'Look back' command. This 'direction' is extremely useful on a hill, and essential should you be fortunate

Starting work - Laddie, son of Garry aged ten weeks

enough to compete at International level.

Start by shedding a few sheep from the flock, and drive them away from the remainder of the sheep. When a suitable distance is reached, stop the dog. Walk in his direction clicking your fingers, and using his name to get his attention away from the sheep he is holding. Ask him firmly to 'look back'. You may need to walk a few paces with the dog. Ask him again 'Can you see them?'. When he does, say slowly and clearly, 'Look back', following it up with a whistled note you have chosen to mean the same.

If you keep calm and persevere he will soon grasp what you require. Before long you will be able to stand him between the sheep he has shed off and the sheep he is to 'Go back' for, and send him from that point, with you in front of the shed sheep.

It helps the dog if you place him on the side of the shed sheep from which you are going to send him back, e.g. Should you intend to send him on a right hand outrun for the remaining sheep, flank him to his left, on the shed sheep first of all, and then ask him to 'look back' from that position. An experienced dog can be asked to 'Go back' from directly in behind the shed sheep, because, should it be necessary, he can be directed by using a slow, opening out, whistled direction.

When working a young inexperienced dog on the hill, it is important that he be asked to fetch the first sheep he encounters right to your feet, before being sent back for those he has missed and those that suddenly appear on the sky-line out of pure nosiness. The reasons being that an impressionable young dog will 'Go back' the moment he hears a stop whistle, without being re-directed, even when there are no more sheep to go for.

When the dog becomes competent at 'going back', gradually increase the distance you send him and discard the verbal 'Look back' command for the whistled signal. Mine is a straight note followed by a curved one. A different whistle will be required when working more than one dog.

At a 'Double lift' trial where two lots of sheep require to be gathered, if they are wild it is often difficult to get a dog's attention away from his first 'packet' of sheep. It is definitely advisable to practise at home, using flighty sheep, prior to a trial of this kind.

When you introduce a young dog to 'Looking back' it is vital you keep calm if at first he appears not to comprehend. Impatience will cause a dog to become confused, sometimes

resulting in him 'burling around with his rudder in the air', or as the sages put it 'waving his flag'. Not only does it look dreadful, it can become an incurable habit.

Driving

Some dogs show a marked reluctance when asked to drive the sheep away from the handler. These dogs must be taught using methods carefully thought out by the trainer, so that the dog eventually grows to enjoy the task. Should it be necessary, the trainer must be prepared over a period of time to walk many miles beside dog and sheep.

Dogs which flatly refuse to settle in behind sheep should be taken to a wall or fence, and be encouraged first to drive them round the field one way, and then the other. The dog must walk behind the sheep, with you walking alongside them covering the open flank. The 'weaving' dog benefits from being kept well back so that he develops the habit of 'following straight'.

Whenever possible the natural driver must be allowed to do his own thing. If he pushes the sheep too hard he can be stopped and told to 'take time'.

If there is a need the trainer should walk slightly in front of the dog to prevent what is known as the glancing habit. There are many reasons why a dog, every now and then, will have a quick glance or even a prolonged stare, in the handler's direction when his concentration should be on the sheep. Youngsters lacking confidence may do it if the trainer drops too far back. As they grow older they usually snap out of it. Working away from home on fast sheep generally doesn't afford them with an opportunity.

Over-commanding by the trainer can be a cause. A timid dog is reassured by a firm voice when he is young, but he should be encouraged to get on with the job himself. It is easy for a handler to get into the habit of over-commanding, especially when working a determined or a soft dog.

An intelligent O.A.P. can be forgiven for glancing. These veterans are simply asking for guidance as their hearing and eyesight may not be as good as it used to be.

Another exercise to improve a dog that is inclined to flank past the point of balance, or 'over-flank' as it is termed, consists of shedding three sheep from a flock and driving them to a suitable distance. The trainer should then walk first of all in a clockwise direction around the remaining sheep, and then in an anti-clockwise direction, leaving the dog to hold the three sheep to him. Should the dog go beyond the point of balance by over-flanking, the sheep will endeavour to break back to the main flock. It is surprising how quickly a dog improves his flanking technique after losing the sheep a couple of times.

Cross Driving

Once a dog has learned the driving habit, teaching it to cross-drive usually presents no problems.

The trainer must position himself in the centre of a field, allowing the dog to drive the sheep around him in a circle, first one way and then the other, gradually increasing the distance by enlarging the circle. At this stage the 'come here to me' whistle is very useful. When the dog learns what is expected of him the 'come here' whistle can be dispensed with, and substituted by the appropriate flank whistles.

Lessons must be repeated regularly as it is through repetition that the dog becomes confident and proficient. However, there is a happy medium. Schooling every other day is perfectly adequate, with dogs being exercised away from stock on their days off.

When, after months of careful schooling, you can work your dog(s) without taking your eyes off the sheep, when you can trust them to flank at the correct speed and distance, in tune with the slightest turn of the lead sheep's head, when your dogs have become an extension of yourself, then and only then are you ready to compete in Open Trials.

It needs to be mentioned that training keen young dogs is a relatively simple task compared with keeping them receptive, enthusiastic and up to trial standard throughout their working lives. Nothing sickens a dog more than rigid, unreasonable repetitive training. A 'class handler' will tell you, 'It's the work that keeps them right'. Meaning normal everyday tasks which allow a dog to do what it is bred for, without constant supervision.

Penning

There is nothing more soul destroying for a young dog than to be flanked round and round a pen when there is no hope of ever putting the sheep inside. Except when competing at a National or a team event, a wise handler would put the sheep away. There are many reasons why sheep refuse to be penned, the pen is too small, the sheep are in a panic due to the dog's abuse around the course and they have been hurried from the last gates. Often sheep are badly herded on their home ground and occasionally instead of easing back out of the way, to encourage the sheep into the mouth of the pen the handler insists on forcing them on to his dog.

Once in the vicinity of the pen mouth, wild sheep need to be allowed to settle and see where they are going. They need to be lulled into a feeling of security which can only be achieved by a well-balanced dog turning 'off the corners' when they attempt to break. When the sheep realise that they cannot escape and the dog means them no harm they will begin to settle. This being the time for the handler, and when necessary the dog, to ease quietly up to them.

Some sheep dog handlers are masters in the art of penning sheep, often winning the trial at the pen. At Kilmartin Scottish National Trials a few years ago, I was fortunate to be seated beside one of the best. The sheep on that particular day were blackface gimmers, that had been proving particularly troublesome to pen. The expert was studying this particular dog, and whispering to himself, 'Lie down, lie down'. As though the dog had heard him, it obligingly lay down and the sheep marched confidently into the pen.

The expert's name? Jim Gilchrist, brother to Jock who owned the famous 'Gilchrist's Spot' featured in pedigrees all over the world.

Sadly, Jimmy and Jock (and Spot) are no longer with us. It was Jock who once confided in me that, although he had been running a dog for over sixty years, he learned something new every time he walked on to a trial field.

11
On Judging Trials

I am often asked by the media, 'How do you judge a Sheep Dog Trial?' In my experience, when it comes to judging, most people hold a totally different view on the 'Acceptable' and the 'Points Deductible'.

I firmly believe that Sheep Dog Trials should only be judged by competitors experienced in the ways of dogs and sheep. They should be judged in a practical manner taking into consideration the behaviour of the sheep and the judge should always have someone to clerk and keep time.

I recognise that luck plays a major role, less in the case of top handlers. These men are few and far between in some areas, while prevalent in others, making getting into the plac-

ings more difficult for the less experienced. The dog in reasonable hands, fortunate enough to draw a reasonable packet of sheep, unfortunately may score higher than a much better dog in novice hands, that has unluckily drawn a bad packet. Should the latter show power and intelligence in the command of difficult sheep I would deduct less from him for good work, e.g. in the mouth of the pen and keeping sheep on the move, than I would a slack type of dog in the hands of a top handler.

There is a danger of too much technicality and insufficient practicality creeping in regarding judging. Especially with the more fanciful judges, who perhaps should leave 'the appliance of science' to the boffins as technicality has no place in practical sheep dog handling.

Regarding the trials themselves, whilst admitting that more hill trials are definitely a step in the right direction because these undoubtedly present a stiffer test than an 'Inbye' trial, one cannot escape from the fact that a dog capable of winning one is not necessarily an exceptional work dog. There will always be the distinction between a good trial dog in good hands, and a genuine powerful working dog. A fifteen minute test whether it be on the hill or inbye cannot be taken as a definite indication that a dog possesses intelligence, stamina, quality or determination. What it indicates is that its handler definitely does!

I often wonder how many trial dogs would be capable of 'Lifting' and 'Fetching' sheep in a straight line to the handler over a big distance without commands, as is required from a working hill dog?

I maintain that it is the ground and the sheep which prove what a dog is made of, and not the wild flying kind, but the awkward, heavy slow type, for these are the sheep that it takes courage to walk up and move. By the word 'move' we do not mean that the dog should use its teeth (unless the sheep use theirs) gripping without provocation is a cowardly dog's method. A good dog should have sufficient presence and determination that the sheep automatically move away when confronted. Unfortunately many collies lack this indefinable presence. It has been lost through breeding and in-breeding with the wrong blood-lines.

Contrary to some people's belief it is possible to breed powerful working dogs which lack aggression. As far back as 400 BC, 'deep-mouthed line-hunting hounds, slow enough to follow on foot, with noses tied to every jink of the hare, in poor scenting conditions, with so little killer instinct, that they could be stopped from their quarry by voice alone' were meticulously bred by Xenophon the Greek.

Regarding sheep dogs 'work must come first' and therefore my preference is for a strong intelligent dog that is kind to the sheep and trustworthy when working out of sight. I like a dog which works on to its sheep with a purpose to one which flies off at the corners or tends to over-flank. It must be capable on a large course, of working with few or no commands, depending on the circumstances. It should know its distance. By 'distance' we mean that the dog should be capable of adapting to the type of sheep that it is working e.g. keeping back off wild sheep. It should have 'Lining up ability' - by this we mean that a dog should be able to fetch and drive sheep in a straight line with few or no commands keeping to the 'heavy side' of them. It should 'bend' off naturally on the corners of a flock, but stop directly at the 'point of balance' e.g. where the work is. The fully trained dog should possess all of these qualities. When I judge I look out for dogs of this calibre, hoping against hope that they get the luck, the sheep and the handler.

THE OUTRUN – worth 20 points

It should be neither too wide nor too tight. I would deduct a lot more points for it being more tight than wide. (Having said this if I were given the choice of two young dogs one of which gathered straight, the other having a tendency to hug the dyke backs, I would prefer the former because I would feel it had a more direct approach).

The perfect OUTRUN, as trial enthusiasts know, is said to be 'pear shape' with the dog arriving either at the twelve o'clock position, or the point of balance, without unduly disturbing its sheep. Before being sent for the sheep the dog should be positioned by the handler on the side it is to be sent from. If positioned too far from the handler, or allowed to cast behind (or in front!) of the handler - the latter recognised as 'Course crossing', points will be lost. Should the dog run straight down the field I deduct half of the Outrun points. If the dog runs around the perimeter of the field it may lose several depending on the shape of the field. Should the handler whistle to the dog on the outrun I would take away one point; if the dog stops on the outrun, two points.

If a dog stops short of the sheep the points deducted would depend on how far short it stopped. If the dog stops 'short' but is facing the sheep at the 'right bit' (i.e. point of balance) I deduct nothing providing the sheep come away 'straight'.

If the dog 'overshoots', running past the sheep on the outrun, points would be lost depending how far it over-shot.

If the dog 'crosses its course' but is brought back, I deduct fifteen points. If the handler fails to get the dog out again and it picks its sheep up on the wrong side, I would take off eighteen points leaving the handler with two points for his dog getting there.

THE LIFT – worth 10 points

'The Lift', if the sheep allow, should be cautious. It is nice but these days a rare occurrence, to see a dog 'Lift' sheep without a command but I would not penalise a handler who halted his dog first.

If the sheep leave the post before the dog arrives I would not deduct points providing the dog picks the sheep up efficiently and brings them in a direct line to the 'Fetch Gates' and in the absence of these, in a line to the handler.

When coming into the 'Lifting Position' I do not object to a dog drifting the last few yards at a steady trot. In doing so I believe it is using its brains and weighing up its charges.

THE FETCH – worth 20 points

On 'The Fetch' every deviation must be taken into account so that the perfect 'Fetch' can be given maximum points.

I prefer that 'Fetch Gates' be dispensed with altogether so that the sheep can be picked up without the hassle of holding them to the post at the top of the field, another advantage being that the dog can be left to bring the sheep without being constantly commanded in order to 'hit the gates', as over commanding a dog used for hill work robs it of initiative.

If there are Fetch Gates, running on four or more sheep, I deduct half a point per sheep for a miss.

THE DRIVE – worth 30 points

I like a tight turn around the handler into 'The Drive', which is split into three sections to make judging easier. Points are deducted for deviations and missed gates, a 'near miss' being preferred to the sheep being fought in all directions. I look for tight turns at all of the gates, with straight lines in between, especially from the last gate up to the mouth of the pen.

I split the drive so - 'Down Drive' eleven points because there is a set of gates to negotiate. 'Cross Drive' same points. The 'Last Leg of the Drive', because there are no gates included merits eight points.

THE PEN – worth 10 points

When running on four or more sheep I deduct half a point per every sheep that breaks around the pen. I always leave a score of half a point per sheep should they eventually go inside. Penning is a skill. It can be the most difficult part of the competition and it is debatable whether ten points suffice.

Should sheep at any time make to run over the top of a dog or turn on the dog at any stage of the trial I would not penalise a dog unduly for 'gripping' providing it lets go of the offender immediately.

THE SHED – worth 10 points

I give five points for the dog coming in and five for the 'Wear'.

In Scotland 'shedding' is still widely practised. A good shedding dog I maintain, is invaluable on the hill or on the farm and yet in England, shedding has largely been abandoned at trials so that more dogs can run, giving them the opportunity to gain points in order to enter the National Trials. I believe that this should not be allowed. Neither should the confusion that Scottish judges cause competitors in saying that they require 'A Split' or 'Any two sheep'.

Another debatable issue is 'should a trial be judged as a whole or as a number of separate tasks?'

At a National a handler can be in the team without com-

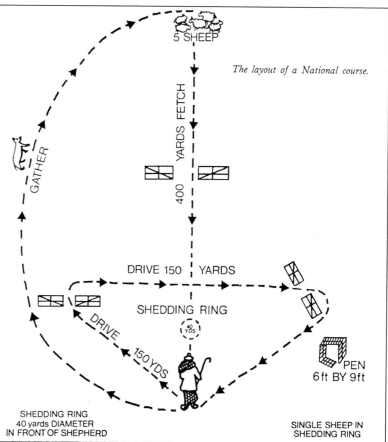

The layout of a National course.

5 SHEEP

400 YARDS FETCH

GATHER

DRIVE 150 YARDS

SHEDDING RING

40 yds

DRIVE 150 YDS

PEN
6ft BY 9ft

SHEDDING RING
40 yards DIAMETER
IN FRONT OF SHEPHERD

SINGLE SHEEP IN
SHEDDING RING

pleting the course, whereas at most Open events if you don't finish you are not included in the prize list.

I favour the former ruling because at home shepherding is split into various tasks. At some trials when sheep are difficult the time limit is not enough to complete the course in a steady dignified manner – and this is what skilful handling should be all about, not chasing sheep at a hundred miles an hour!

I also believe that penning which is the most difficult task, should be done last.

12
Nursery Trials

Nurseries in Scotland allow dogs up to the age of $2^1/_2$ years on the first day of October, to compete. Commencing in October, weather permitting, there are usually several trials held at various venues throughout the region. At the end of the season, the five highest pointed dogs from each region go forward to the Nursery Final, held in March.

In order that the young dogs be given a confident introduction into the art of trialling, a great deal of thought must go into the construction of courses. A good idea is to place a bale of sweet hay beside the lifting post (which ideally should be painted white). This encourages the sheep to stay put without the attendance of either man or dog. The less the young dog is distracted the better. The letting out pen should be well hidden from the dog's view and the outrun should not exceed 300 yards, gradually increasing the distance of the outrun as the season advances.

When competing in his first trials, an intelligent young dog can, on being asked if he can see his sheep, become agitated or confused. The reason is that of course he's seen them and thinks that there must be others that he cannot see. Should this situation occur, try to set him off with the appropriate flank not asking if he can see the sheep.

At some local Nursery trials, fetch gates are dispensed with to enable the dogs to bring and line up their sheep with as few commands as possible. I feel that fetch gates are unnecessary at any trial. Granted a dog must flank to put sheep together on a hill, although a capable dog should be able to achieve this virtually unaided, as he will be much happier doing it for a valid reason. Throwing a dog about, here, there and everywhere, when he is attempting to bring sheep to you will not only go against his natural instinct but also dampen his initiative and enthusiasm.

The average trial course is far too short for the use of fetch gates to serve any practical purpose. Wild sheep are upset further by the shepherd at the letting out pen being required to hold them to the post — a skill at which few men are adept, even with well behaved sheep. Without 'fetch gates' sheep can be picked up from any position with less cause for concern on the part of the handler.

The 'easy' type of dog would quickly become more proficient through not being over-commanded in the initial stages of a 'run'. A handler whose views I normally respect, except on this issue, argues that a dog is expected to flank on command

T here are many valid arguments both for and against the running of young dogs in Nursery trials. Some say Nurseries ruin a young dog. Certainly training a dog in such a way as to expect him to win will dampen a young dog's enthusiasm. I have seen many heartily sick by the last Nursery of the season, and a high percentage are never to be seen again on a trial field.

However, providing the handler takes the right attitude, which should be to use the facilities provided for the benefit of the dog and not for the benefit of himself, i.e. to give the dog confidence and valuable experience to prepare him to run in Open trials, I cannot see much harm in Nursery trials. Local when fetching sheep over a distance and driving them through gates at home. He misses the point completely. A dog with any brains at all (if he is allowed to use them!) quickly learns where all the gates are situated and is quite capable of bringing the sheep through them on his own — a relatively simple task in fields with a fence at either side of the gates!

From fetch gates we come to the starting post which should be positioned, preferably, well to the fore of the judge's car so as to allow plenty of room to turn the sheep behind the handler. A large pen is provided, to put the sheep in and sufficient time allowed in the hope that every young dog has a good chance of penning and completing the course. If there is a rope on the gate it should be positioned to be held in the handler's left hand.

Partners in grime

At the shed any two sheep (regardless of which way they are facing) can be taken off. Much to the amusement of spectators and fellow-handlers this sometimes results in the handler shedding and walking away in one direction whilst the dog drives the 'last' two sheep in the other!

It is nigh impossible to judge a young dog's merits on one showing. Consistency over a long period is what counts. At a trial you will hear spectators state emphatically: 'That is the best young dog I have ever seen!' By the following event they will probably have had a complete change of heart and be making exactly the same statement about a completely different one. There is only one person who really knows the dog and that person is his owner. In the long run it is often the dog which suffers the most criticism which ends up the best of the bunch.

If you own a dog which is being discussed by the media, favourably or otherwise, it is often a useful dog. It is not what a young dog is capable of achieving that is important; it is the way that he goes about it. In certain circumstances, it is wiser to allow offending traits so that you are given the opportunity, eventually, to discourage them. We should all realise that if we are prepared to learn, every dog that we own will teach us something new and beneficial in the training and handling of our future dogs.

Some tips for Open trials:

Trial sheep which are handled quietly with care and consideration within the letting out pen often behave reasonably well on the course compared with sheep which are handled roughly and noisily. It is when the letting out pen begins to empty of sheep that the few remaining inevitably become upset and suspicious, causing the rot to set in.

Rain often settles sheep, whereas wind stirs them up. A combination of hot sun and annoying flies will send them scurrying for the shade! Often the first and last sheep of the day are inclined to be the easiest to handle. There is an exception to this rule, in the shape of gimmers who (so I've been lead to believe) become frisky of an evening!

On an average-sized trial course it helps the dog to see the sheep and gather them correctly if both he and his handler walk on to the course in a direct line with the starting post, and

'Nursery trials' - working brace

from behind the judge's car. On a big International-type course it is helpful to the dog if he is walked on at a slant from the opposite side from where you plan to send him for the sheep. This way his nose should be pointing in the right direction for a wide outrun.

It is always common sense to study a trial course carefully, and to see as many runs as possible before your turn comes in order to watch sheep's behaviour, and tactics (especially those of the 'top' handlers) although mimicking them is often another kettle of fish. More often than not fewer points will be deducted by an efficient judge for a missed set of gates than would be for sheep which are chased and fought in order to put them through.

Some time ago, in the late Doctor Sheila Grew's marvellous magazine *Working Sheep Dog News*, there appeared a letter from a Swedish trialist seeking advice on how to cure his nerves because they had a serious effect on his ability when handling his dog amongst other competitors. Psychologists tell us the reflexes of a slightly nervous person are much sharper than those of someone who is in a relaxed frame of mind. However, a handler who is absolutely petrified is bound to transfer his fear to the dog who, I believe, due to his primitive instincts, can actually scent the agitation his master feels and thus reacts unfavourably. Espinar said in 1644: 'Partridges lie much better to the dog that finds them not by foot-scent but by body scent, and measures his distance by their tameness or wildness, for he can tell by the body-scent if they are restless or tranquil.'

Running a dog in a team event is always nerve-racking, owing to the fact that there is always the worry that you may let your side down. When running for Scotland, and doing badly, I attempted to walk off the course, but was hurriedly chased back by irate team mates. Because I was dreadfully nervous on this occasion, I completely forgot that my points, no matter how few, were still necessary.

I have found that running a strong determined dog, once you are actually out on the course, will often keep you so busy that you tend to forget your nerves. Working a slack, easily-handled type of dog, you become all too aware of what is going on, and what is being said around you. I believe that what helps nervous handlers most is that if they fail to pull themselves together they inadvertently fail their dogs and they must tell themselves just that, prior to competing.

When and if you ever receive compliments about your dog, or handling ability, it is wise to remember that within the trialling fraternity you can be discussed and have your praises sung from John O'Groats to Land's End one season, and be completely forgotten by the next! It is very easy to come to believe that your dog's faults are practically non-existent, but very foolish considering there is no such thing as perfection. All dogs have faults – you hope that, with age and experience, these will tend to lessen as do the faults of their handlers. The sensitive dog develops more confidence, the weak dog acquires adequate power to get by and the very determined dog (providing he has a patient handler) will gain enough sheep sense nine times out of ten.

13

The Flock

There were fifty blackface 'aged' ewes and 720 south country Cheviots in my husband's care, running in fields near the house and on two hills, known as the Swindon and the Whitelaw.

To the uninitiated, blackfaces are a hardy, heather eating breed of noble appearance. Both the rams and the ewes possess horns. The long, sweeping rams' horns are used by shepherds in the art of stick dressing.

South country Cheviots are a medium sized pretty sheep - white faced, prick lugged but rather short in the leg when it comes to travelling through deep snow. This shortness of leg can and does have another disadvantage for when the weather

is warm and humid sheep enjoy a good roll in order to relieve their itchy backs. The Cheviots, due to their 'affliction' often have great difficulty in righting themselves, and if they are not discovered by the shepherd almost immediately, will die of heart failure or have their eyes removed by crows which are on constant lookout for sheep stranded in this manner.

To help counteract this problem and get more size about them generally, a north country Cheviot ram was introduced, longer legged and slightly coarser in its features, but much more active and resourceful, which had its advantages come lambing time when the extra vigour was very much in evidence in the newborn lambs.

The rams or tups as they are called, (don't ask me why) normally go out amongst the ewes on November 18th and come home on New Year's Day.

I had a 'special' ewe of my very own. Lu-Lu is of the blue-faced Leicester breed. It had been years since I owned one of these parrot-nosed, blue skinned sheep and I was looking forward to her lambing. Lu-Lu never failed to breed triplets. They were sired by a Suffolk tup and we kept all of the ram lambs for breeding, they boosted our lambing average from 175% to over 200% in-bye. Mated to a mule or half-bred ewe the lambs were rarely less than 120 lbs live weight and some by the following Easter were 148 lbs when they went to market.

At mating time each tup was given his own harem which meant up to eighty ewes, which I considered were more than enough.

When 'the boys' came up the glen I liked to study their appearance: Ideally a ram should look like a ram but there are numerous variations and age also had to be taken into consideration. Strong tup lambs do on occasion grow into masculine adults but it doesn't always follow. Some rams are distinctly effeminate, others border-line. Some are naturally polled whilst others sport stumpy horns, remnants of a past defence mechanism.

The rams that I like most carry masculine heads, have Roman noses and flat dominant eyes. Their backs are long and their bodies thick set and heavy. I like them square in appearance with plenty of width between their quarters and strong shoulders. Unfortunately this type of sheep is getting few and far between. Inbreeding, and breeding for show purposes has begun to take its toll.

When we first turned the rams out amongst the ewes the

sight of those blundering beasties lumbering around excitedly amongst their wives had me in stitches. They reminded me of little boys playing aeroplanes, running hither and thither with their short necks comically outstretched and heavy heads held to the side like dive bombers dipping their imaginary wings, they leaned towards whichever ewe their fancy took, then even before she had a chance to introduce herself she was dealt a hefty blow along the ribs by a mighty cloven hoof.

When the tups had been running with the ewes for nine days they were strapped into a harness, rather like the one a sled dog wears. A red crayon was slotted into the harness and the ewes that were mated branded Scarlet Women on their woolly rumps. Nine days later ten fresh tups were brought in to finish off the job, this time wearing a crayon of a different hue.

The reason for this palaver was so that the shepherd would 'ken' which ewes will lamb first and could bring them nearer home. However, it doesn't always work out that way – like all best laid plans. For as we ladies know only too well some babies choose to arrive early, whilst others choose to arrive late. So unfortunately you can have a situation where some reds lamb before some whites (un-marked sheep) and some blues lamb before some reds ... This problem was more prevalent in stormy weather when the dragging weight of a wet fleece caused ewes to lamb before their time. Nowadays scanning the ewes with a type of X-ray machine is becoming more and more popular as this enables the shepherd to know who is carrying twins and who isn't. The benefit of scanning is two-fold. Ewes that are carrying twins can be drawn out and placed in a separate field where they can receive extra nourishment.

When all of the ewes are left running together the twins and their mothers have to be walked from amongst the flock by an already overworked shepherd and his dog whose time could be spent better elsewhere.

Ewes with twins cannot be left running with ewes that have single lambs and ewes that are still expecting a happy event. Believe it or not lambnapping is common practice amongst sheep that have a particularly strong mothering instinct, especially when they have a full udder. I remember one occasion when I was attacked and chased down a steep hill by three irate lambnappers as I attempted to rescue stolen babies. When lambs are taken in this manner should they be away from their real mothers for any length of time the real mother will often refuse to take them back again.

Extracts from a shepherdess's diary ...
Ringing in The New

So here we are on New Year's Day 1985 after eleven happy years living at Swindon in the valley of the Bowmont.

As I hurry downstairs to prepare breakfast for my husband and son I cannot help but wonder what 1985 will bring. '84 had certainly been the most exciting and rewarding year of our lives, for much to my surprise and delight a book I had written in my spare time was published, *One Woman and her Dog*, about our lives in the country and sheep dog trial experiences.

There then followed what can only be described as a very hectic summer doing book signings, newspaper interviews, television appearances and radio chats. Until then we had lived fairly quietly except for our trialling and at first we found all the publicity a bit overwhelming. I had to keep pinching myself to make sure that it wasn't all a dream.

Once we had all eaten breakfast, shared with avidity by T C, Little Geoff's ginger cat and my dog Garry, who resides in the kitchen due to a kennel shortage, GWB stepped outside to water and feed Tarka our mare, so named due to her otter-like colouring.

Afterwards the kennel doors were thrown open to allow dear old Jed and Trim, now in their fifteenth year and nick-named the old aged pensioners, out for exercise. Nowadays these sprightly stout old ladies, are beginning to lose their sight and hearing, but their scenting ability however remains intact. They can still smell their suppers a mile away!

GWB has acquired two new, smooth-coated replacements, again sisters, but they will not become proficient overnight because it can take years before two dogs learn to run as one.

The newcomers, Jan and Bett live solely for their master, he is the light of their lives.

Their coats shine like satin, black as night. They have white waistcoats and feet and their large fox-like ears, give them an alert appearance.

As GWB strides up the Whitelaw Hill, with Jan and Bett at his heels, to gather the tups from amongst the ewes I cannot help thinking how totally dedicated shepherds are. For on this New Year's Day, throughout the land hundreds of shepherds and their faithful collies will be performing their duties as on

Laddie babysitting

for the often foul and freezing weeks that lie ahead.

Although most shepherds prefer to breed and train their own dogs purely for the interest, breeding collies is a risky and expensive business and their training time consuming. Although they are predominantly a tool of the trade, a useful hill dog can cost a shepherd several hundred pounds or more.

Should a dog fall ill or sustain injury during working hours it is the shepherd who must count the cost.

Puppies require injections against disease, with boosters given annually throughout their lives, and on many farms kennelling leaves a lot to be desired.

You may conclude that a shepherd's lot is not a happy one, but you would be wrong because shepherding to these resolute characters, their home loving, industrious wives and happy children, isn't just a job. It is a cheerfully accepted, much appreciated, highly respected, way of life.

In September '85 it became law that shepherds would be supplied with rainwear by their employers.

Happy New Year

And so, with January 1st over and done with for yet another year, we climb slowly upstairs to bed, we three tightly clutching bulging hot-water bottles after an extremely enjoyable day eating stuffed turkey, roast potatoes, plum pud, apple-pie, ice-cream and the remnants of the Christmas cake that my naughty cat Greystoke sampled first.

What a delightful day of relaxation, fun and laughter. Little Geoff relished every precious moment. As we clambered sleepily into our welcoming beds I heard the first sleet of winter spatter on the window pane and observed its slow progress as it slid almost reluctantly down the glass to form an uneven line of wet slush, and as we drifted into dreamland we were brought momentarily back to reality by a faint voice, calling out to us from along the landing 'Goodnight mum, goodnight dad' and as an afterthought 'A Happy New Year'.

January 2nd

There is a decided chill in the air this morning. Winter has finally arrived with a vengeance after months of mildness and damp.

any other day.

Over the Christmas and New Year period shepherds have stock to 'look' and feed, and in a snow storm they are fortunate to be home for lunch. No shepherd worth his salt would dream of abandoning his flock to the elements to take a holiday during winter and many are hard pressed during summer for who would 'look' their charges as efficiently as themselves?

When I hear of workers coming out on strike I cannot help but wonder what their attitude would be if their work necessitated turning out seven days a week during the winter months and at lambing time working from dawn 'til dark with no paid overtime. Ewes do not choose to lamb between the hours of nine and five, five days a week. At this busy time protective clothing - raincoats, leggings, rubber and leather boots – provided by the shepherd, often need replenishing in preparation

The month of November had been the wettest that anyone could remember. The Bowmont overflowed its banks flooding the whole of the valley and causing a vast amount of damage. Gates, fencing posts and yards of wire, all were swept away by the fast flowing current. Even the wooden bridge down at the old school house collapsed into the murky torrent, leaving the occupants cut off from the outside world. The moody unpredictable Bowmont Water had on this occasion taken everyone by surprise, excelling in ferocity as it gushed by, brown and angry with the tang of peat on its frothy breath.

Thank goodness the present Swindon house is built on high ground. It wasn't always so, for not half a mile away standing in the haugh where the old road used to be, are the ruins of the original shepherds' house.

Today we have a covering of snow, the wet soggy variety that is accompanied by a damp mist.

After breakfast I set off to drive the ewes back to the Swindon Hill from out of the fields, where hopefully they have all been mated during the past six weeks. As I follow in their wake their red and blue crayon-marked rear ends gleam like flashing beacons, from out of the swirling mist.

I am using Laddie for this little job. His sire Garry has been left at home in the warmth of the kitchen, snoozing happily on his tartan rug under the table.

After completing the task we set off home, to find that the mushy peas I had left simmering gently in the pressure cooker have boiled dry and are now spattered all over the ceiling, walls and floor. Beneath the table dear old Garry slumbers on, blissfully unaware of the sticky mess around him.

January 3rd

It is 7 am. I hurry along the landing to Little Geoff's bedroom to waken him. He has had his hair cropped by his father the previous evening, using sheep shears. It stands up like a hedgehog's prickles. How sweet and vulnerable sleeping children look. It seems such a pity to disturb him.

'Good morning Geoff,' I call out from the doorway. He sits up in bed and rubs the sleep from his eyes. 'What's the weather like, mum?' he asks, hoping against hope that he will not have to attend school. I glance upward at the skylight in the ceiling. It is covered completely with snow and in my mind I make a mental note to knock down the cobwebs gracefully adorning it.

'Better get up and see,' I reply, making my way downstairs. As I enter the kitchen Garry yawns and stretches as he greets me, his tail wagging nineteen to the dozen. What a difference a dog's presence makes to the temperature in the kitchen. Perhaps I should fetch Laddie in too. I open the door to allow Garry out for a few minutes, then on with the Calor gas heater, and the bacon and eggs. When I call Garry he races quickly indoors leaving a trail of snowy paw marks, closely followed by the cats Jemima, Top Cat, Greystoke, and little Silver, who at the last moment because of shyness, changes her mind and dashes back outside.

Heavy snow is falling and the world outside is cold and crisp. As I pour out the tea I wonder if the school mini-bus will make it up the valley. The two Geoffs appear, hungry as the mewing cats. As they eat I turn the radio way down low in protest, for I am deeply mourning the loss of D.J. Terry Wogan's show and wondering how I will survive without his constant banter.

The animals' usual circus tricks will have to suffice. Garry is half-heartedly scolded for pulling at GWB's sleeve over enthusiastically, begging as usual for titbits. Greystoke is brushed yet again from my shoulder where he is intent on perching to warm his cold feet, and ever mischievous Top Cat gets his knuckles rapped for reaching with his paw over the edge of the table, for small pieces of toast strategically placed there for him by Little Geoff.

With breakfast over, up goes the cry for shorts, boots and rugby shirt. In this weather? There then follows a frantic search, whilst Little Geoff scurries off to feed his rabbits.

Father has all of his dogs out, and is watering and feeding Tarka my horse. The school bus sails by on its way up to the top of the valley to collect the older children in order to transport them to Morebattle, where they are then picked up by another bus and taken to the High School at Kelso. Geoff will be collected on the way down. He has been at the High School since the summer holidays. John, the driver, does a wonderful job in all weathers. Later, a second bus will travel up the valley to pick up the younger primary school children from Sourhope, the Agricultural Research Farm, and take them to school at Yetholm six miles away. Geoff's journey involves a round trip of over twenty miles.

Our son rushes indoors for his schoolbag, then with a

quick peck on the cheek and a 'Goodbye, mum' he's gone for his first day's schooling of 1985.

I don waterproof trousers and coat, my head and hands warmed and protected by a bright coloured woolly hat and mitts. I silently thank my mother for her endless supply of woolly jumpers hats and mitts that she has knitted over the years, smiling as I remember the first hat, complete with a large many coloured pom-pom. I even wore it in bed I was so delighted with it.

Today our six hens remain imprisoned inside the hen house where they perch snug and warm, the draughts blocked off by snow.

I feed and water them. The two ducks, Daisy and Cheeky, are allowed out to play in the snow, for unlike the hens they are capable of finding their way home in a storm.

Laddie and dear old Garry accompany me eagerly to the Whitelaw Hill for some exercise, stopping every so often to chew at lumps of frozen snow trapped between their toes.

As we return to the house snowflakes block out the sky and cover the ground with a fresh blanket. I wonder if it would have been wiser to have kept Little Geoff at home.

Greystoke sits on the doorstep watching snow, the first he's ever seen, whilst Top Cat chases his tail.

GWB suggests an early lunch so that we can set off to Kelso in good time to collect a mammoth supply of groceries - things like bread, meat, milk, flour, sugar, tea and dog meal, in case we get snowed in.

As we drive down the narrow winding road toward the second cattle grid I see one of our neighbours heading in our direction. 'There's a car coming', I warn GWB in good time because the road up ahead is pretty treacherous. His reflexes are sharper than I thought and he jams on the brakes and we start to skid.

Luckily, we only travel for a couple of yards before stopping but it brings to mind a similar happening on the same stretch of road a mile further on at the bottom of the bank. It was during a severe blizzard when off on a very necessary shopping spree. The icy conditions had been with us for a number of weeks and it was necessary to venture forth for provisions. I had been about to drive up the bank when over the horizon drove a large grey, snow covered monster looking like something out of Star Wars, but in reality turning out to be nothing more menacing than the local refuse cart! It kept on coming

and I hadn't the sense to realise that the driver was braking gently, for had he braked severely he would have run into me. Naturally I panicked, pressing my foot down hard on the pedal with the result that I was the one who very nearly skidded into him. Luckily, at the last moment the car turned sharply to the side ending up with the front wheels off the road up a steep bank.

Before I could say anything, up rushed two burly refuse men, and without the slightest hesitation bodily lifted the front of the car back on to the road. Ever since that day I have been particularly careful when leaving the valley in dubious weather.

As we reach Attonburn, a part of the estate where a tractor driver, two shepherds and their families reside we observe that there are three 'strange' vehicles parked by the roadside. The 'shooters' are about! I can't help smiling guiltily to myself as I remember what happened when they were here last. At that time I knew nothing of the procedure of shooting for pleasure. In my ignorance it never dawned on me that when a pheasant fell out of the sky and plopped down on the road in front of the car, it wasn't manna from heaven – it was a shot bird. Being of a somewhat tender nature where the unfortunate are concerned, I jumped out of the car and caught the half extinguished bird, laying it gently on the seat. I then turned in the direction of home and the man of the house. He was busy sawing logs when I drove into the yard. I called out that I had found a badly injured bird, and please could he do anything to help? 'Yes, of course,' he replied, reaching into the car. After giving it the once over and before I could say a word, he promptly wrung its neck.

The poor thing was full of shot. I know because I'm ashamed to admit that after it was hung I helped to eat it.

The historic town of Kelso is a bustling busy place that bears no resemblance whatsoever to the sparsely populated hills we've left behind. Throughout the summer months Kelso swarms with tourists, who quickly melt away come autumn, making shopping less of a nightmare for the locals.

Today it looks as though everyone has come in to shop and finding a parking space proves difficult.

People from outlying areas are stocking up with much needed provisions after the New Year, in preparation for fiercer winter weather.

Margaret and Sheila, the girls who work on the tills in the supermarket where I regularly shop, double up with mirth and

Viv and Geoff with
their dogs at
Bowmont Water

stare in amazement at my heavily laden trolley bulging to capacity with long life milk, and large white loaves, as well as many other necessities.

We pass quickly through the checkout. GWB goes off to fetch the car and very soon the boxes of groceries are securely loaded in the back and we are homeward bound, steadily round the Square, over the gently flowing Tweed, and up the bank back towards Yetholm.

We drive by flat close-cropped fields, grazed by Suffolk crosses and Scotch half-bred ewes, heavy in-lamb. Unlike hill sheep they enjoy a kinder environment and drop their lambs much earlier.

In the vast open spaces and thickets an abundance of vivid pheasants strut, such lovely birds. No 'shooters' tread this way today.

Ahead of us, high rounded hills merge with the sky. Clothed in snow they resemble mountains on the moon.

It is a different world in there, once you've learned to abide by the rules and got to know the ground. Snug, safe, and secure when you've battled against the elements, and come out on top.

It's easy to imagine what it must have been like centuries ago in these wild Border hills, where hunted people sought refuge away from prying eyes, their wits honed to a sharpness not unlike that of the fox and deer that abound in these secret places.

As we reach the homeward stretch that runs between Yetholm and the narrow road end leading to the Bowmont, we wave gaily to 'The Last of The Summer Wine' a frisky, fresh-faced flock of retired shepherds, on their weekly pilgrimage past the cemetery. Their days are greatly enhanced by each other's jovial company, discussing avidly the local Hatches, Matches and Despatches, and taking time to study nature at its best, as the ever changing seasons wax and wane before their eager eyes.

Fresh routes abound around these 'herds' for there are highways and byways too numerous to mention leading in and out of Yetholm for this growing bevy of energetic gentlemen, with cheerful smiles and a wealth of untapped knowledge penned within their minds to explore.

January 5th

Today I allowed our six hens out for a jaunt and had great difficulty herding them back into the hen house until Laddie came to my rescue. The snow doesn't appear to make any difference whatsoever to the ducks, who slide down the hill like penguins for their morning dip in the burn.

January 9th - Market day

With the Blue-grey suckler cows filled to capacity with soft sweet hay and Geoff Jnr Safely on his journey to school, we set forth bright and early in the LandRover on our way to Wooler cattle market, a stone's throw over the Scottish Border, in the county of Northumberland, the rattling trailer in our wake loaded to the roof with hardy blackfaced sheep from neighbouring Cocklawfoot, a mile or so higher up the valley, and plump rounded south country Cheviots with snow encrusted fleeces from Swindon.

We quickly leave meandering Bowmont Water behind us, happily exchanging a harsh vast environment of crispy, whiteness for a world of gently rolling green fields, rusted bracken fronds and stark frost-blackened hedgerows. Stalwart dry-stone dykes and steep dramatic hills fade fast into the background as we look forward to an all too infrequent 'away day'.

The twisting narrow road from Kirk Yetholm to Wooler winds and undulates through breathtaking countryside. In the distance to the right of us are the glistening Cheviot Hills and to the left deep hidden valleys, dully illuminated with a pale yellow glow on this cold grey Wednesday morning, as a wintry sun climbs slowly in a dull and heavy, snow-laden sky.

On reaching the sprawling market place we turn sharp left along a muddy rutted lane, slowly passing a long grey line of enormous cattle floats patiently waiting to unload their living cargoes of unwilling passengers, some collected long before dawn from outlying weather-bound farms, set deep in the hills.

Weary waggon drivers sit with engines ticking over, starved expressions on their faces, sipping steaming cups of coffee from a flask or reading a newspaper whilst others yawn with fingers drumming on the dash, or snatch forty winks.

We join the ever growing queue, our noisy, gasping engine muffling the raucous sounds of loudly bellowing cattle and the constant bleating of anxious sheep. Through the open window wafts the pungent aroma of wet wool and dung intermingled with exhaust fumes.

Ever so slowly we inch forward until finally comes our turn

to reverse into the unloading bay. Suddenly, from out of the blue a tyre appears and rolls comically by us down the centre of the highway. We watch incredulously, then wave down the driver of the oncoming vehicle. The erring tyre has come off a rear wheel on his trailer. Hurriedly, an observant mart employee steps forward, a broad smile lighting up his face. We all stare after the tyre in disbelief. Eventually the 'runaway' collides with the kerb, pirouetting slowly to a halt as two elderly ladies in an ancient car, completely oblivious to what is happening, weave cautiously in and out of the stationary vehicles – 'like two pullets on the point of lay' remarks the highly amused mart employee.

At long last we are guided in reverse into the 'dock' where we quickly unload our sheep. They are herded carefully into a pen where they hurriedly merge into a vast sea of bobbing faces. Black ones, white ones, some with patches, others speckled. Cheviots - north and south, Scottish half-breds, lanky Leicesters - Suffolks and their crosses, to name but a few. Marching proudly down a distant alleyway are a dragoon of blackfaced rams. Their heads held high, nobly displaying their majestic sweeping horns that most certainly will not have gone un-noticed by the local stick dressing enthusiasts. These days suitable horns are few and far between and therefore greatly sought after.

By 11 am, thousands of sheep have arrived. The previous week's sale was the first following the New Year and the public were by that time tired of turkey, chicken and pork with the result that the price of sheep has risen hence today's large entry.

I think of cattle markets as sad places and would much prefer if animals must be slaughtered that they went directly to the abattoir from the farm, which would be a lot less stressful for them.

All around me I witness hundreds of pairs of eyes. Some, usually the elderly, exhibit complacent expressions, whilst others appear curious, uneasy or afraid, looking for all the world like children in a dentist's waiting room. There are decrepit rams, broken bellied ewes, their gaunt frames sagging through carrying their heavy burden of lambs over several seasons; plump rounded hoggets and sleek fat beasts of different shapes, sizes and hues, their thick winter coats lick-marked into delicate wavy patterns. All awaiting the same inevitable fate.

Around noon GWB and I partake of lunch in the mart canteen, steaming pea and ham broth, followed by thick crusted apple-pie and cream, washed down with a scalding mug of tea. Then follows stimulating conversation (mostly about sheep dogs) with friends we haven't seen since 1984. After exchanging good wishes for the New Year, we leave to sit awhile at the ringside, my husband noting the various weights and prices of sheep as they come under the auctioneer's hammer. Soon it is the turn of our own hoggs. Reluctantly I follow them over the weighbridge after they have been graded, then stand back whilst they are being sold. Afterwards my husband informs me that due to the enormous entry the price is less than expected. Fortunately the government subsidy will recompense our loss.

Outside the temperature has fallen rapidly. We stamp our freezing feet and blow on our hands to warm them and stand for a moment with me showing child-like fascination at the clouds of steaming breath hanging in the air above our heads.

To the left of us, along a narrow alleyway ambles an ancient hobbling Suffolk ewe, with long drooping black ears that give her a dejected and forlorn appearance. 'Sow-mouthed', her lower jaw much shorter than her upper, she shuffles slowly by and is ushered carefully into a large spacious cattle pen that already contains two skinny yearling sheep that have been rejected by the grader. Following hastily in her wake trots an elderly man with a craggy kindly face, dressed in baggy blue overalls and carrying what proves to be a precious burden. For nestling in the crook of his arm lies a wet and shivering mucus-coated new-born lamb. His mother had dropped him moments earlier into an inhospitable world of slurry and cold concrete and in doing so had not only saved his life but her own for she was destined for the butcher's knife.

I watch captivated as she licks and nuzzles his steaming body, all the while making low mutterings of encouragement. She looks to be one of the patient long-suffering kind, plain ewes often are as thin as a rake and brimming over with character – as is her soulful offspring. However, no simpering softie have we here, for within moments he is up on to his coal black feet and at the business end, his little wet tail wriggling fiercely like an eel. Enchanted I carefully watch his heaving flanks fill up with mother's milk, then satisfied, he lies down in one complete movement, yawns, then falls fast asleep. His belly filled, he sighs and shudders with utter contentment whilst Mum stands guard with head bowed low and eyes half closed,

Tarka takes a well earned rest

contentedly chewing her cud with a look of absolute bliss on her wise old face.

January 15th

Today is GWB's birthday. He says he is 21 again.

So far we have endured fourteen days of snow and below zero temperatures, so I gave my husband his birthday gift a week early - a thick woolly jumper, military style, to keep out the cold.

I rise at 6.45 am. The insides of the windows are thickly covered with ice and it is pitch black outside.

Hidden inside the wardrobe are three birthday cards. Originally I bought two, one from Geoff Jnr, and one from me. Then as always happens I espied another that I liked even more. It depicts a shepherd and his two dogs, watching over a flock of white faced ewes. Inside this card I have written from Jed, Trim, Jan and Bett. Downstairs I arrange the cards carefully on the kitchen table, GWB is at the back door. I can hear him kicking the snow off his boots.

Little Geoff arrives downstairs, just in time to join me in wishing his father a 'Happy Birthday'.

I enquire about the weather and am invited to take a look outside. So leaving the two Geoffs eating breakfast, I go off in search of the cat dish. Eventually, I discover it buried beneath a pile of fresh snow that has slid down off the roof.

As dawn approaches the sky grows lighter and is filled with masses of giant fluttering snowflakes. Every landmark is obliterated by a vast mantle of undulating whiteness. The blackened mountain ash, the grey stone walls, wooden fencing posts and barbed wire. All are covered, hidden from my sight by an all-engulfing blanket. Thankfully, the wild east wind has not as yet put in an appearance, blocking the road, burying the sheep, and preventing a certain young man from getting his education.

A bevy of cats meow hungrily around my freezing feet, whilst tiny sparrows and a robin redbreast wait in the background to clear up the crumbs, their feathers fluffed to keep out the gnawing cold, their heads sunk deep inside their chests. Suddenly alert, they rise into the air as cats scatter. There is a stranger in the camp. John, who drives the school bus, strides into the yard. The steep bank leading to our house, is much too slippery to attempt, so will we telephone Sourhope and ask them to bring the children down in the Land Rover?

John sips a hot mug of tea in front of the heater. He looks cold and is to be admired. Collecting children from remote areas in the worst weather imaginable is not for the faint hearted.

We wait and chat until the sound of a running engine tells us the children have arrived.

'Don't forget to bake a cake and make a trifle for dad's birthday' is Little Geoff's farewell plea as he vanishes in John's wake.

GWB calls to Jan and Bett, before setting off to feed the ever-hungry ewes, scattered around the low lying ground at the foot of Swindon and Whitelaw.

He crosses over the burn, stumbling through deep snow as he makes his way to the hayshed where his tractor is housed, then, loaded up with the sweetest of hay, he chugs along the haugh to where the blue-grey cows and their multi-coloured calves eagerly await their breakfast.

Garry and Laddie whine in anticipation. It's time for their walk. Together we trudge along the valley in the direction of the old school house which once long ago rang with the childish laughter of local children and now provides a cosy home for our nearest neighbours, Maisie and Gil Telpher. In the distance I espy a flock of ewes that have strayed to the boundary fence. I send the dogs off to retrieve them before the swirling snow gets any deeper. Then with lolling tongues and coats that are spangled with silver frost they drive the wanderers homeward, their bellies trailing in the snow.

Time for a cup of coffee before I mix the all important birthday cake. Barking dogs herald the postman and I retrieve the cards and letters from the porch.

Excitement prevails! One of the envelopes contains an invitation from Ethel Conrad of White Post, Virginia, USA to judge her sheep dog trial in May. I had heard a whisper at the Scottish National Trial that there might be a possibility and at last here it was confirmed. I would need a new suitcase, clothes and a passport.

Happily I set to and make a fruit cake, followed by a chocolate sponge and some walnut and ginger buns, then I cross my fingers, remembering previous culinary ventures, that when they were good they were just passable but when they were bad they were awful! A new oven wouldn't come amiss!

Thankfully, on this occasion my efforts prove passable, and

come 4.30 we are ready to blow out the single candle that is wallowing in a bed of chocolate flavoured butter icing in the centre of the table.

February 11th : Back With A Vengeance

Taps freeze, emulsion flakes off walls, kitchen curtains billow, black damp creeps in all directions as powdered snow filters through invisible gaps in window frames, driven there by the bitter east wind.

Outside the door, a century old stone flour barrel that I have cherished all of fifteen years, is cracked all down one side. I shall miss it in the spring for planting seedlings in.

The 'real' winter is now upon us, and in order to blot it out I close my eyes and dream of lush green meadows and summer sun.

This morning there's a glow lighting up the sky, after three days in a row of raging blizzards, which smothered roads and covered up dog kennels, drifted into doorways and blocked the drains. Now at last there is a respite and time to unwind.

Over the radio we are told that there are three people 'snowbound on Mount Cheviot' and that last night's rescue attempt failed, so they plan to try again this morning. Sure enough, outside we hear a helicopter's throbbing drone. I ask myself how can those people be so foolish as to risk the lives of others? If a shepherd is unfortunate enough to lose his life it is in the pursuit of his duties, whereas with hikers it is in pursuit of pleasure.

Thankfully, rarely is a shepherd lost, for he knows the ground and his limitations, and, surprisingly, very few suffer from hypothermia considering that their apparel is much less sophisticated than that of a mountaineer.

An hour later comes the news that the rescue is a success and the culprits are on their way to hospital. Relieved, I dig out the dogs and together we set out to walk to the boundary wall that divides us from Gil Telfer's 'blackie' herding.

It is a long steep haul uphill, hindered by a flurry of snow, but at the end of it a rewarding sight, as the sun peeps through the clouds illuminating distant Cheviot, bathing it in gold. Bowmont Water, winding along the valley bottom like a silver thread, glints and sparkles down below, reminding me of a Christmas scene.

In front close by the wall I perceive a bizarre sight. A wild rabbit that is surely dead appears to move across the snow at speed whilst lying on its side. Meanwhile, there comes distraction overhead, as a skein of geese winging south in V-formation make music in the sky. Perhaps someone should tell them that the weather is the same elsewhere. I pause to watch and listen and in doing so, lose sight of the moving rabbit.

As we wander downhill once again the dogs pick up the scent, and after changing direction the rabbit suddenly appears and this time it's quite clear that it's being towed by a sharp toothed chestnut weasel, with bright darting eyes, and a breast which blends with the scenery. He shows no fear of us and continues on his way, trailing his weighty lunch up and over a mountainous drift, that unfortunately lies in his path.

Much reduced in size to his cousin the stoat, I marvel at the weasel's strength, for the rabbit must be at least three times heavier than himself.

The stoat at this time of the year is easy to recognise, but not so easy to catch a glimpse of in this kind of weather, for he wears a suit of snowy ermine. Only the tip of his tail remains the customary black.

Weasels are commonplace in the valley, and are known to virtually charm the birds down from the trees. Like most vermin they are cunning creatures living on their wits, and once they've marked their prey will pursue it uphill and down dale, until finally, paralysed with fear, the prey forfeits its life.

A favourite trick with some of their kind, is to provide a floor show beside a teeming rabbit warren, where they will cavort and dance, building up to a crescendo of backward somersaults, before their enraptured audience then, when the bunnies' curiosity is aroused, and they feel confident in the company of the clowns, suddenly they pounce, capture and kill amongst a sea of fast disappearing cottontails.

In the distance by the stell, with a trailer loaded up with hay, I see GWB warming his hands on the tractor exhaust pipe, lucky him being tall. I have to stand on the wheel when participating in this all important shepherd's ritual.

(Above)
The *One Man and His Dog* trophy

(Left)
The two Geoffs, Viv and Garry waiting to compete in *One Man and His Dog*

(Above)
Garry at the pen

(Right)
Garry with his trophies

14
Spring is in the Air

February 22nd

GWB sets off early, walking on ground that is soft and yielding, with not a trace of frost.

In the corner of the garden snowdrops flourish, raising their bent heads as high as they are able, in order to greet the sun. Hens scratch in the earth, shake and ruffle their feathers before standing contentedly on one leg, their heads to the side watching curiously while cats yawn and stretch on the window ledge. How quickly some semblance of order returns when the weather gets back to normal.

I lead Tarka out to bask, and see that she is slightly lame,

her near fore tendon strained from slipping on the hill. I make to lead her back inside but she looks so disappointed that I relent and turn her loose. The limp miraculously disappears as she makes for her 'patch' at speed and rolls her stale bulk in delicious clinging mud. I call out to her in anguish. She rises, shakes off a huge cloud of dust before emitting a happy squeal, and gallops off towards the burn, bucking, and kicking out her hind legs, delighted to be free. Then, splashing through the water, she makes for the furthest wall to see what is happening on the hill.

The days are growing longer, tonight it's still light at 6 pm. In the wood a blackbird sings his warbling song, the first I've heard this year, rejoicing at the thaw.

February 25th

This morning I detect the smell of spring in the air. Spring really does have an aroma all its own that floats on air wafted by a warm and gentle breeze.

The balmy perfume grows richer and stronger day by day. It is the scent of growing things, given off by plants and trees and strangely this exotic elixir of life which tantalizes and excites can start emanating long before new buds and swards actually put in an appearance, as though advertising to the countryside the expected birth of a brand new season. The knowing shepherd must step warily here. There is always the danger of being lulled into false complacency for inevitably there is still yet to come the fierce lambing storms of the 'pees-weep' and the 'warp'.

Poor Tarka's lameness has returned these past three days. There is heat and swelling of the fetlock joint. I stood her in the burn for all of half an hour and this morning she is nearly sound. I believe the ice cold torrent, besides reducing swelling, has healing propensities all of its own.

I once owned an Anglo Arab mare, a fiery but harmless beast who, one roasting hot day, when she was tired coming back from the hill, slipped on the tarmac and badly gashed her knees right down to the bone. Three times a day, for a week, I led her into a deep part of the burn. Except for a tiny pin prick of white on her offside knee, she healed perfectly within a couple of weeks and bore no ill effects whatsoever.

With the advent of fine weather comes the instinctive urge to make a clean sweep, by that I mean spring cleaning, for as this globe changes her angle bringing sunlight to our valley, it shines in through previously darkened window panes, highlighting dust, dirt, and cobwebs that mysteriously materialise as if from out of nowhere.

I see new growth beginning to appear on gaunt geranium stems and feel excitement. In the airing cupboard my precious Busy Lizzie has survived yet another winter, and perking up its transparent stalks and watery limp leaves, begs to be back in its familiar haunt on the window ledge, but I dare not carry it out as yet, as a sharp and unexpected frost could lead to its demise.

February 25th

Many of the hill ewes are walking lame through spending the night in wet sheep pens prior to scanning.

It is years since I witnessed so many limping sheep, and on that occasion it was caused by being 'worried' by dogs.

I was working for Ernest Crisp at the time. It was a fortnight before lambing was due to start and the ewes were running in three different flocks dotted about the farm.

The two furthest flocks were grazing in a field called Cinderkiln where many years previously horses had been raced on a cinder track beside a kiln and in the Ewe Hills, a large undulating field with a deep valley running through it. Both these fields had corn bins in them that were filled twice a week.

The third, and nearest lot of sheep were grazing a reseeded corn stubble, in what was known as the East Field. As this field was next door to the farmyard their feed was carried to them from a heap in the granary in a much prized item, namely 'my corn bag'. I describe it as being 'much prized' because a genuine corn bag of the correct shape, size and texture is not easily come by.

I remember that on that particular morning as I walked towards the troughs with my collie Shep, I was surprised to notice that many of the ewes trotting in our direction were limping badly in their hind feet. I put it down to the fact that they were heavy in lamb because sheep are often prone to lameness at this time, but not usually in such large numbers.

After walking along the long row of troughs evenly tipping out the sheep's breakfast I made a quick count and realised that one ewe was missing. I immediately set off to seek her. A trail of wool led me over the brow of the hill to where I witnessed a pitiful sight – an old ewe not quite as nimble as the rest, lay torn and mutilated about her hindquarters.

I quickly returned to the farm and explained what had happened before continuing on to feed the rest of the ewes.

In Cinderkiln two fine ewes lay dead, their throats and faces bloodied and I later discovered a third, lying drowned in a ditch where she had run to escape.

A careful count of the Ewe Hills sheep showed that there was one short. It was Hannah, an old pet that I had reared artificially on powdered milk. She was at that time around eight years old, and walked with an ambling gait.

Shep and I set off in search of her, fearing the worst. A walk around the perimeter of the field proved fruitless. Perhaps she had escaped underneath the fence? I began to feel hopeful.

Before returning home I asked Shep to 'Go find Hannah'.

A lick and a promise

Viv and Garry

Viv asking Garry to stand

Viv and Tarka, Bowmont Water

He had often been sent to fetch her as she trailed miles behind the other ewes on their way to the troughs.

He immediately ran off in search of her and quickly located 'the lost sheep'. No wonder I had failed to discover her where-abouts, for she had tumbled backwards into a large deep fox earth set in the side of the hill and was stuck fast with only her head visible. As I made to pull her out, her large eyes, one pale yellow in colour, the other dark brown, rolled in fear until I sent Shep away to the other side of the field in order to pacify her. It was now obvious that the poor sheep had spent a dread-ful night being chased and worried by killer dogs. I say dogs, because it is usually two or more, one dog not daring to tackle sheep on its own.

Luckily for Hannah her only injury was a torn flap of skin, which hung limply down around her nose.

I pulled her from her refuge and drove her gently back home where, with the aid of some lint and a pair of old tights, repairs were soon completed. Thankfully she survived and within days gave birth to a strong pair of lambs.

The rest of the flock did not get off so lightly as many of them aborted during the following weeks.

Eventually the culprits, a pet collie, and a terrier, were caught after killing and maiming over thirty sheep in the area.

I couldn't help feeling that their foolish owner was to blame for it was disclosed that when he went on night shift, he left them outside until morning 'to amuse themselves'.

March 1st
'In Like a Lamb'

On this first day of March a white mist rolls gently up the valley enveloping the lower ground in an ethereal quality, leaving the hill tops suspended in the sky like enormous mole hills.

On sloping ground outside the back door, miriads of dark green daffodil shoots have mysteriously appeared overnight, their vivid 'spikes' in contrast with the faded grass.

By the stone wall in the corner of the garden, standing out starkly against a backcloth of pale vapour, on the topmost branch of a rowan, a single blackbird sweetly heralds the dawn quickly followed by others perched out of sight in the forest across the burn, vigorously announcing their presence and lay-ing claim to their territory, until the still morning air vibrates with the sound of bird song.

Inside the wooden hen house the poultry cluck and cackle animatedly to one another. The lengthening daylight encour-ages them to start laying their creamy white medium sized eggs that glisten like giant pearls, lying in the nesting boxes.

The sight of them brings to mind that this time last year we had an ebony coloured bantam whose tiny eggs were green. She was much prized, especially at Easter but was unfortunately carried away by a fox.

The mist clears after tea and at long last in these more favourable conditions I am able to give Garry and Laddie a much enjoyed refresher course in the art of working sheep 'trial style'.

We are accompanied on our journey to the haugh by the effervescent Top Cat who on nearing the mature age of two years has developed into a solid bundle of handsome muscle. Some moments later we are joined by GWB with Bett and Cap, this new acquisition, as yet a bit of a male chauvinist where women are concerned, held securely on a long string.

After giving Garry and Laddie a 'run' I am treated to watch-ing first of all Cap being put through his paces whilst the 'sharp edge' keen Bett trails the string at her master's heels, with TC stalking and pouncing on the end of it as she eagerly awaits her turn.

And afterwards the vital, all important 'clap' along the ribs is lavished on both dog and bitch by their grateful master, as a reward for their efforts.

As we cross over the bridge on our way home, with panti-ng collies running on before us, an inevitable short, sharp shower of sleet ensures that this third month of March comes in not unlike 'a sheepish lion'.

March 2nd
The Nursery Final

Great excitement! We are going to the Nursery Final, this year held at Oxton, not far from the town of Kelso. Throughout the season, commencing last October, sheep dog trials have been taking place for the benefit of the young inexperienced dogs.

Scotland is divided into eight regions for today's prestigious event. The highest pointed five dogs from each region have the honour of competing in the Nursery Final for the title of Top Nursery Dog, the John Ferguson silver cup, and the Robert Wallace Shield which is presented to the highest pointed team.

It is a cold dull day and so we use this as an excuse to fill hip flasks with whisky and wrap up warm, especially in the feet department!

The trial commenced at 9 am sharp. We arrive at 10.30 after feeding sheep and beasts. This year, like most years, we have no nursery dogs to run. We tend to keep our dogs on until they grow old and therefore cannot keep too many.

The judge of the final is a friend of ours, Bob Short, who bred Old Meg the mother of Jed and Trim.

On the course, north country Cheviot hoggs test and tantalise young dogs, especially up the sloping 'drive' and at the 'pen'.

We pay our dues and park the car amongst the long line of enthusiasts. Luckily for us, there's a vacant space directly in line with the 'Fetch'. We could not have timed it better.

Without a doubt trials are the most fascinating of affairs, and this one proves no exception. It is six long months since the summer trial season ended and it is wonderful to glimpse so many familiar faces.

If you can close your eyes for a moment and imagine a peaceful undulating setting where numerous people intermingle in a warm and friendly manner, discussing in an animated fashion each and every young dog, its method, breeding and potential, excluding the past hardships of winter work and dreaming of the comradeship of summer, then you have captured some of this compelling atmosphere. As I glance around me I note that every available plot of ground is taken up by competitors and spectators alike, studying and observing the proceedings with an exhausting concentration.

To the rear a huge barn dominates the landscape, inside of which is the all important bar, where 'dog men' congregate to wet their whistles and occasionally to drown their sorrows, sup hot soup and munch tasty sausage rolls and meat pies, their ever hopeful collies cleaning up the crumbs.

As the day wears on the excitement builds. Farmers and shepherds intermingle crossing each other's paths like ants, pausing occasionally to speak with long lost friends. Their heavy tweeds, worn caps, horn handled sticks and rugged weatherbeaten faces betraying their trade. Their conversation comprises of 'Who's standing at the top now?' 'Did so and so manage to get penned?' 'What do you think of such and such a dog?'

Young collie dogs and bitches of all descriptions peer out of the rears of cars and vans. Some roam free or follow at their master's heels, whilst others are chained apart along the fence. Some lie sleeping, some sit quivering with anticipation. The more faithful stand with tails wagging slowly, eagerly awaiting their master's return. Occasionally one or two delinquents, whinge and bark in annoyance at being left behind.

Into this fascinating hub of activity we merge, filled with delight at being part of it all, and at the end of a long day it is Adam Waugh of Glenluce's fox-masked Liz who wears the crown and carries the well earned title of Miss Nursery Sheep Dog Champion of 1985. Her sire, Davy Guild's black and tan, rough coated Tweed, is a dog greatly admired for his balance and intelligent method of working sheep. Liz scored 91 points out of a possible hundred, her Outrun, Lift and Fetch bringing her a decisive victory. North Ayr carried off the team shield.

To end a perfect day we and some friends retreat to a nearby tavern, where open roaring fires and delicious bar snacks await us, before settling down with a round of drinks in anticipation of the highlight of the evening, a sing song from Andy Mclymont, of Traqhuain, the gentle, rosy featured, 'herd whose lovely tenor voice fills every corner of the room and holds the occupants enthralled until the final note runs clear, then the whole place erupts with tumultuous applause from an appreciative audience.

Finally before we leave for home I have the privilege of being seated at his side, listening enraptured by his sweet rendering of my favourite melody *The Londonderry Air*, or *Danny Boy* as it is known, the sound of which never fails to awaken happy childhood memories of my Irish schooldays and as I glance around at the rapt faces of dear friends and well known sheep dog handlers, I swear there isn't a dry eye in the house.

Reluctantly we say our goodbyes then set off for home deliciously tired and deep in thought, in our minds savouring just one more time Traqhuain Andy's songs, whilst outside on the shadowy verges sleepy snowdrops, their delicate fragile beauty enhanced by our headlights, scatter the muddied banks.

March 5th
Spring Cleaning

It is a simply glorious spring day and the sun's warm penetrating rays shining in through the kitchen window make me duty bound to begin my annual spring clean. For when the better weather arrives the days pass all too quickly and before we

(Above)
Tweedhopefoot steading

(Right)
Viv and Geoff are in business!

Charlie is our darling

know it the lambing will be upon us and if I am to leave for my trip to America (the very mention of the word America gives me butterflies!) in May, it is important to me that I leave a clean home.

Before I climb the stairs with creaking step-ladder under my arm, and my old friend the can of brilliant white emulsion in my free hand, I must finally release my precious Busy Lizzie from her cosy sanctuary in the airing cupboard, where she has spent her eleventh winter safe from the elements. After polishing her pot with a damp cloth I place her alongside the geraniums on the window ledge, and after removing a few crinkly dead leaves I ascend the stairs with dragging feet and a long face, feeling not unlike Geoff when he leaves for school in a morning.

By noon, with half the bedroom ceiling whitened I decide that enough is definitely enough on this fine day so I release the dogs and escape somewhat guiltily up the Whitelaw adopting 'Out of sight, out of mind' for my motto, (at least until tomorrow.)

Slowly we wend our way upwards to my favourite spot, huffing and puffing. It feels really warm here on the south side of the hill where it is sheltered from the wind.

We quicken our paces eagerly as the cairn at the summit comes into view. The Top of The World I call this, my favourite haunt from where I can see the most marvellous and dramatic view imaginable. For on a clear day such as this I can look quite easily into several deep mysterious valleys that were gouged out of the Cheviots in the Ice Age by vast glaciers forming flows of freezing water.

As I reach the cairn, the dogs already there before me are resting, panting laboriously, their eyes mere slits. Relieved, I drop down beside them and as I joyfully gaze out on acre upon acre of lonely, beautiful countryside it is easy to imagine what it must be like to be an eagle poised for flight ready to soar high into a clear never ending blue sky and then hover for a while before sliding luxuriously down a thermal back to earth.

Instead I must be satisfied to sit and reap contentment from within my imagination as I look upon this vast panorama of ancient now peaceful hills that are steeped in a violent and bloodied history.

Seated here beside the stone cairn on Whitelaw it is easy to relive an ancient time when the valleys rang with the sound of clashing swords, the thudding hooves of vast armies and the dreadful screams of injured and dying men and horses.

It's time to leave but before making my way home I hungrily cast my eyes in a wide circle, first to the east, then northwards, westward and finally to the south, drinking in the scenic splendour of first of all the bleak and desolate Windy Gyle from where it is reputed that on a clear day you can gaze upon all of seventeen counties scattered both sides of the meandering Border. Then to the impressive King's Seat, an enormous deep hollow flanked on either side by high ridges that from this distance make it look like a massive armchair.

After the King's seat comes Mallie Side, and Auchope looking on Hen Hole and the wild grandeur of Cheviot's broad snow capped summit down to Fasset. Then I seek out Blackdean Curr overshadowed by its mighty big brother, The Curr.

Then onwards to the Shoulder Hill and Percy Law before crossing the Bowmont to Cushat End, Hownam Law, Elisheugh, Place Hill, and The Kip, Wondrum, Greenknowe, Hopehead and Belshaws swinging round to the appropriately named Pudding Law, Crock Law and finally into the familiar gentle sheep dotted lower reaches of the Swindon herding, and the haugh.

And in below these towering hills, shelter the dwelling places of Kelso Cleugh, Cocklawfoot, Sourhope, Blakedean, Attonburn, Cliftoncote, Belford, Mowhaugh, Calroust and finally Swindon, in that order.

All of these wild hills and dwellings over the years I explored on horseback with the late Wattie Little, shepherd of Cocklawfoot, and I remember clearly how on these memorable occasions Wattie painstakingly tried to instil in me the geography of the area, a task for which I am greatly indebted to him.

As we make to walk downhill through the narrow gulley called Lavender Syke, the fiery afternoon sun's reflection is caught for a moment in the burn turning its ice cold water into liquid gold, and as we near home on sighting me Tarka whinneys for her tea from the far side of the wicket gate, a deep throaty welcome that causes her whole being to quiver.

15
Mad March

March 11th

It's a bright clear sky overhead and a keen frost underfoot as I set out on Tarka to 'look the hill'. She is casting her winter woollies for a sleeker shinier look and there is horse hair everywhere, sufficient to stuff a sofa!

We trot quickly along the haugh, Garry and Laddie racing ahead. Once through the hurdle that leads to the hill, Tarka breaks into a brisk canter until we reach the top of Swindon where she stands blowing gently whilst I look around for any sheep that may be in trouble.

Above our heads a solitary skylark hovers, fluttering her tiny wings and singing her enchanting anthem as though her very being depended on it. I sit quietly in the saddle, enthralled by the clear sweet tones whilst the inquisitive Garry cocks his head first to one side, then the other. Suddenly, impatient to be off, Tarka pulls the reins through my fingers, snatches at a clump of bent and ambles on her way.

She breaks into a fast gallop along the 'tops' for it is smooth and safe with no deep drains or rabbit holes to catch her out.

Garry and Laddie, their mouths agape, fall back a hundred yards or so, ever ready to drop out of sight down a gulley in order to take a short cut. They know the surrounding countryside like the backs of their paws.

Riding swiftly downhill, the sun is in my eyes, but to the right standing close by the fence in the shade of the forest I observe a group of young sheep and send Laddie to retrieve them. Unexpectedly he cuts his course and vanishes into a hollow refusing to re-cast despite my frantic whistles. Eventually realising that he has discovered something I ride over and find a poor Cheviot ewe lying 'holed' on her back with a swollen belly and bulging, frightened eyes. Judging by her size she has lain in the hollow undetected for quite some time and is lucky to be alive for had a wandering fox or a foraging family of crows passed by they would undoubtedly have made a meal of her.

I dismount quickly and haul the poor inoffensive creature to her feet. There follows what can only be compared with a ride on 'The Magic Roundabout', as she gallops wildly lop-sided in a circle, with me hanging on to her neck wool and rump. If I were to set her free before she has regained her balance she would immediately roll on to her back again, a dangerous practice for an in-lamb ewe.

Eventually I release her and after a few staggering steps she races off downhill to rejoin her companions.

Much relieved by her recovery I turn Tarka's head for home. She is ready for off! So much so that, full of the joys of spring she attempts a few feeble bucks. When I roar with merriment at her foolish antics she takes it as an intimation that she can bolt, with flattened back, and ears, she takes hold of the bit and flies faster than the wind, only prevented from further mischief by a muddy bog. Thankfully, once the steam is out of her she settles to a sedate lady-like walk, as though butter would not melt in her mouth, her heaving flanks glistening with sweat

Left to right: Glen, Holly, Garry and Laddie, Tweedhope pensioners

Tweedhope puppies

Holly and Glen (foreground)
at Tweedhopefoot

in the morning sun.

Nearly home, I take a last look at the ewes. They are beginning to look heavy now, but fit and sprightly, licking at their feed blocks and nibbling on their hay. Tarka shies half heartedly as a wisp of it rolls along the ground beneath her feet. I scold her gently for I do not wish to topple off today. Tomorrow is my umpty tumpth birthday and a lady who works in the Kelso cake shop who shares my special day, has phoned to say that as a gift she has baked me a birthday cake, a mouth-watering affair, covered in delicious pink and white icing decorated with a blackface ewe, her lamb, and a collie dog. How kind of her.

As I enter the back door I note that Tarka is not the only one filled with the joys of spring for young Geoff's pet rabbits, Pixie, Dixie and Caroline are leaping and playing in the garden like mad March hares. How pretty they look against a background of purple and yellow crocus.

March 16th

Alas! The dreaded winter scourge has returned to torment us, dampen our rising spirits and chill us to the very marrow.

More snow has fallen during the previous night than has fallen all winter, engulfing the house in a giant snowball, smothering the landscape, piling high on the window ledges, and blocking out the daylight.

My poor Busy Lizzie is immediately relegated back to the safety of the airing cupboard, leaving me contemplating as to whether the hint of spring that we had enjoyed of late had merely been 'a window' in the winter weather. However, on opening the kitchen door I am treated to the uplifting colourful sight of primulas – red, blue and gold, gloriously blooming, in old jam pans in the porch. A very definite sign that spring is surely just around the corner.

Outside, on the far side of the burn, tall fir trees, their branches heavily laden, bend in an unnatural curtsey as far as the eye can see.

When I call for the cats to come for their breakfast, the poor bemused creatures crawl out from beneath the dog kennels, shaking the sleep from their eyes before taking giant leaps and bounds across the yard in my direction, vanishing beneath the snow with each soft landing, only their long tails sticking comically skyward as proof of their existence.

Through the garden wicket the wooden rabbit hutch has completely disappeared, under a mantle of white, and so I leave young Geoff to dig out the bunnies whilst GWB and I set forth on the tractor to find and feed the ewes, for it is with them that our sympathy lies, stranded high in the hills where they wended their way the previous fine evening, heavily weighed down with unborn lambs. This 'weather' could not have come at a worse time with the ewes already stressed due to the long hard spell they've endured.

We journey on, loaded up with 'foisty' hay, for the stocks are dwindling fast. The last of the 'good stuff' is unfortunately finished. Nearly 1,000 head of sheep, plus 29 adult cattle and their calves make huge in-roads in the fodder rations when fed seven days a week since the new year.

Along the way, we cast our eyes repeatedly to the hill-tops seeking grey dots on the landscape. Nothing visible stirs, not a sound pierces the quiet except the endless chugging of the tractor engine. We pause, calling out to the sheep hoping that they will eventually wander down the steep brae under their own steam. To forcibly 'dog' heavily pregnant animals through deep snow would play havoc with their well-being.

We space hay out in a long line for the ravenous cows and calves then armed with a bright yellow can of thick black treacle, which helps prevent pregnancy toxaemia, we approach the inbye blackface O.A.P.s who come running at the double at the sight and scent of the container, their eyes round and hungry, their pink tongues protruding from their mouths darting in and out licking their lips, eagerly anticipating the sweet, sticky liquid.

Over the skyline, long straggling lines of little Cheviot ewes begin to appear, gathering speed as the sheep bringing up the rear force those at the front to reluctantly quicken their paces.

I leave GWB to make a rough count and give them their breakfast whilst I trudge home to prepare lunch and finish my spring cleaning. How relieved I am when finally cupboards are tidy, drawers neat, shelves and ceilings whitened, black damp obliterated (if only for a while) and the place is spick-and-span.

Tomorrow is Mothering Sunday and we have saved the snowy-white iced cake decorated with pink dog roses, that Eileen from the Kelso cake shop kindly baked for me because the 'Sheep Dog Boys' are coming to tea.

Alistair, Dougie, Jimmy and Joe are journeying up the valley on their annual visit to Swindon to assess our young dogs, and weigh up the competition —or is it the other way around?

I do hope that the present weather improves because I don't think that we could bear not cutting the birthday cake another day.

March 17th : Mother's Day

Four inches of fresh snow fell overnight and so, to my great disappointment GWB reluctantly telephones Joe to explain the weather situation and suggest that both he and 'the Sheep Dog Boys' come another day.

Joe tells us in surprised tones that his part of the world is relatively free from snow, that 'they' are greatly looking forward to their visit and despite the atrocious conditions at our end they will endeavour to arrive as planned, directly after lunch, (especially since Moira, Joe's wife, has baked a delicious 'Granny Cake' for the auspicious occasion).

Joe will be accompanied by Doug and Alistair. Unfortunately our good friend Jimmy Wilson, who dwells on the hill place of Mayshiel, has to meet a long lost pal he hasn't seen in thirty years. He sends his commiserations and the message that he will see us at the trials once 'The Busy Time', (lambing) is over.

Outside the back door young Geoff's bicycle stands, covered in snow with Silver and Greystoke wrestling for supremacy on the snow-laden cross bar. Surprisingly it is the normally reticent Silver that emerges the victor, neatly toppling Greystoke backwards. He makes a perfect landing on all fours and after mewing plaintively dodges expertly past my legs, eager for the comfort of the armchair and the welcoming warmth of the kitchen.

Delighted that 'The Boys' will come after all, I speedily make half a gallon of quick-set jelly, the strawberry flavoured kind, a trifle and a huge pile of sandwiches encasing them in tin foil to ensure that they stay fresh, before accompanying GWB to feed the stock.

A distant rumble heralds the arrival of the council gritter complete with snow plough. My prayers are answered and miraculously the heavy bales of hay seem lighter as I lift them on to the cart.

Soon after lunch 'The Boys' arrive and we rush outside to greet them with the sound of slamming car doors and wildly barking dogs ringing in our ears.

Alistair steps forward first, carefully carrying a pretty plant followed by Joe bouncing Moira's granny cake up and down like a yo-yo, in a 'stretch' string bag. Under his arm the traditional 'magical' Pandora's Box, loaded with a host of delights including the medicinal kind. Last but not least comes Dougie Lamb, winner of last year's Bowmont Water sheepdog trial, young Geoff's 'special friend' since his toddler days.

Doug humps an enormous brown paper sack bulging to capacity with swedes, leeks and the largest carrots and potatoes that I have ever seen! To me it seems just like Christmas all over again, with modern day shepherds generously bearing gifts. After handshakes all round we go inside the house to warm ourselves, both inside - and out!

The granny cake is rescued and placed out of harm's way, then we unpack THE BOX sharing sweets and chocolates, arranging 'THE MEDICINE' on the drinks trolley and admiring Geoff's new Easter egg.

We settle down comfortably for an hour or so to chat, joke, laugh and tease before taking the customary jaunt down to the Bull Park with keen youngsters Jan Mk. II, her sister Bett and brother Cap. By now the cloud has cleared and a warm sun brightens up the sky.

The dogs are put through their paces on our hoggs, discussed, assessed, praised and criticised mischievously. Afterwards we make for home and tea. Assessing the young dogs is hungry work for man and boy alike and young Geoff is anxious to sample the cake.

As we return the dogs to their kennels I swear that they sigh with relief that no pound notes have been exchanged, assuring them of a home at Swindon.

Finally, we sit down to eat and when the enormous birthday cake is cut and sampled our opinion is unanimous – 'Delicious!'

After a truly happy day amongst friends I go to fasten in the ducks, and find guess what? – a large cream coloured egg, laid by Daisy duck (or was it Cheeky?).

March 21st

Ahead lies a busy week for GWB. All the sheep must be gathered off the hills, dosed for worms and the ewes injected to provide their unborn lambs with immunity against disease and whilst they are in the fields, the thin ewes and those expecting

With Tarka the hill horse at
Tweedhopefoot

twins will be drawn out and kept back in order that they receive adequate nutrition.

With the weather the way it is the less robust ewes would lose condition resulting in death or lack of milk at lambing time.

How shepherds keep their strength up God only knows. Working all hours in the most appalling weather, often getting soaked to the skin and chilled to the very marrow. Come summer - even then there is no respite with hay to get, sheep to shear, dip and drench, cattle to attend to and later on the lambs to wean. Still - these days one must be grateful to be in work at all.

This evening young Geoff, the dogs and I walk along the burn where newly arrived oyster catchers cover the banks. Their pied bodies, bright orange legs and feet, stand out in sharp contrast against the clear deep water and faded background.

Overhead, one of my favourites flashes through the sky on delta wings, uttering its yodelling plaintive cry, long drawn out for the benefit of its mate standing sentinel-like upon a distant rock, with curved rapier like beak pointing in our direction. How I love the sound and sight of curlews whether they be busy in the air, darting over the moorland, brooding their chicks or standing in corn, an amusing sight with only their heads and beaks visible to the onlooker.

Sadly, little Trimmy – sister to Jed, is failing. Now in her fifteenth year, for the first time in her life she refuses to leave her kennel and lies staring up into our faces with sad eyes that are filled with pain. We wonder if this is the beginning of the end.

We live in hope that it is just a taste of arthritis and feed her duck eggs whisked with milk to which we add some sugar for what would Jed do without her? Right from birth they've lived their lives as one, sleeping, eating, running brace and even mothering each other's offspring.

16
April 1st

April Fool

March certainly went out like a lion, with a gust of wind so strong it blew the guttering down from the top of the house.

This morning I easily April fooled GWB telling him that Sue-Ellen, a hefty Cheviot ewe, had given birth to triplets during the night. He asked if I had put them in a pen, to which I replied 'April Fool' and in return received a quiet smile. Young Geoff wasn't so easily caught out.

We do have lambs though, they arrived two days ago, cross Suffolks that positively ooze quality with their pearly white coats, sturdy limbs and inquisitive speckled faces, looking for all the world like naughty children who have jumped into a muddy puddle.

We mated our own twenty ewes to a Suffolk, an enormous hefty chap with a coal black nobbly face. These twenty include Lu Lu, my bluefaced Leicester, who surprisingly has wintered well despite the fact that 'the experts' told me that the breed is soft.

The second of our lambs to be born was dead. Fortunately we were able to obtain a premature blackface lamb and when covered in the dead lamb's skin it was accepted without question. Cheviot ewes are without a doubt the most instinctive mothers and will very often take a new born lamb without a skin on it at all.

We are tube feeding one pair because the ewe is poor and not producing milk. What a boon this gadget is. You simply hold the lamb between your legs, insert a long rubber tube carefully down its throat and into its stomach, then pour the milk into the attached plastic container. By using this method of feeding many lambs can be fed in a short space of time.

The clocks went forward yesterday. Thankfully we have an hour longer of daylight in the evening, which suits us fine now that the lambs are coming.

At night we herd our own ewes into the now empty hay-shed, inside it's warm and dry, with plenty of clean straw to lie amongst.

It has rained solidly for almost three days. Everywhere is sticky mud, the oozing, clinging kind. On a happier note the daffodil buds are opening out and little Trim is much improved. Wagging her tail, she is now helping herself to duck eggs, straight from the nest. I would not have guessed but for the tell-tale yolk adhering to her chin and whiskers.

Now I've been 'April fooled' by young Geoff, who told me that Jemima cat was sitting on my primulas in the porch!

He is cheerful because he's broken up from school for two weeks' Easter holidays.

April 2nd

On my way to the lambing field something bright catches my eye, a sparkling shimmering spider's web soaked in minute droplets of translucent dew. I pause so that I can examine more closely this one of my favourite things. As I gaze on its intricate delicate beauty, marvelling at the complexity and sheer ingenuity of its design and attachment between two strands of wire, one barbed and the other plain, an enormous, fat, long-legged, spider scuttles hurriedly to its fragile edge where it dangles precariously for a moment until a sudden mischievous puff of wind billows its gossamer trampoline inside out.

This morning the air is warm and thick, like soup. Elusive spring has returned. My ewe Lu Lu has gone and blotted her copybook by producing in the dead of night a male, spotty, single child. A massive donkey of a lamb and to think that I kept telling myself when I looked at his mother's sylph like form that Leicesters ALWAYS carry their lambs light, and that at least she would bear two. Perhaps it was the change of ground? I excuse her, maybe next year?

After breakfast I drive to Kelso to pick up a dear friend Eve Edminson, who's husband Frank is now retired. From south of the Border they are a delightful couple.

Eve paints beautiful pictures of wild birds in watercolours. They adorn the walls of every room in her lovely home, whilst Frank's hobby is his large garden.

Eve and I are on an important mission to the woollen mills in Jedburgh to pick out a special 'going-away outfit' for when I depart to the States. I've invested in a new swimsuit too. It's black and white, marked like a collie dog, one of those cut back affairs, that expose everything you've got (and everything you haven't!)

At the mill, everything is arranged in rows on rails. There's kilts and skirts, with coats to match, hats, blouses, shirts and woollies too, in blues, greys, pinks and greens - all the colours of the rainbow. Oh! How I wish I could take the whole store home.

After numerous fittings I settle for three outfits in pink, turquoise and brown that will mix and match. Then, delighted with our choice - Eve's dress sense is impeccable - we have lunch in a nearby restaurant. We have salad and, as a special treat, strawberry flan washed down with sparkling wine, whilst Eve shares with me, secret mouth-watering recipes. And I am on a diet!

Then back to Kelso where Eve produces the most attractive hat in 'ashes of roses pink' for me to wear with my new clothes.

I drive home with a full shopping bag and an empty purse to face the music.

April 8th Easter Monday

It is all systems go on this dank and misty Easter Monday morning.

The shepherds at Attonburn are about to prepare the buildings for housing their ewes at lambing time.

GWB was hoping to put up pens and wire nets in readiness for our 'busy time' but instead must help castrate calves off the Swindon Hill, a task that previously there has been no time to perform.

The yard and garden are a mass of nodding yellow trumpets as daffodils explode in all directions. This morning their golden heads droop low weighed down by the damp, touching what was yesterday scarred and winter-battered earth. Today the air is filled with birdsong, the roar of rushing Bowmont Water and the sound of baby lamb bleats as the ground heals, and sprouts vigorous green grass shoots.

Easter was a happy time - we ate our eggs plus half a surplus turkey that we bought at cut price from a local shepherd.

Our twenty ewes have gone on strike regarding lambs. So far only eight have produced offspring.

On Sunday the little blackface 'set on' lamb finally breathed his last. He caught pneumonia and in spite of every care succumbed.

On a much happier note a blackface pensioner at death's door miraculously revived after a hurried injection of calcium. She had been severely exhausted by the atrocious weather.

This morning GWB leaves our in-lamb ewes fastened in the hayshed to prevent them from harassment when the cows and calves rush in from the hills to be castrated.

Lu-Lu Leicester, much to my surprise, proves extremely aggressive in caring for her spotty son, but old campaigners such as Garry and Laddie refuse to be provoked and give her ample room. They have seen it all before! Young sheep and bought-in sheep usually take a couple of seasons before they settle down.

It is imperative that flocks be gathered together regularly throughout the year by dogs with a quiet authority, ensuring that a bond of trust and respect develops which provides a stress-free environment at the all important time of giving birth.

A 'well-herded' flock eventually accepts their canine guardians as part and parcel of their existence.

The greatest compliment that a hill flock can pay its shepherd at lambing time is to remain lying down contentedly chewing their cud whilst both he and his dogs walk quietly among them. It is certainly worth bearing in mind that a gentle docile ewe invariably rears a gentle docile lamb.

17
Rural Ladies and Lambing Time

April 9th

I awaken early to the steady drip of water and rush downstairs in search of my red plastic bucket - last seen at the back of the pan cupboard.

The skylight in the annexe on the landing is leaking. I've had it stuffed with plastic bags for years but occasionally they drop out and then a damp patch appears downstairs which sends me racing for my pail. The ceiling caved in once. What a memorable occasion that was!

How I wish the rain would cease - it's rained on and off for a week now. What was it that we used to chant as children?

'Rain, rain go away, come back mother's washing day!' It always worked then, every day seemed to be sunny when I was a child.

Young Geoff has got the sniffles, no wonder he's never free from chills and sneezes.

After lunch I bake two large apple pies (his favourites) filled with sweet, delicious golden apples from Frank Edminson's tiny but bountiful tree, plus a date and walnut and a cherry cake. What a pity I am on a diet, wishing to look slim and elegant for my visit to the United States!

Then I face the ironing, a task along with window cleaning I'm forever putting off.

Young Geoff has gone with his dad to learn how to make hurdles for the lambing pens that are suddenly appearing in each field.

Before tea I am invited to come and view a particular ewe that every time 'dad' bends down, she smothers him in kisses. Disbelieving I walk down to the haugh and sure enough there she stands as brazen as can be. A truly amorous ewe. She really is a love and at feeding times when the sheep receive a few 'nuts' she leaps into the trailer and stands there looking regal while she takes a ride.

We christen her Miss Ellie, for already on the Swindon side we have a Pamela and a Sue-Ellen.

Tonight I wear my best bib and tucker and with Garry and Laddie looking solemn and clean, sitting in the rear of the car we embark on a foray to St Boswells, three quarters of an hour's journey away, where I have been invited by the Ladies' Rural, to give a talk on my favourite theme – 'Sheep Dogs'.

On the way, a bedraggled tho' active red squirrel darts across the road. How pleasing it is to see these dear creatures on the increase. I now know of two places where they can be located, one of which is on the way to Kelso from Yetholm.

On our arrival at the village hall we are warmly welcomed by Margaret Rutter, the local secretary. Ten other Rurals in the area have each sent a car load of representatives. We are greeted by a sea of smiling faces which helps dispel my nerves and calm my shaky knees.

The hall looks lovely, the stage decorated with a mass of pink azaleas still wet and freshened by the rain, provided for the occasion by Mrs Anne Gordon of White Hill, where the St Boswells annual sheep dog trial is held.

There are tables everywhere around the room neatly set for supper.

I am asked to chat about our lives as shepherds, for at least 45 minutes. Thankfully, facing me there is a clock set high up on the wall. I hope that I can manage to speak for all that length of time. Now what was the much appreciated advice that I received just last week? I know, it was 'look for a smiling face in the crowd, and speak to that person'. So I look. They are all smiling, I need not have worried. Both Garry and Laddie provide a certain amount of amusement behind me on the stage snoozing amongst the azalea blossoms, looking quite bored except when during my talk I mention them by name. Then they raise their heads and happily wag their tails.

I enjoy speaking about my little family, sheep and dogs and soon my nerves dispel.

Afterwards I am invited to help judge 'The Border Tarts' and am much relieved to discover that they are the oven baked variety.

Mrs Mabel Bisset is the expert and so I leave the decision to her – learning, and listening to what she has to say. Apparently the rules state that the tarts must sport a latticed top. What a pity that some of the contestants didn't realise this. Their efforts look marvellous otherwise.

I am asked to sample the tarts, hang the diet. Who wants to look slim and elegant anyway?

We eat a delicious supper provided by the local ladies for their guests and as a special treat Garry and Laddie, watching hopefully from the stage, are fed biscuits. Their frequent reproachful glances in my direction tell me that it is past their usual supper time.

The Harvesting of the Lambs

Once more the all important harvesting of the lamb crop is upon us.

My husband's two hills amount to some nine hundred acres of ground to cover. These hills are known as The Swindon and The Whitelaw.

Each lambing season I help him lamb fifty blackfaced ewes and seven hundred and twenty south country Cheviots.

One week before the first lambs are expected the ewes are gathered in from the hills and placed in several large fields situated near our house.

Thanks to scanning – those that are expecting twins have been pulled out earlier and driven to a sheltered area - namely the acreage known as The School Field because it lies next door to what was once a school for shepherds' children. In a quiet corner, a long stretch of wire netting has been unrolled to provide a sizeable enclosure where ewes and their young lambs can run in unfavourable weather conditions.

Small pens, covered with corrugated sheets, snugly surrounded by bales of straw have been erected in order to house ewes that give birth late into the evening, and to restrain ewes that have unfortunately borne a dead lamb and require another 'setting on'.

The lambing season is a culmination of the shepherd's skill and effort throughout the previous year and given favourable weather conditions in which to harvest his lively crop the 'good shepherd' inevitably reaps his just reward merely by being aware of the fact that the precious charges in his care have produced a 'guid average'.

Lambing time is very often the most exasperating few weeks on his calendar. For me it is a happy/sad season covering six extremely arduous weeks that are brimful of highs, lows, blood, sweat and tears. In other words lambing can be a pain in the neck or on extremely rare occasions a golden opportunity to develop an enviable sun tan.

Without a doubt a great deal of a shepherd's time is taken up 'wi' studyin'', which is akin to worryin'. Therefore, a good worrier is often a good studier, and visa versa. At this busy time you cannot beat this studying of the sheep in order to be able to pace oneself and last out the distance. For instance a starving lamb that is on its feet can be 'spotted' from a distance of at least two hundred yards. A lambless ewe that should not be, and a eweless lamb that might not be, must be 'kenned' at not less than a hundred.

Lambs that are lying down must unfortunately, as we say, be 'poked' up in order to observe whether or not their bellies are full, and should they rise and stretch after being gently prodded by the shepherd's most essential asset – his crook, the happy 'herd can breath a sigh of relief and happily journey on his way, content in the knowledge that 'the wee mite has sooked'.

A great deal of one's time is unavoidably spent on fruitless – yet necessary – excursions, and strangely no-one is more relieved than the shepherd when his journey does prove fruit-

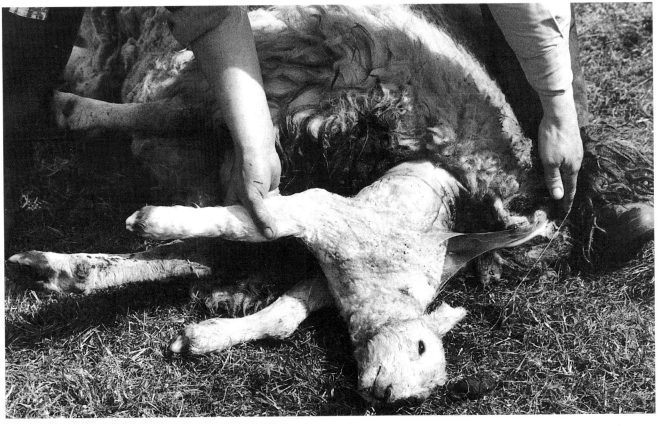

A normal birth

less. For example, when a distant ewe is thought to have a dead lamb lying by her side which suddenly leaps up and springs to life at his approach, and when a sheep considered to be in difficulty proves on closer examination to be giving birth in a normal fashion.

Throughout this busy time the shepherd's greatest attribute is patience as he faces the inevitable storm ridden days ahead when icy rain lashes mercilessly down upon him and the bitter east wind furiously howls around him. With stick in hand and faithful collie beside him he'll pause with his back to the wind in order to turn up his collar and adjust his weather worn cap before plodding doggedly on with a wry smile of acceptance playing about his lips. The attitude being 'the hotter the war, the sooner the peace'.

At the onset of lambing, coloured marker sprays plus a small 'poke' of milk powder are delivered to our door by the farm manager.

Today I prepare for yet another lambing season, with my carefully chosen tools of the trade packed neatly inside that essential commodity, the 'lambing bag'. In the front compartment there is a large ball of string for the purpose of trailing home any unfortunate perished lambs, necessary when the ewe is young and of a flighty disposition – which is quite often when dealing with south country Cheviots. Also in the front compartment – a sharp knife, for skinning of same.

Marking fluid for marking twin lambs identically, and each individual pair differently so I can tell who belongs to whom. Penicillin, to be administered BEFORE a difficult, assisted birth, iodine to prevent joint-ill, a plastic bottle containing lambing oil, and a length of clean cord to loop around mis-presented lambs' slippery feet; protein drink for exhaustion; calcium for deficiency and stress and last – but not least – a prepared mixture for enteritis. The bag is lined with sheep's wool in order to provide a cosy draught proof nest in which to shelter a chilled lamb on the long walk home.

An indispensable 'tool', if it can be called that, is the long shanked shepherd's crook, or stick, no self respecting shepherd would be seen without one. Preferably light and well balanced, its ram's horn handle is fashioned exactly to fit the neck of an erring lamb making escape impossible, as there is nothing more annoying than to catch a lamb then lose it.

Although during a normal working week our dogs receive one good meal a day – usually at bedtime, during lambing they are given a little milk at breakfast and their evening meal supplemented with a beaten egg and part of a carcass of a still-born lamb, when there is one available. There is nothing to compare with fresh meat for putting a collie on its mettle, providing it is free from drugs.

On cold wet days the kennels are filled each evening with clean straw and the dogs rubbed down with an old towel.

At lambing time I am oft accused of being a workaholic - driven on by an inexplicable force I have little choice but to throw myself into each and every task. Unfortunately, being completely unable to pace myself inevitably leads to what can only be described as a 'burn-out'. At such a time I have become so utterly exhausted that after my last rounds of the evening I tumble fully clothed into bed in order that my batteries be given the opportunity to recharge in readiness for the onslaught of the following day.

During this anxious, busy time I am afraid that the house must be given the go-by, for with lives at stake the lambs must come first.

Icy cold weather invariably takes its toll, young lambs cannot stand constant rain upon their backs. However, weather that is dry and cold appears not to affect them unduly. Hill lambs will often naturally find a sheltered place in which to lie. Inside a wooden trough, behind a stone wall, a tussock of grass or their mother's woolly bulk, all of these will suffice.

Small lively hill-bred lambs are more hardy than their larger softer lowland cousins. Too much in the way of cold winds will however only serve to 'knock the milk' off their dams and so supplementary feed in the way of concentrates, feed blocks and when available good quality hay must be fed in sheltered places, and lambs with arched backs and empty bellies topped up with milk last thing.

Cheviot ewes have an above average flocking instinct which makes them eminently suitable for training young dogs. However, just like shop stewards, their attitude of 'one out all out' can prove extremely exasperating at times, especially when one endeavours to extract two or three sheep from the rest. Their nosey, anxious friends and relations invariably insist on accompanying them and despite being 'dogged' away in the opposite direction follow expectantly, eagerly awaiting the slightest opportunity to swallow up and rescue the captives.

Now that all the ewes expecting twins are enclosed together what a tremendous saving of energy there should be in not having to walk each ewe with a pair from out amongst the flock. This way less pressure is put upon the ewe and work is less exhausting for the dogs.

Some of the south country Cheviots have been mated with a north country Cheviot ram. The resulting progeny prove extremely 'wick' for want of a better expression – meaning sharp and lively. Being long and narrow certainly makes their entry into the world much easier for the ewe.

All in all these 'cross-breds' may not be quite as attractive as their pure bred contemporaries but appearances aren't everything.

April 21st Atrocious Sunday

I wonder why bad weather invariably appears at the weekend? On this particular Sunday there is a biting north east wind accompanied by freezing rain.

I leave the house at 5.30 am, rubbing the sleep from my eyes, to find the lambing park looking like a battlefield with frozen corpses lying everywhere. When I lift them they feel like soggy sponges.

Maybe it is not such a good idea to confine sheep in fields. For in this crowded state many lambs are mis-mothered or abandoned. I have always believed that timid Cheviot ewes need space and seclusion in order to produce and get to know their offspring. Neither of these conditions can be met when ewes that are expecting twins are confined together in a small area.

Eight lambs have perished on this cold and bitter morning. After finding and penning their mothers I skin the dead lambs but leave the 'setting on' of fresh lambs until after breakfast when the ewes will be all the keener to sign the adoption papers!

I spend a couple of hours feeding starving lambs. How quickly the milk has gone off their mothers in this atrocious weather.

I do most of my travelling on horseback. It's much faster that way. How patient Tarka my mare is, standing slurping the sheep's 'energy giving' treacle in the rain. How comical she looks with the heavy sticky liquid dripping from her velvety lips, not unlike an ad for black lipstick! I ride Tarka out at least five times each day, always gentle, always willing, big and at this time of the year, raw-boned. I don't know how I would manage without her.

All around us many lambs are being born, popping out like champagne corks, the weight of water soaked up by their mothers' fleeces forcing them out prematurely into this inhospitable world.

Only the greedy ewes arrive for their concentrates, the rest too miserable to leave the shelter of the walls. I dare not walk amongst them for fear they will abandon their lambs.

In many parts of the country there exists a high mortality rate amongst young lambs. Thousands perish every spring. Causes vary. Many are killed or injured by predators, some by careless motorists and others suffer from malnutrition - when a lamb loses its mother on the hill or the ewe is a poor milker. Then there are losses due to pneumonia but, without a doubt, the most common cause of loss is exposure to the elements which can only be avoided by housing in suitable buildings. This inevitably results in extremely high feed bills.

It is unavoidable following a long cold winter, not to lose some of the older ewes. Causes vary, the most common include pregnancy toxaemia, pneumonia, post natal infection, mineral deficiency, mastitis and getting 'couped' so those of you contemplating keeping sheep, be warned!

This evening the kitchen floor is aswim with saturated steaming lambs and soaking outdoor clothing. Should we fail to get the latter dry there will be nothing else for it but to step out in our Sunday best!

Some unfortunates lie trembling inside cardboard boxes placed in rows in front of the Calor gas heater, whilst those on the verge of recovery slither and slide on slippery linoleum, their woolly legs splayed wide.

High on the bleak hillside above the banks of raging Bowmont Water, protected by glistening dry-stone walls, sprightly heavy-coated lambs born of blackface matrons, race back and forth unperturbed by the constant deluge, whilst their hardy dams graze earnestly close by - as yet untouched by human hands.

There is a lot to be said for the 'blackie-ewe'. My husband once lambed six hundred and never laid a finger on any of them. They are of exceptional intelligence and excellent mothers. A truly worthy breed.

I am fast coming to the conclusion that because of their lack of hardiness the south country Cheviot could become a rich man's hobby. Fortunately when crossed with a 'northy' the resulting progeny is much easier to lamb, and crossed with a Suffolk the lambs make a superb butcher's sheep.

Entering the lambing field, especially at the commencement of the season, can be an extremely sobering experience. I often feel that some of the 'mums-to-be' should be wearing 'self destruct' labels. There they stand looking a picture of innocence. You give them their breakfasts then check on those which fail to arrive, only to find lambs dangling from their rears with swollen heads flopping back and forth as the ewes beat a hurried retreat. Sometimes the lambs are mis-presented with one or two legs trapped inside, but even when perfectly presented some Cheviot ewes make no effort whatsoever to push out their lambs, much preferring to spend their time 'borrowing' someone else's, or pulling grass with a completely blasé expression on their faces.

At this busy time collie dogs pick up all manner of bad habits such as 'gripping' because they are constantly being required to catch and hold ewes for the shepherd to lamb. They will also stop short of the sheep they have been sent for, because they are weary of angry confrontations with stroppy ewes. 'Cutting in' on one or two sheep is another problem because during lambing it is rarely required that the whole field be gathered.

All of these faults must be eradicated before the start of the all important trial season, a near impossibility in the case of the

Tarka, the lamb-napper

hill dog who lambs two or three months later than his lowland cousin.

April 27th

I awaken at 5 am after a restless night, with cut infected hands and aching swollen joints – the lambing shepherd's bane, and as I creak out of bed I ask myself for the umpteenth time why do I do it? Certainly not because of monetary gain. Perhaps it is out of habit? Or maybe I feel a sense of duty toward these helpless woolly-backed creatures? No, I think the real truth is that I am just a glutton for punishment.

On rising I am quick to note the rain has ceased and the wind has dropped. Bird song heralds this particular dawn.

Downstairs the hungry lyrical bleat of a lamb that I had given up for dead urges me to hurry and prepare his breakfast. The knowledge that he is still in the land of the living greatly cheers me. No time for self pity or to lick my wounds. Outside there's work to do.

I wonder if Tarka and the dogs groan inwardly at the thought of yet another hectic day. How long-suffering they all are. I will always be grateful for the work that they do on my behalf, always willing, loving and forgiving, never seeking any reward.

Thank goodness it's fine and warm again. The hardy redcurrant in the centre of the garden has made a remarkable recovery from yesterday's battering and is ablaze with tiny blossoms. Beneath the fir trees, in sheltered secret places, clusters of my favourite golden primroses decorate the mossy banks.

This morning there are several new pairs to tend. It is always exciting when first setting eyes on them as very occasionally a 'Brockie' or badger-coloured lamb is born.

I note that there are two single lambs among the twins. Scanning is not infallible.

I hastily tuck Tarka's reins into her bridle, leaving her to graze, whilst I kneel and relieve a poor ewe of two dead lambs both coming at once. Nearby a blackface ewe easily gives birth to a pair of tiny tup lambs. I give one of them, the wettest, to my bereft ewe who happily accepts him as her own. Relieved, I creep away to drag an unwilling Tarka away from the treacle dispenser.

On mounting up, to my consternation I realise that I've mislaid my wedding ring. No time to search for it now and anyway, perhaps it slipped off my finger and is lost inside the ewe I lambed! Off we gallop to the field below the house, the one we call the Hospital Field, where my husband and I put all the waifs, strays, and invalids.

I am warmly welcomed by 'Little Twerp', who by rights should be taken away from his mother, an ancient toothless ewe with a heavy sagging jaw, but she dotes on 'Twerp' so much that I am loath to do it. It will be necessary to supplement his feeds until the grass comes through for 'old Mary' is rearing her last lamb, and must be allowed this final privilege.

In the far corner skips 'Woolly Trousers' who once was 'weakly' and had to spend his nights in the byre, sleeping in an old chest freezer which usually acts as a corn bin.

'Peter Pumpkin', a large fat pompous lamb, stiffly goose-steps by his mum's side. He's recently recovered from a swollen head.

'Horace the second' had watery mouth. An aspirin put him right.

'The Milky Bar Kid' comes galloping up. He's still limping slightly from a broken leg.

Last but not least I discover my favourites, sleeping soundly beside the burn. Barely visible behind a giant tuft of grass I find the miniature pair. A third of the size of normal lambs their own mother abandoned them at birth because she hadn't enough milk to sustain them. Fortunately my husband had a ewe with a dead single lamb so he skinned it, cut the skin in half and gave her two offspring for the price of one 'Tweedle Dum' and 'Tweedle Dee' as we call them, will remain in the Hospital Field for at least a few more days.

18
The American Experience

Saturday 4th of May

It's D Day. My new leather suitcase is standing conspicuously beside the back door. There are one hundred ewes left to lamb. This week the tailing and castration will begin at Attonburn. I do hope that GWB will find time to 'look' the Hospital Field in my absence.

We leave home at 3 am Sunday the 5th day of May stifling yawns and turning up coat collars to keep out the chill morning air.

My flight from Newcastle doesn't leave until 7.30 am but GWB must be home in good time in order to tend the remaining in-lamb ewes.

The car exhaust has a hole in it and bubbles noisily whilst I check for the umpteenth time that I have brought along my passport and purse containing all important American dollars as well as British currency - just in case I need money to spend during the journey.

I am wearing my pink tweed outfit crowned by Eve Edminson's delightful round hat, plus a thick grey woolly jumper depicting sheepdogs, Cheviot sheep and shepherd's crooks, worked in white so I should be warm enough. For once I'm taking my mother's advice to 'never cast a clout until May is out'. When my sister Jenifer and I were children It was vests, liberty bodices and long socks whatever the weather until the first day of June!

Besides my suitcase and hand luggage I tightly clutch a delicately carved shepherd's crook. A gift for one Paul Coy, from Dave McTeir of Peebles - one of Scotland's top sheepdog handlers.

As we leave the valley my thoughts are with young Geoff sleeping soundly in his bed. We had said our goodbyes the previous evening. What I wouldn't give for him to accompany me on this trip of a lifetime. 'One day,' I promised him. He will have a great deal of responsibility heaped on to his shoulders whilst I am away. I do hope that I am not overburdening them.

The fridge, freezer and store cupboard are all full and he has a list as long as his arm to remind him of his chores.

We bypass Wooler, then on down the A1 in the direction of Ponteland and the airport, arriving within the hour to find the place in semi-darkness. I have visions of finding the doors closed and locked but as we head towards them they obligingly slide open. Once inside we make towards the upstairs lounge past smiling cleaners who wish us 'Good morning.' You cannot beat 'Geordies' when it comes to friendliness, even at this time of day.

I can sense the anxiety that GWB feels for the ewes at home so I wish him a hurried goodbye telling him to drive carefully, inwardly wishing that he could stay a little while longer. He turns and walks away, stopping, pausing and smiling reassuringly, waving whilst I blow kisses. Then he's gone from sight and I'm on my own, watching the airport clock and thinking how much more wonderful the 'American Experience' might have been if shared.

Alone, all of a sudden my nerves get the better of me.

President Eisenhower's dog, Robbie

lighting, their excited spouses wearing summer slacks with white shoes, or track suits and trainers. I begin to feel quaint and stuffy in my Border tweeds and smart hat, but not for long for in a far off corner I spot a lady similarly clad. We smile politely towards one another thinking similar thoughts. 'Bing-Bong' ... flights for Malaga and Malta are announced giving flavour to the scene in front of me. I strain my ears listening hopefully for mention of Heathrow – my destination. How I long for a cup of coffee as the aroma wafts by. If only I had remembered to bring loose change. Silly me, sat here clutching a twenty pound note that no-one has change for.

My suitcase weighs a ton. Why didn't I buy one with wheels? Better go in search of the loo, oops, there goes the shepherd's crook falling on to the polished floor with a clatter. Thank goodness it's OK. As I make my way to the Ladies Room the announcement that I've been waiting for comes over the intercom. The visit to the loo will have to wait. I pick up my suitcase and stagger with it en-route for the departure lounge.

Downstairs there is such a sweet man on the desk, both helpful and kind. He offers to send my burden right on through to Dulles, Washington where my hostess Ethel Conrad will meet me.

My hand luggage is placed on a conveyor belt that is surrounded by stern faced policemen whose job it is to check for anything untold. 'Place your walking stick on as well madam' says a voice. Walking stick? Madam? On it goes, then out of sight before reappearing at the other end.

Now I'm being scrutinised intently by half a dozen wary pairs of eyes - making me feel guilty until proven innocent.

I smile nervously in their direction. The response from my surveyors is surprisingly warm. I'm sure that underneath they all realise that I am a complete novice at all this.

I pick up my belongings and make haste to gate 11, down the stairs and through the glass doors out on to the tarmac where the huge monster, a blue and silver Boeing, is waiting to devour me! I am the last to board. Foolishly I enquire of the stewardess following in my wake 'Is this it?' to which she laughingly replies, 'Well, it's the only one.' Attempting to put

What on earth am I doing leaving home and loved ones? Me, who is absolutely petrified of flying. Why it's very nearly as bad as being wheeled on a trolley down to the operating theatre! Suddenly, I want to run after my husband and call after him 'Wait, I'm coming home with you'. STOP IT - compose yourself. Now I feel sick! This place is dark and lonely, only the clock shows any sign of life.

As if by magic, on come the lights as dawn breaks, grey and misty. It's 7 am and people begin to appear as though from nowhere. They are for the most dressed casually - the ladies wearing baggy, comfy, trouser suits, in pastel shades, their newly permed and tinted hair gleaming under the artificial on a brave face and pretending that I do this every day and twice on Sundays I run up the gangway and inside the aircraft to be confronted by row upon row of seats, some pink, some blue. Mine, I am quick to note, is a garish pink that clashes dreadfully with my outfit.

I quickly stow my hand luggage and place the walking stick in the locker overhead, at the same time sighing with relief that my seat is an aisle one - handy for a quick getaway.

I plonk myself down and the stewardesses give out the safety drill.

We are asked to stop smoking and fasten our seat belts before the 'silver bird' swings first of all into reverse and then eases forward smoothly down the long runway. I daren't lean sideways in order to look out. Instead I grip the arms of my seat and tightly close my eyes as the plane breaks into a trot followed instantly by a fast gallop. My heart leaps into my mouth as suddenly with a mighty thrusting surge of power we are finally airborne; rapidly ascending into a brooding cloud-filled sky, in the general direction of heaven - making that particular journey much shorter should anything untoward befall us I reassure myself.

Turbulence is announced. I think to myself, this is definitely the end as the aircraft begins to shudder, and the floor beneath my feet vibrates. I tell myself to stop being a 'cowardy custard' as bright sunlight streams unexpectedly in through the left hand porthole. We are above the cloud, the plane levels out and the lighted sign says that we can now undo our seat belts.

Across the aisle a tall lady hurriedly squeezes by her grinning husband, her face the colour of puce. She quickly disappears towards the rear of the plane.

Breakfast is served, which helps take my mind off my surroundings (or lack of them). Never too scared to eat! For starters there is grapefruit with half a giant strawberry stuck on top, followed by fruit juice, a roll and marmalade, cheese and biscuits plus coffee. What could be better?

The lady re-appears but doesn't eat anything at all.

Bing-Bong, the pilot wishes us good morning and announces that we are now travelling at a height of 27,000 ft at 400 mph. If only he's waited until breakfast was over.

Bing-Bong – fasten seat belts we are approaching Heathrow.

Gosh, that didn't take long, did it?

The plane rolls gently from side to side before touching down, then on go the brakes as we skid carefully to a halt and before I know it I am standing outside, anxiously holding on to Eve's hat lest it be whisked away in the stiff breeze. How chilly it is and how glad I am of my winter woollies.

What a vast exciting airport Heathrow proves to be - and as a special bus whisks me away to terminal 3, I note that I have precisely six hours to kill before my plane leaves for Washington.

Once safely inside the terminal I take a trip around 'Sky Shops' where I replace my lost wedding ring with a stunning replica which costs the princely sum of £2.50. It will probably colour my finger green but I feel undressed without one. I wonder if at home the ewe that 'swallowed' mine has managed to 'spit' it out again.

There are delicious ices on sale, every variety and colour under the sun. I ask for one that doesn't clash with my outfit. Then settle myself into a comfy seat preparing for the inevitable long wait.

What a busy bustling vantage point this proves to be with all the various nationalities hurrying to and fro. Some carrying, others trailing tired fractious infants by the hand, exact miniatures of their handsome parents. I am pleased to note that just like different breeds of sheep we humans come in many colours, shapes and sizes.

To my mind to be black or coloured with flashing eyes and a dazzling smile is to be born truly beautiful and how totally insipid and out of shape some whites appear in comparison to these lissome, swaggering people.

The vivid colours, unusual fashions, different hair styles, languages and gesticulations intermingling peaceably hold me absolutely spell-bound.

I wonder what time of day it is, my eyes seek out a clock. When finally they come to rest it is such a large one, rather like a giant rubic cube, bright yellow in colour, dangling from the ceiling on a long slender stem, that I wonder how I didn't discover it much sooner. What an enthralling pastime studying humans is, wondering at their cause or mission, and where destiny will lead them.

Two young lovers embrace beneath the yellow clock, one black the other white, kissing, laughing, pulling away from one another then coming together again. Finally he has to go. Tearfully, they make their last farewells. How quickly time flies, it's noon already. Suddenly I feel quite old.

Phew, it is getting warm in here, off with the grey woolly jumper and unaccustomed high heels.

An elderly Indian lady is wheeled by in a chair followed by an entourage of anxious chattering relatives, and in their wake a stout American blonde dressed in a noticeable flared trouser suit, that without a doubt is made from rose patterned curtain material. I fan myself with a magazine as two Asian ladies hurry by wearing mink coats, then two young men (holding hands).

I strike up a conversation with a girl sat next to me. In a strong American accent she tells me that Virginia is suffering a heat wave. Oh no! My suitcase is full of winter clothes.

A pretty Japanese girl glides by cradling an enormous bunch of wilting blossoms. Time stands still as the temperature soars. I quickly become mesmerised by the everchanging sights, moods and fashions. Stripes, checks, flowers, covered heads, bared heads, plaited hair, pony-tails, bunches, corded, beaded and ridged tresses. A plump Chinese girl wearing patent leather shoes gobbles down her third pea green ice and is promptly sick.

I observe delightful reunions. Relations and friends hugging, kissing, laughing – shedding tears of joy. Sweet babies are held aloft for inspection by their adoring parents, whilst toddlers chase around their feet in endless circles.

At long last it's 3 pm. Time to leave this riveting kaleidoscope of colour for the last leg of my journey but before boarding a final treat, a quick trip around the duty free.

Well, I'm finally on board – it's positively ginormous! Much bigger than our house. A massive Jumbo 747 that holds approximately four hundred people and is capable of travelling at 550 mph. '700 in a strong tail wind' the steward informs me with a twinkle in his eye.

The large plane stands placidly on the tarmac blowing gently sounding for all the world like a giant grain dryer.

Right next to me a talkative athletic lady sits nursing a broken toe. She informs me that she broke it floating down some rapids in Madagascar when living dangerously, then enquires of the steward if she can have two seats instead of one - to make her toe more comfortable on the long flight ahead.

I'm seated in a bright orange seat this time, the floor is carpeted in royal blue, while the curtain cutting us off from 1st class passengers, blocking off the film screen is striped, pink, orange, purple and blue. I'll bet a MAN is responsible for the décor!

Safety regulations have been read, seat belts fastened and headsets and film programmes given out. At long last we are taxi-ing smoothly down the runway, past many different coloured aircraft from all over the world. The sun is shining brightly and there is enough blue in the sky to make a sailor suit - always a good sign. We slowly turn left handed on to the main runway and with a quick surge of power off we go faster, faster, faster, ooh, for me this is by far the worst bit.

I'm almost sure we're airborne, better take a peek. Yes, up we go at an almost vertical angle. I hear a squeak followed by a click as the wheels come up. Perhaps they need a drop of oil?

We are climbing steadily now. The engine sounds lovely, purring away just like Top Cat on a full belly. I wonder what everyone at home is doing at this moment?

I am seated above a wing. It's rocking but only slightly. America here I come!

We are flying over Bristol, the M4 and the River Severn in that order. I know because we've just been told by the captain.

Drinks are being served. I have my favourite tipple drowned in lemonade on a little folding tray in front of me.

Behind the 1st class curtain the film is in progress. My attention is commanded by someone of much more interest than the film, which happens to be one I've seen anyway. Across the aisle in front of me a gorgeous little girl - obviously a seasoned traveller - with long curling dark hair and eyes like saucers is playing peek-a-boo and giggling at me. A much more amusing pastime.

After a truly marvellous lunch I slip off my shoes and take a welcome snooze. Sheer luxury this. I could possibly grow to enjoy this mode of transport?

We are informed over the intercom that we will be landing at approximately 6.15 pm American time, and that the temperature in Dulles is in the high 80s.

We are nearing our destination so I think I'll pop along to the ladies room for a quick wash and brush up. I reach for my shoes. Cripes! They won't fit. My feet have swollen to twice their normal size. What am I to do? I can't very well leave the plane without any shoes. I know, I'll fill the sink with cold water and dip my feet in it.

I trot along and do just that, but what a difficult task it proves to be in the narrow confines of the loo. I am not a contortionist but somehow manage to hoist my right foot high above my shoulder and place it in the ice cool water, at the same time hopping on one leg in order to keep my balance. That's much better. Suddenly a sign lights up, there's one in here too? It proclaims that there's turbulence up ahead. I must go directly to my seat. BUT – no way am I going anywhere. After all of this tricky complicated manoeuvring my feet are staying put. So I hastily cross my fingers and tightly close my eyes as the floor begins to vibrate and immediately begin to visualise being discovered, should something untoward happen, in this somewhat peculiar position.

Thankfully, by the end of the turbulence my feet are beginning to return to their normal size and when the plane lands I am able to disembark wearing my shoes.

Ethel is waiting to greet me just beyond customs. How reassuring it is to see her smiling countenance amongst a sea of eager welcoming faces. She waves and welcomes me with a hug. An extremely attractive lady of Swedish descent whose startling brilliant blue eyes and outdoor complexion belie her 62 years.

We go in search of a porter to man-handle my heavy suitcase, then I am invited to wait on the 'sidewalk' whilst she fetches her enormous station waggon.

On noticing the registration I have to laugh, the lettering reads GRRR 6, Ethel owns six Border collies!

We load up and I make to get in. On the wrong side, of course, almost colliding with poor Ethel who 'Whoa's' me and directs me to the correct side. I wipe the beads of perspiration from my brow. It's 87° in the shade and I'm dressed for winter!

After hurriedly stripping down to blouse and skirt I am driven off in the direction of the Blue Ridge Mountains of Virginia, but alas not on the trail of the lonesome pine - not today anyway.

It's at least one hour's drive to Sunnybrook, Ethel's farm. dogwood trees laden with brilliant white blossom, Virginia's emblem, mark the route - what a change from Britain's leafless trees.

It is almost dark when we reach the house which Ethel and her late husband Bryan Conrad bought in a dilapidated state some 31 years previously. Bryan was a Brigadier General in the American army and the first American military observer to be sent to Britain in '39, later to become Head of Intelligence, G2.

Inside we are leapt upon by Ethel's black and white army,

Tess aged seven and easily the leader of the pack, Jan who is six, a recent import from Scotland, the lovely Mig, so much like our breed in both looks and temperament. Old Bahnie, wirey coated and recuperating from a caesarian, the sensitive Flo and last but not least the baby of the bunch nine-month-old Belle, whose mother Nan sold for a record price of eight thousand dollars and of whom great things are expected.

These six boisterous Border collies form the nucleus of Ethel's immediate family – apart that is from Bryan, her only son who is married to Tammy and lives a few miles down the road with their adorable two-year-old son William. Another 'happy event' is imminent.

Bryan farms Ethel's land in partnership with his brother-in-law Justin Mackay Smith. The two of them operate a profitable feed lot at Montana Hall, one of Virginia's vast estates where Justin's aunt resides. Three hundred head of cattle are fattened in the yards at the push of a button whilst a further three hundred await their turn in the surrounding parkland.

At Sunnybrook, Henry, Gladys and Mac assist with the running of things – all coloured, warm happy folk who worship the ground Ethel walks on.

Ethel is the first to admit that she would be absolutely lost without her mainstays. Henry has been with her for thirty years and his mother, described by Ethel as a wonderful person, was employed for twenty years until her death. Originally Henry was hired as a groom for the Conrads' eighteen horses. These consisted of retirals, brood mares, hunters and young stock. Of him Ethel says, 'You can't buy his kind of loyalty and devotion, nowadays he helps Bryan with the cattle but still finds time to fetch me the morning papers and check on me at the same time.'

Gladys does the household chores. She immediately took me under her ample wing for the duration of my visit calling me her 'Little Bo-Peep', and nurturing me like a mother. She's taken care of the Sunnybrook household for twelve years.

Mac is 'head gardener'. 'He's a marvellous carpenter when he's there,' Ethel laughs. She explains that poor Mac frequently suffers Monday morning sickness.

I am shown around the spacious house. The walls are covered with paintings of hunting scenes and collie dogs and it is tastefully furnished and decorated in the old colonial style, with gleaming wood floors that are scattered with colourful rugs, and huge carpets brought over from China in 1917 by Ethel's mother-in-law.

When Ethel and Bryan purchased Sunnybrook it was so full of bugs, bats and nests of ticks that they debated whether or not to renovate it, or tear the place down and start all over again. Finally they decided on the former and renovation plus extensions took place with the Conrads acting as chief architects.

To the rear of the main house stands a small school that nowadays acts as a guest house. Once the children from three farming families gleaned their education within its creeper covered walls.

Most of the houses in this part of Virginia are predominantly made of wood. Ethel's is painted a gleaming white, with dark green shutters. Along the front a shady verandah overlooks smooth sloping lawns, tidy flower beds and a kidney shaped swimming pool. The whole area is surrounded by trees - weeping willows, silver maple, cedars, golden rain, mulberry – all planted by Ethel and her late husband.

I settled down for a chat about the forthcoming sheep dog trial and a welcoming Scotch on the rocks, much to Ethel's horror, diluted with orange juice. (They don't have fizzy lemonade in Virginia). Exhausted but surprisingly not one bit hungry, we retire to our beds, Ethel to a four poster accompanied by her entire flock of dogs and me to an enchanting room at the end of a long highly polished landing. After unpacking, within moments of my head touching the pillow I was sound asleep lulled by the sweet notes of a mocking bird from its bower in the mulberry tree outside my window.

The air is warm and filled with the heady perfume of honeysuckle. I sleep deeply, covered by a single sheet, blissfully unaware of the many night noises that are to be heard in this part of the world and the fact that miriads of bugs of all shapes and sizes are clamouring to be in, only prevented from doing so by the fine wire mesh which covers the outsides of the

Lewis, Ethel and the author at the presentation of the prizes

open windows.

I am awakened at 6 am, dawn. The air is bursting with birdsong, magnified more than I have ever heard it previously. (Everything's big in America!).

Through the cane blinds shading the four windows in my room, the sky is alight with a vivid pink glow which spreads rapidly from the horizon, its deepening reflection reaching in, caressing the solid wooden antique furniture and highlighting the enormous oak bed with its ornately carved posts and intricate headboard. The snowy white coverlet and primrose and marigold patterned sheets take on a soft roseate tinge as the morning sky deepens gradually to indigo, and a fiery red sun rises over the skyline.

At the windows hang long silk drapes in a pastel shade of green. The walls are milky white, in sharp contrast to the heavy furnishings that comprise of a walnut writing desk, rosewood dressing table and a sturdy chest of drawers.

On top of the writing desk an imposing brass lamp dominates the room. Paintings and photographs abound and from the wall opposite a portrait of Bryan Conrad Snr. gazes down on me with a kind authoritative expression.

I begin to doze feeling secure in this comfy sunlit haven but I am brought rapidly wide awake by the thunderous patter of tiny feet along the wooden landing as Ethel vacates her bedchamber to take her family 'walkies'. I do a hasty calculation, six dogs mean 24 paws, mean 96 claws all hitting the floor at once, well almost, for Ethel explained to me the previous evening that poor Tessie had recently had a toe amputated due to injury.

Ethel returns minus the dogs and begins to batter mercilessly on her typewriter. I wonder where on earth she gets her vitality from. Later on I am to learn that she derives her energy from drinking gallons of 'battery acid', a secret concoction made from iced tea, lemon and mint. What a slogger she is and in her day a brilliant horsewoman, judging by the many photographs of her riding over impossible fences with a mischievous grin on her face and a determined glint in her eye.

Her main sport had been polo, closely followed by hunting across the vast often densely wooded Virginian countryside, where people like John F. Kennedy kept a country retreat.

Ethel's greatest moment came in 1969 when she won the Virginia Field Hunter Championship riding her homebred horse 'Prodigy', now a sprightly 26-year-old who runs out with his half brother, a chestnut named Snob who is a mere 24-year-old. Snob was born with a slightly deformed leg and it was suggested that he should be destroyed. However the groom was optimistic that his deformity would not deter him from making a useful hunter. Thankfully he was proved correct and Snob made a wonderful riding horse.

Nowadays Ethel must be content to compete with her dogs in sheep dog trials. An accomplishment at which she is no mean hand.

In her spare time she fulfils her duties as president of the United States Border Collie Club - truly a woman of substance.

May 6th

After a leisurely breakfast Ethel takes me on a guided tour of Sunnybrook Farm - 'Ethel's kingdom' as I am wont to call it.

We return to the house hot and sticky and after consuming large quantities of 'battery acid' we spend what's left of the morning working her dogs on a small flock of Barbados black bellied sheep, kept by Ethel for just that purpose. A rich red in colour, closely resembling deer in appearance, if handled quietly, contrary to popular belief, they are not as unmanageable as their reputation would lead one to believe - providing you can discover their whereabouts in the first place. For like deer they are capable of clearing great heights from a standing position. Therefore the average fence presents no problem to them whatsoever.

In order to discover their hiding place more quickly Ethel has hung bells around the necks of the ring-leaders.

Why keep this particular breed at all when there are many others to choose from? The answer is simple. In Virginia the summers tend to be hot. Already the earth is parched and dry. Coming from the island of Barbados these black bellied sheep are used to high temperatures and shine above all others in regard to stamina.

We take a look at the field where the Blue Ridge Sheep Dog Trials are to be held on May 11th and 12th. Ethel smoothly skims over the grass in her electronically charged golf car – a mode of travel necessitated by a bad fall the previous winter when she broke her ankle whilst trying to prevent a dog fight.

It is immediately obvious that the ground will provide a good challenge to both the handlers and their dogs, with dips and gulleys abounding – should a dog be directed right handed for its sheep there is every possibility that it will lose sight of them on the outrun or run too wide, because there is a lot more acreage in that direction.

A left hand outrun is definitely preferable, and even then there is a chance that the sheep may have run downhill and out of sight before the dog reaches them.

If the sheep are picked up successfully they will be fetched into a valley, then between two large trees in the direction of the handler. I have decided not to have any Fetch hurdles in order that the sheep can be lifted more easily should they stray.

The Drive Away is down a steep hill and halfway up another, therefore it will require to be carefully negotiated before turning into the Cross Drive, the last part of which passes close to an outcrop of rocks and trees.

After attempting the last gates the sheep will be brought uphill to the pen, which is an ample 6ft by 8ft, carefully constructed of wood covered by a fine wire mesh.

Due to the expected high temperature we decide against including a sawdust marked Shedding Ring in the course.

Following lunch, with Ethel's blessing I give her two youngest bitches two-year-old Flo and nine-month-old Belle, a short schooling session. Both bitches prove promising, Flo slightly more inhibited than Belle, rather strong of eye but stylish and intelligent. Belle at first refuses even to give the sheep as much as a glance until we attempt to leave the field, then as if fired from a rocket she sprung into action, working for all she was worth. At first with neither eye nor style, but I know that it will begin to creep in eventually for I have seen her work the other dogs in a very classy manner as they followed Ethel's golf cart.

Occasionally, I pause to breathe in the sweet air and gaze on the wooded landscape and rolling green hills set against a backcloth of steely blue, for today the visibility is excellent and the Blue Ridge Mountains really live up to their name. If it wasn't for a brilliant red cardinal, Virginia's chosen bird, flitting back and forth among the trees, I would swear that I was back home in Britain.

I begin to melt in the sweltering atmosphere, and feel the need to blink at least twice to convince myself that it isn't all a dream, that I am really here in a green meadow with a sheep dog working sheep, in one of the United States of America. Later in the day, after a short nap, at Ethel's insistence we take a ride in the car to White Post, Ethel's nearest town, so named because of a stalwart white post erected at the crossroads by George Washington in 1750 under the direction of Lord Fairfax. It was originally used as a survey marker and guide post to direct strangers on the old Dutch waggon trail to Greenway Court, home of Lord Fairfax.

We return to the house for a shower, dinner and 'drinkies', in that order. Until naughty Ethel suggests that we've earned a 'dressing drink'.

An afternoon nap, a dip in the pool should I desire it, a dressing drink? This could easily become an extremely pleasurable ritual. How on earth am I going to slip back into the old routine when I return home?

Two exciting events occur the following day. The first being the arrival of twins. No, not to Ethel's son Bryan and his wife Tammy, but to a Barbados gimmer (two-year-old sheep). Normally I would call her a shearling or once sheared ewe, but one doesn't shear black bellied sheep, one plucks them!

Henry and I shepherd the 'new Mom' and her two lambs into the barn where we could keep a close eye on them for a couple of days to ensure that they get plenty of milk.

The second bit of excitement was the arrival of the trial sheep. Ethel had hired them at two dollars per head, plus an extra dollar for shipping! Her own flock is no way large enough to provide runs for seventy plus competitors.

19
Preparing for the Trial

The ewes for the trial, Corriedales accompanied by their young lambs, are delivered and enclosed in a lush pasture in order to get some meat on their bones in preparation for the ordeal ahead.

I telephone the two Geoffs, and I'm relieved to find that all is well at home.

Thursday 9th Preparing for the Trial:

What a hot and hectic day this proves to be. I rise at the crack of dawn and with dear obliging Tessie's help return 'the lodgers', as I've nick-named the Corriedale sheep, to their field,

from out of the fold where they reside at night so that we can watch over them for any signs of ill health.

When I first set eyes on them I panic because they appear to have 'runny' noses. However I am quickly re-assured by Ethel that their apparent sniffles are caused not by rampant pneumonia but by a minute insect called the bot fly which invades the nasal passages. I am tempted to enquire with a name like that shouldn't their business be at the other end but refrain from doing so.

There is much to accomplish on this sweltering Thursday. The trial course must be erected, a task that is not as simple as it sounds as a great deal of thought must go into the positioning of the hurdles and the pen if the trial is to be a success. Perhaps I should have said pens for Ethel explains to me that at most trials in the States instead of one man and his dog holding the sheep to the post at the far end of the field, they are held in a collapsible pen and released when the competing dog approaches them.

The thought of this method of release fills me with disappointment. I have had experience with these contraptions and feel that they interfere with a dog's Lift. Ethel points out that conditions in America are different because of the heat making it impossible for a man and a dog to hold the sheep as is done at most trials in Britain. By placing them in a collapsible pen a child can be seated in a deckchair under a parasol with orders to pull a string as a competing dog approaches. Providing the child is attired in clothing that tones in with the background there are usually no problems.

The pen or 'Bird cage' as I call it proves better constructed than most, only the front drops down to release the occupants.

Once we have placed it in a suitable position we give Tessie a practice shot to see how it will function.

When she gets to the 11 o'clock position I swiftly pull the string then collapse laughing at her antics for the sheep refuse to leave the pen until she walks to the back of it and taps twice with her nose. What a wise old bird she is for even though she will accompany me almost anywhere, in her mind she is working independently.

This type of release causes a dog to get into the habit of coming in too tightly behind the sheep and often they cannot fathom out which way the sheep will lean with the result that they start the Fetch off course. I make a mental note to allow for all these possibilities, and to arrange for someone to walk forward and quietly put the sheep out of the pen should they refuse to budge.

Sam, a neighbouring farmer's son and I put up the course - with him kindly offering to do the heavy work. We carefully position the other pen at this end with its gate in a direct line with the last hurdle. Afterwards we lead a truck-load of straw bales to the top of the field to camouflage the main holding pen so that the competing dogs will not be distracted by the wrong sheep.

Some of the competitors begin to arrive in their luxurious mobile homes. All throughout the season they will travel thousands of miles in order to compete in this their chosen sport.

Big Joe Lawson is a dairy farmer from Creek Farm, Shady Dale who introduces himself and his three collies Gael, Mirk and Drift.

Between us there is an instant rapport for he reminds me so much of Hoss Cartwright, of Ponderosa fame, a favourite childhood TV star – and in the days that follow this big sweet man who spent 25 years shoeing horses before milking cows, becomes known to everyone as Cuddles.

Cuddles imparts some useful advice regarding the pen. He has run on ewes before which were newly separated from their young lambs. (For we must shed them off each morning before the trial). The advice is that we turn the pen completely around so that when penning the dog will be on the 'heavy-side' of the sheep, thus preventing anxious mothers from bolting off the course and returning to their young.

Walt Jagger is another super chap, who addresses his dogs as 'my little girls' and croons to them on his lap. His tall daughter's name is Cheryl, a lovely girl who alternates her voice beautifully when she commands her dogs. 'Mom' has come along too, accompanied by her pet sheltie who is capable of getting up to more tricks than a circus dog. Both they and their dogs have travelled from Sheepy Hollow, Hop Bottom, Pennsylvania.

Cheryl's friend is Bruce, a professional sheep dog trainer and a great chap – I would not have missed meeting them and others like them for the world. Even though it is All Systems Go!

May 11th The Great Day at Last

The great day has arrived at last. The Blue Ridge Open Sheep Dog Trials are due to commence at 8 am sharp!

Hopefully everything down to the smallest detail has been catered for. There is even a bath of cold water for the dogs to cool off in once they have completed their run – though wise guys immerse theirs beforehand.

Candace and Gerald Terry have provided a roomy horse trailer for the judge and attendants, Pam Plummer on pencil and Gail Dapogne on stop-watch. The trailer comes complete with all mod cons including a fitted commode and a pail of ice to place my feet in when the temperature soars.

Candace is dark haired, tall and willowy, a pretty girl who will be competing with her imported Welsh bitch Gwen, in the Open Class. I first made her acquaintance last summer when she visited us with Gail Dapogny to attend the International Trials at York.

When I asked Candace how she first became interested in sheep dogs she told me that it all started when she was teaching school. She took a trip into the desert where she met Gerry then a bachelor, working as a Secret Service agent, assigned to the General Eisenhower detail.

Love blossomed – and Candace eventually became Mrs Gerald Terry. Together they lived happily on the outskirts of Eisenhower's Gettysburgh Farm in Pennsylvania.

When the General suffered a heart attack he was taken to the Walter Reed Military Hospital leaving a treasured possession at home on the farm, Robbie, a one-year-old Border collie puppy bred from Scottish stock. When Candace went to check on Robbie she found him desperately ill with pneumonia so she took him home and nursed him back to health. He was a beautifully marked, rough coated, black and white dog that had been given to Eisenhower as a gift. He received many gifts of animals for his farm from well known dignitaries. President Khrushchev sent him mules – of all things.

When Candace visited her husband who was standing vigil at the hospital, General Eisenhower asked to see her. First of all he thanked her, then he gave her Robbie for her very own saying, ' As I have your husband you may have my dog'.

Candace has never forgotten those words and though Robbie her collie is long since dead, she will never forget him, either.

There are three other classes besides the Open, entered in the trial. The first is called the Novice Novice, which consists of a shortened course plus penning, for dogs and handlers who have never run in an Open Class. The second class, known as the Professional Novice, consists of a shortened course, and includes one set of gates plus penning, for professional handlers competing with novice dogs.

The third is called Open Ranch. This includes a full course without a Shed, where either the dog or the handler can have competed in the Open Class, but not both.

Before the commencement of the trial I was invited to give a short talk regarding what I would be looking for concerning the handling of the sheep around the course. I hope I explained clearly that apart from straight lines and tight turns I was hoping to see practical work plus a good working partnership between man and dog (or woman and dog).

I also said that I judged hard, meaning that I would be looking for perfection and that everyone would be judged exactly the same regardless of sex, then in case it would be misinterpreted changed it to regardless of what sex they were !

8 am. Kick Off. Dick Karrasch a veteran sheep dog enthusiast, had been elected beforehand as Master of Ceremonies, and throughout both days did a marvellous job on the microphone keeping everyone informed as to who was at the post and who followed who, interlacing his perky commentary with subtle American humour – the Bob Hope kind using baseball jargon that consisted of 'There's so and so at the post, one on the deck – and one in the hole'.

In Britain it has been said that we keep dogs to work sheep, and in America they keep sheep to work dogs.

I found that in most cases this tended to be true. Competing in the Blue Ridge Open, there were people from all walks of life. A dentist, a lawyer, a garage owner, a nutrition expert, an insurance salesman, an author, a builder, a carpenter, a nurse, a barber, a school teacher, a nuclear plant worker as well as a whole host of domestic engineers. (Candace's name for housewives.) Of course there were farmers too, but these tended to be in the minority. It was soon obvious that in most cases the farmers' dogs had a bigger advantage over the rest regarding stock sense and the ability to keep the sheep 'on course'.

Throughout the long day I made the acquaintance of many an old friend – four footed ones that is. There was Rod from Wales who won *One Man and his Dog*, Jan from yon side of Yetholm, Ben, Meg, Queen, Shep, Drift, Midge and Tess, to name but a few. Some had greatly benefited from their newly found freedom and new high protein diet, whilst others still betrayed the same old hang-ups they exhibited back home. Personally I would like to see more dogs being bred and trained in America as I am sure the handlers would find it both rewarding and beneficial to produce their own trial dogs.

To export a sensitive dog is to cause it untold misery and heartache, however I have to admit that friendly out-going types appear to suffer little or no ill effects from what undoubtedly must be a long and traumatic journey for them.

Most of the male handlers appeared tall and handsome, dressed like cowboys in their stetsons and high-heeled boots. They brought back happy childhood memories of my erstwhile hero Roy Rogers – who fell rapidly in my estimation when he had his beautiful palomino horse Trigger stuffed. However it didn't stop me eating at one of his many restaurants, scattered about the countryside like gold dust.

Throughout the day the penning of the sheep proved a great source of amusement to us three girls slowly baking like jacket potatoes within the confines of the horse box. Because of the intense heat no amount of skilled dog work, short of a quick nip which could result in disqualification, would persuade those poor sheep to enter that 6ft by 8ft pen so in sheer exasperation the handlers resorted to what can only be described as an Indian war dance, leaping up and down in the air, causing the parched earth to vibrate so as to encourage the ewes to take those few vital steps that meant the gain or loss of those vital points.

Some handlers even resorted to blowing hot breaths of air into stubborn sheep's faces.

However, over the two days I was pleasantly surprised by both the ability of the dogs and the handlers. I can honestly say that nowhere have I seen such enthusiasm. Healthwise the dogs were a great credit to their owners – they fairly bloomed, and it became very obvious that in order to compete in the extreme weather conditions their diet would have to consist of the best nutritional value available.

I cannot speak highly enough of those concerned in releasing the sheep from 'The Birdcage' and those transporting them to same. For the sheep were handled expertly, just like grandmother's china. It is this all important task that ensures whether or not a trial is a success or a failure.

With the exception of one unsound packet of sheep I felt that the trial had been a truly great success and at the culmination of two days' rigorous shepherding, Lewis Pulpher and his tri-coloured imported Moss were well and truly the outright winning combination at the Blue Ridge Open Sheep Dog Trials.

Moss impressed me greatly, not only by his class and method of working, but also by his breeding. His sire is David Guild's Tweed, a dog which I greatly admire.

Lewis and Moss

Moss is a rough coated five-year-old dog imported in '83 from Scotland bred out of a daughter of Willie Welsh's Don. His first home was with Bob Childress in Texas. Bob originally sent him to Ohio so that Lewis could put some 'polish' on him. After the polish was on he shone so much that Lewis wanted to keep him, and eventually he managed to buy him from Bob.

Lewis took a liking to Moss mainly because of his quiet authority over sheep, his intelligence, balance, steady pace and the fact that he could line sheep up on his own – all of these qualities I have seen in Moss's sire Tweed.

Lewis had neglected the trial scene for quite a while due to pressure of work. He farms 550 acres of cropland singlehanded.

He obtained his first Border collie pup in '58 after watching a trial at Peebles (Ohio, not Scotland) never dreaming that one day he would compete against, and beat the best.

Although Lewis's pup was American bred the first trial dog that he owned came from the late John Brownlee of Inchgall, Scotland. Of the dog, Lewis says that he was an honest, old-fashioned type with plenty of brains and power.

The tradition of buying Brownlee dogs has continued with Lewis's recent acquisition Meg, a $3^1/_2$-year-old bitch trained by Ian Brownlee, son of John who is following admirably in his father's footsteps.

Two days after the trial was over, much to our surprise one of the ewes that participated, produced a perfectly healthy, long legged, grey coloured Corriedale lamb, a comical ungainly creature encumbered by loose folds of skin which he would hopefully eventually grow into. This birth, after what the mother sheep had experienced over the last couple of days, only goes to show the toughness and resilience of this particular breed of sheep.

On Ethel's lush pasture the ewe's udder had become full to bursting, resulting in it hanging so low to the ground that the lamb was unable to suckle. When first discovered he was in a sorry state and suffering badly from dehydration.

After a couple of feeds with the ewe sat firmly on her rump, both he and his mum were despatched for home with Henry in attendance.

Americans are great believers in holding seminars, or 'clinics' as they are now called. They are organised to cover practically every subject under the sun.

While I was there Ethel organised a three day Sheep Dog Clinic at Sunnybrook, to take place on the second day after her Blue Ridge Trials to give me a chance to recuperate.

Twenty-five handlers and dogs participated in what I can only describe as three days of pure pleasure and enlightenment except for the overpowering heat.

I was called upon to preach what I try to practise regarding methods of sheepdog training back home.

Each dog and handler were encouraged to demonstrate their capabilities within the confines of a well fenced area, after first of all being asked to allow their dog to work without commands in order to run off steam. Most of the handlers insisted their dogs were 'hyper' (hyper-active to the uninitiated). I hope that I was able to convince them that their canine partners were merely keen, through lack of work.

After both dogs and handlers were put through their paces we retired to the shade to discuss any problems which had arisen or phases of training about which they wanted advice.

Each dog and handler were allowed to 'perform' with the sheep for approximately ten minutes twice daily – meaning roughly that over a three day period I would walk out to sheep 150 times. By the evening of Day Two not only had I practically lost my voice, I could hardly put one foot in front of the other.

Noticing my predicament, Ethel packed me off to my room for a nap. On waking I glanced at my watch. It said 7 o'clock, so after a refreshing wash and brush up I went down to supper only to find much to everyone's amusement that breakfast was being served. Afterwards I returned to the clinic much refreshed and determined to pace myself more carefully, but by lunch time rain had stopped play so we adjourned to the comfort of Ethel's spacious verandah for a discussion which included not particularly artistic diagrams chalked by me on a blackboard borrowed from the little school. While I chalked I wondered how many school marms were turning in their graves.

On the Friday after the clinic, Ethel and I found ourselves loaded up with dogs and friends, on the road heading in the direction of the Fairhill Sheep Dog Trial, where the prodigious World Championship won by a Scottish handler had taken place a few years previously. We had approximately 150 miles to travel in order to reach our destination near Wormington, Delaware.

Our journey took us across the fast flowing Potomac River which joins with the famous Shenandoah at Harpers Ferry. Then over the wide Susquehanna until finally we reached our destination – a swish motel where unlike some eating places in Britain, everyone is given a menu at table!

The following morning we arrived at the trial in good time to find guess what? Kilted pipers plus massed pipe bands, to greatly enhance the already electric atmosphere.

This particular sheep dog trial was entirely different to any that I had experienced previously, the results being worked out by a points system – the idea being that instead of points being deducted around the course, points were awarded for weaving in and out of obstacles.

Both myself and a number of other handlers felt that to compete in this type of trial with a young dog was to rob it of any initiative it might have, so they put their views to the organisers and it is hoped that next year the course may be changed to the conventional style.

I must admit that while watching I did quite fancy having a go - if only to see the expression on Garry's face when asked to exert himself in this manner, (especially on a hot day!).

At the conclusion of the competition the first prize could not have been presented to a nicer person or a sweeter dog, for Walt Jagger, of Sheepy Hollow, Hop Bottom won the event with one of his 'little girls'.

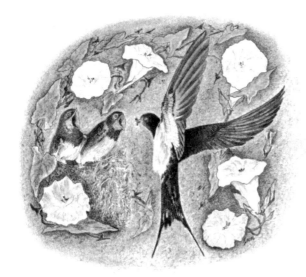

20
Sheep Dog
Fanatics

Don MCraig

Don McCaig is a well known American author whose novel *Nop's Trials*, a tale about a fictional Border collie may be made into a film.

Ethel Conrad and Don are close friends. In fact one of the characters in Don's book is loosely based on Ethel.

I was extremely fortunate in making Don's acquaintance at the Blue Ridge Trials where he was competing with his collie, Pip and again at the clinic where he participated with a splendid mottled, prick lugged bitch named Silk. After the Fairhill Trial Don kindly invited me to stay with him and his wife Anne at their home set deep in the Alleghany Mountains, an offer that I was excited to accept when he explained that the area had once been a favourite buffalo hunting ground used by an off-shoot of the Cherokee Indian tribe.

Ethel obligingly arranged to meet Don halfway, so we set off driving through the Shenandoah Valley on a glorious day in this the second week of my three week stay.

As arranged we met up with Don at an attractive farmhouse set amidst rolling green hills where we enjoyed a super lunch with the occupants Leo, Judy and their delightful though somewhat damp baby son.

After lunch Don and I hit the trail, travelling cautiously along steep mountain tracks, passing through dense forests where black bear, puma and bob cats lurk but thankfully the only critter to cross our path today is a harmless scurrying grey squirrel and the only roadside casualties are possums and the occasional raccoon, for no hedgehogs reside here.

On arrival at my host's Yucatec Farm (nearest town Williamsville) which started out as a log house, in 1879, we are greeted by Don's pretty wife Anne, dressed in working garb for she is busy lambing their one hundred Rambouillet cross-bred ewes.

I was soon made to feel very much at home and after supper, before hitting the hay, Anne introduced me to their puppy Mac, Pip and Silk's lively three-month-old son.

'Why did you call him Mac?' I asked fully expecting to be told that it was because of his ancestors' Scottish connections. She grinned and explained to me that she was a basketball fanatic and had wanted the pup named after her favourite player Bob McAdoo. Don of course refused, so Anne decided to pull a fast one on him by suggesting that they call the dog Mac, and like most of us girls she got her way in the end.

Prior to climbing the steep wooden stairs to bed I stepped outside for a brief moment to stand underneath the stars, feeling a little homesick. America is such a vast land compared to our small secure island of Great Britain.

Tonight I lie cosy and warm beneath a gaily coloured patchwork quilt in a little wooden bed known in these parts as a sleigh bed, because of its shape. I am slowly being lulled to sleep by the sound of a large congregation of giant frogs croaking to one another in the meadow. Thunder, and electric blue lightening rend the sky, providing occasional background music to their song, and lighting up the room, illuminating the pretty gingham yellow checked curtains and reflecting on the saffron coloured wooden door.

The following morning as dawn breaks, I glance out of the tiny window, my confidence permanently restored by the sound and sight of my favourite birds, swallows, the first I've seen this year darting, diving, and swooping for flies whilst their ever-hungry young twitter in the nest. How I love these courageous little travellers with their chattering voices, steely blue bodies, cream waistcoats and delicately forked tails.

After breakfast, in between caring for her precious ewes, Anne tells me that before 1978 she knew absolutely nothing at all about sheep. Raised in the state of New Jersey she had been employed both as a social worker and as a teacher with a degree in English teaching in a day care centre for working mothers in New York.

After marrying Don and moving to Yucatec, the first sheep which they kept were purely as lawn mowers to keep the grass down in the yard.

Later on in the day Don proudly shows me over their domain. We walk through acres of shady forest, gaze deeply into the creek's clear waters, examine plant life and brightly coloured insects and partake of wild mint and chives. The only animal life that we encounter is when I accidentally step on a small red-necked turtle who was shuffling slowly through the undergrowth to a secret destination that he shared with no-one but himself. After examining him carefully to ascertain he's all right we send him on his way.

Don explains that in these parts lady-bugs (ladybirds at home) are collected from the redwood trees in California and released from gallon jars on to dewy alfalfa grass where they are protected overnight by a covering of straw. The following day these small red armies, replete and rested, set about destroying the local weevil population with gusto.

A massive pale yellow and black monarch butterfly flutters gaily beside us. Don tells me that they are known to fly thousands of miles, alighting every year on certain trees to rest. One of the most beautiful sights he ever witnessed was an enormous tree covered by these delicate, fragile creatures.

Wild turkeys, lunar moths with crescent moons embroidering their wings, coyotes, foxes red and grey, all frequent these hills.

We return gladly to the house to rest in the cool tranquility of Don's impressive library, left to him by an elderly uncle

whom he admired greatly as a child. His uncle's books and chiming clocks impressed him to such an extent that nowadays Don lives in a similar style, surrounded by both books and clocks.

The following day we say our goodbyes, but before I leave, Anne bestows upon me her favourite wide brimmed straw hat - truly a most appreciated gift.

As I depart dramatic Highland County that is a part of the Appalachian Chain, I whisper a fond farewell to this beauteous naturalist's haven, situated 25 miles from the nearest supermarket, with my scalp mercifully intact.

After an exhilarating ride through 'rebel' country we finally return to Sunnybrook and an Ethel style welcome, driving en-route through the town of Lexington, population 5,000.

It's 130 miles to White Post, 130 miles of green fields and forests, wooden houses with garlands of straw hats with flower-bedecked brims as a summer decoration, hanging on their front doors. The long drive was made blissful by the heady perfume of mile upon mile of honeysuckle hedgerows. As we near the lane that leads to Ethel's, ground hogs, or wood chucks as they are affectionately known, scurry for the safety of the under-growth. This large brown rodent with a punk hairstyle is to be seen almost everywhere, except during wintertime when it hibernates deep beneath the ground, emerging in the month of March and on that day should it catch sight of its own shadow the winter will surely last another six weeks or more, or so the saying goes.

No sooner have I arrived and settled in than Ethel relates some exciting news. Cathie Leslie of Las Cruces, New Mexico and Dr Kelli Caprile of Baton Rouge, Louisiana, friends of mine of several years standing, are flying in to see me the very next day!

We originally met in Scotland where Cathie had been extremely impressed by Jed and Trim's performance running Brace at Earlston Scottish National Trials.

Cathie ordered a bitch puppy out of Trim for which she had to wait two years but finally Whitelaw Ceilidh put in her appearance and was duly despatched to the USA.

In 1984 Cathie married Ian, a professor at the New Mexico State University, their ambition being to own some land and keep some sheep.

Kelli gained her doctrate in 1981 and is now a professor at a school of veterinary medicine.

The girls arrive at Sunnybrook early, in a hired car and after hugs all round and excited prolonged chatter, for we have much to tell one another, we decide to travel further afield and on my behalf make a nostalgic journey to Pittsburgh in Pennsylvania so that I can fulfil a lifelong ambition and visit the Stoebe family. For these marvellous people, although we have never met them, have continued over a period of forty years to correspond with my mother. The alliance began soon after the Second World War when commodities, though plentiful in America, were extremely scarce in Britain. During that period my mother made friends with three dear old ladies who lived up the road from us. Their names were Madge, Nan and Effie and when we met they liked nothing better than to kiss my sister Jenifer and I, as we were at the toddling stage. The friendship blossomed and the ladies asked my mother if she would care to write to their niece who lived in Pittsburgh, as she had two daughters, Dianne and Jean who were of a similar age to us. From that day on the thrill and excitement of THE AMERICAN PARCEL came into our lives and remained with us for sixteen years. Of course we reciprocated with a British version but it was never on such a grand scale as the one that arrived each Christmas from the USA containing toys, clothes, and sweeties which somehow had an entirely different scent and flavour from the meagre ration that we bought with pennies and coupons on our weekly trip into town.

A much prized item of clothing I distinctly remember wearing throughout at least two cold winters was all-in-one pyjamas, complete with hood, mitts and feet.

Kelli, Cathie and I wave goodbye to Ethel as we set off on a journey that will take us at least five hours. I have spoken to Marge Stoebe by telephone and she can't wait until we get there.

After what seems an age finally we cross the wide Monongahela River into Pittsburgh and my first impression is that it is a massive awe inspiring place. Loud sirens scream, skyscrapers scrape the heavens and one even wears sharp pointed turrets, proudly like a crown.

· We drive cautiously through the wide streets, completely lost until at last we find guess what? A traffic cop, I believe they're called. And as we gingerly approach him as he leans on his enormous powerful, gleaming motor cycle, he proclaims out loud, according to Cathie, in an inner city accent, 'THE ANSWER IS NO!' Unabashed I blurt out that I have come all

the way from Scotland and we are lost. I then produce my address book and show him where the Stoebes are to be located.

To me he looks like a cross between the film star Joel McCrae and the late Sid James, and at this particular moment his expression is completely dead-pan. He stares earnestly into our anxious faces then slowly, beginning at the corners of his mouth, his face creases into a wide smile and his round brilliant blue eyes twinkle and crinkle at the corners. It's then I know without a doubt that we have won him over. He radios through to head office, wherever that might be, and as we wait for the information we need, my eyes inadvertently wander to the low slung gun belt strapped around his waist, containing the heavy holstered pistol which glints in the hot afternoon sun. For a brief moment an amusing vision flashes through my mind. If only I could transport him gun belt, bike and all into the market square at Kelso, what a show stopper he would prove to be. I am hurriedly brought to my senses as he gives us directions, dismisses us with a slight wave of his hand and goes off to direct the traffic, but as we turn to walk away an all too familiar catch phrase drifts in our wake. 'Have a nice day!'

We soon find the place we are searching for and it's really quite beautiful – just like I knew it would be. Peaceful, on a hill sheltered by lots of trees.

Down the steps rushes a lovely lady with tears in her eyes. I am hugged oh so tightly and held in a warm embrace before being introduced to husband Bob who is standing shyly in the background, a gentle kindly faced man with a deep mahogany sun tan.

Cathie and Kelli are welcomed before we all go inside the spacious spotless kitchen, where we partake of supper and afterwards talk late into the evening of the intervening years whilst Madge rocks gently back and forth in her ancient rocking chair – a picture of contentment.

Before saying our 'goodnights' we eagerly sample Bob's delicious homemade strawberry wine, then climb steep wooden stairs to bed underneath the eaves, in a low ceilinged sweet smelling, pine panelled room.

The following morning Madge tells me that her mother was born in the north east of England and that her father built this house they live in and the others round about it for their close relations.

Bob and Madge's interests range from country pursuits to

gardening, travelling, camping and hunting. Devout Methodists, their vacations are spent mostly on the island of Haiti with a church group, helping to build schools and taking part in community projects.

At lunch time daughter Dianne arrives with her husband and only daughter. Unfortunately Dianne's sister Jean lives too far away but manages to telephone instead. Various cousins and their dogs call in to say hello and so we eat together on the lawn before heading back to Virginia, led by our hosts via the Squirrel Hill tunnel, – one of many in and around Pittsburgh, safely out to the Pennsylvania Turnpike Toll Road, then after waving a frantic farewell we are on our own, listening while Kelli tells a funny doggie yarn.

Kelli's mother lives in Roseville, on the western edge of the Sierra Nevada mountains, Californian gold country. In her spare time she loves visiting the original settlements of the gold rush miners. In one such town she was walking along the raised wooden sidewalk when she came across a man sitting in a rocking chair in front of the general store. Beside him sat a larger than life black and white Border collie, and as there were lots of sheep in the area she stopped to talk to him. Admiring his dog she asked whether or not he worked. The man thought for a while then looking her straight in the eye he drawled 'No, ma'am, my dog doesn't need to work. I earn enough money to support the both of us.'

Sunday 26th May. Last Day But One:

It's open day at the local stud farms and stables. Ethel, Cathie, Kelli and I set off on a sight seeing spree around Paul Mellon's famous Rokeby Stud, Virginia's premier horse farm where the famous stallion Mill Reef 'stands' worked in bronze, in the centre of a spacious courtyard.

After multiple oohs and aahs at the sight of various priceless mares and foals standing quietly inside cool clean loose boxes, we decide to adjourn to Ethel's turquoise pool for a refreshing dip before dining out.

The dinner is Kelli's treat, so we dress up to the nines for this our last evening together.

We have booked a table at a charming restaurant with a decidedly French flavour known as L'auberge Provencal, which to the uninitiated like myself means Country Inn. The menu proves excellent and varied. Unfortunately there is none of my favourite curry available so I have to be satisfied with duck breast and fiddle head fern, amusingly described by the imaginative Cathie as 'Duck boobs and weeds.'

The food was delicious, the atmosphere divine and in the background soft guitar music gave the place a happy relaxed atmosphere, so much so that I half expected Toulouse Latrec to come shuffling through the room.

Later, wallowing in contentment after a perfect evening we are reminded by Ethel that 'Early to bed early to rise, makes a gal healthy, wealthy and wise'.

Homeward Bound:

'Goodbye dear friends. Goodbye southern hospitality, goodbye dogs, goodbye Virginia green and pleasant land' and a fond farewell to you Ethel, 'hostess with the mostess'. 'Hello Geoffs, how I've missed you both.'

My flight leaves Dulles at 6.30 pm. Due to the time change we are heading smoothly into daylight. The journey so far is uneventful. How quickly the hours pass. We no sooner eat dinner than it is time to eat breakfast and in no time at all we are flying over vivid green fields of young corn and acre upon acre of brilliant yellow oil-seed rape. How beautiful it looks rippling golden in the wind which is so strong that it rocks the Boeing from side to side like a baby's cradle – but having got this far what do I care about its reeling?

We touch down at speed, whizzing jubilantly along the Newcastle Airport runway, excitement surging within me and also if I was absolutely honest, more than a hint of relief.

GWB is waiting to welcome me in the airport lounge with open arms, tall, tanned, smiling reassuringly, bedecked in his best tweeds. It's true what they say, absence really does make the heart grow fonder.

We collect my suitcase as it bobs around with the rest on the conveyor belt then set off for home. I am quick to note that the car has been cleaned both inside and out in honour of my return. I can hardly wait to unpack my case and give young Geoff his gift, a blue rubber dinghy to sail on the burn, and for my husband there's a silver belt buckle embellished with a cowboy riding a rearing horse. I realise that he'll never wear it but I'm sure it will suffice as an amusing memento.

It's a good hour's drive from the airport to Yetholm, through vigorous Northumbrian countryside, past woods and fields, over bleak heather clad hills teeming with snowy flocks of ewes, racing thriving lambs and sleek black cattle nursing plump bright-eyed calves, standing knee deep in grass.

As we cross the meandering Border into Scotland, I enquire about the stock at home and learn that the only casualties during the time I've been away are three hens taken by a fox.

Within minutes we reach the picturesque entrance to the Bowmont Valley. I am pleased to note that the stark spring bareness that I left behind has miraculously disappeared and in its place green swards abound. Alongside gently flowing Bowmont Water blooms golden gorse, nodding gaily in the stiff breeze whilst by the roadside wind-buffeted hawthorns scatter their pink and white fragile flower petals like a welcoming carpet. Larks hover in the clear sky overhead and agile swallows provide us with an escort. Suddenly it's summer and I am home and dry!

Later, in the gentleness of evening we three and our pack of collie dogs walk beside the burn, watching lively shoals of brown trout endlessly chasing wriggling tadpoles in shallow pools of bright water. Beneath our feet pale bracken thrusts tightly furled fronds whilst from a nearby forest comes an all too familiar call 'Cuckoo, cuckoo' reminding me of an ancient rhyme taught to me many moons ago by Ernest Crisp.

If the cuckoo comes to the bare thorn,
Sell your cow and keep your corn.
If the cuckoo comes to the rough leaf,
Sell your corn and keep your sheep.

I smile, content in the knowledge that for me The American Experience turned out to be not only a totally worthwhile endeavour but also, a truly memorable excursion that I would remember for the rest of my days.

21
Life after Bowmont

In September of 1983, after ten years with Roxburghe Estates, my husband was informed that because of a reduction in staff he was to be made redundant. Eventually, due to 'a change in farm policy', he was reinstated. There then followed what can only be described as three insecure years. Finally, in May 1986, he informed the management of his resignation.

At the time shepherding jobs were few and far between – practically none-existent if you were over forty years of age. So there we were, living in a tied house with few options to choose from. In the months that followed accommodation was offered, but it proved unsuitable from the point of view of the dogs. Numerous positions of employment were applied for. We waited in vain for a favourable reply.

Throughout all of this my faith never wavered. I am a great believer that as one door closes another door opens.

In view of the insecurity of our occupation we decided to try to find a suitable location where we might endeavour to preserve what we had come to believe was a dedicated and rewarding way of life, as well as sharing our interests and skills with others.

It was an enormous step on our part. The fact that many of our contemporaries had recently become unemployed due to afforestation, spurred us on.

We discovered Tweenhopefoot purely by chance, when making a documentary in the area for the National Geographic Society entitled *A Shepherd and Shepherdess*. The small hill farm was situated on a major tourist route, far enough off the road so as not to endanger our animals. Its eighty acres would provide a perfect environment in which the dogs might display their natural skills. Besides the farmhouse there was also a derelict cottage and a useful range of buildings which would suffice for kennels.

Five miles north of Tweedhopefoot following in the direction of the meandering Tweed, against a backcloth of towering hills now emptied of sheep and wearing a cloak of sitka spruce, lay the quiet hamlet of Tweedsmuir with its ancient stone brig welcoming visitors to a school that is nowadays bereft of shepherds' children and a kirk still used occasionally, crowned by a tall steeple and surrounded by a peaceful kirkyard where:

Around me wrapped in silence strange and deep
'Neath mounds of green whereon the sunbeams play,
The hillmen rest in God's untroubled sleep,
And glory gilds this sweet autumnal day.

From hills above the purple heather waves
September greetings to the hearts of men.
And gentle Tweed beside these quiet graves
Flows softly in its passage through the glen.

Here at the base of the eternal hills
My soul uplifts the calm expectant prayer
And borne in sweetness from enchanting rills
The Border song fills all the valley there.

And ever more where Tweed and Talla flow
Like guardian angels round these gates of rest,
To keep their tryst the shepherds homeward go
And sleep at last beside the river's breast.

Anon

The farm appeared ideal for our purpose and I immediately fell in love with it.

Following what can only be described as strenuous negotiations, much to our great delight, 'Tweedhope Sheep Dogs' progressed from a wishful dream into reality as one by one, the jig-saw pieces which had been floating in mid-air began to come together.

Our date of entry into 'Tweedupfit', as it is known locally, was arranged for December 18, 1986.

At last the great day arrived. We were awake and ready at the crack of dawn, anxiously waiting for the enormous cattle waggon that was to transport all our worldly goods except Tarka our shepherding horse, who was coming along later. For the first time in our lives, we would be living under our very own roof: the acreage, three quarters of a mile of the River Tweed, the view, all of these were bonuses.

It was time to reflect, time to broaden our horizons, time to move on. We had outgrown Bowmont and were ready to exchange one lifestyle for another. The famous Tweed Valley, steeped as it is in history, is a dream of a place; our new home a fairytale come true and had I been invited to paint a picture of my idea of heaven – including all the necessary attributes, I would not be able to portray so aptly what nature herself had already generously provided.

I was clearing away the last of the breakfast dishes at Swindon when George, Young of Yetholm's driver, reversed his waggon carefully through the gate and along the drive to the sound of barking dogs. Outside the back door our seven cats and three ducks were already lined up in wooden crates, whilst the dogs waited patiently inside their kennels. They would be the last to be loaded into the already rapidly filling truck.

At long last the waggon was loaded, mirrors skilfully padded with mattresses and larger heavier pieces of furniture tied down firmly – a professional operation performed by George. Strangely, that morning I opened the door to find a family of six chattering magpies had landed on the grass out-side, the first that we had seen in the area in the fourteen years we had lived there. The birds unexpected appearance brought to mind a childhood rhyme:

One for sorrow, two for joy,
Three for a girl, four for a boy,
Five for silver, six for gold,
Seven for a secret never to be told.

I had agreed to ride in the back with our eleven collies to quell any bickering. A comfortable armchair had been strategically placed there on my behalf. I clambered inside and wrapped myself in a large blanket followed by the inquisitive dogs. Once seated the tailboard was hurriedly raised, just in case any of the occupants should have second thoughts and try to escape. A couple of minutes later we were on our way. Young Geoff was sad at losing his school friends and the only home he had ever known. I was sorry to leave the sheep and the scenery, but enormously looking forward to the warm, dry cottage awaiting us in peaceful Peebleshire. There was time for one last fleeting glance at fast receding Bowmont Water through a narrow aperture in the side of the waggon.

As we rattled down the familiar winding road I whispered a fond farewell to mighty Cheviot as it disappeared behind round sheep-dotted hills, while pulling the blanket more tightly around my shoulders to keep our winter's chill. I slept for a couple of hours, then pinched myself to keep awake, eagerly awaiting the vibrations that would tell me that we had reached the lane into Tweedhopefoot.

Three hours later we arrived at our destination in a raging blizzard. The dogs, apart from a minor squabble, had been well behaved, stretched snoring at my feet like recumbent crocodiles.

As we bumped and shook down the farm track my first view was of dancing white flakes, and the uppermost branches of spruce heavily laden with snow. We reversed up to the gate and the tailboard was quickly lowered. To the amusement of everyone I half-walked, half-fell out of the waggon after completely seizing up with cold whilst I had slept. Joe, our new neighbour, was waiting to welcome us with a roaring fire. He immediately telephoned his wife, Moira, who quickly came to the rescue and in no time at all thawed me out with a hot drink. Fortunately most of the carpets had been laid the previous week, so it was just a matter of carrying in the furniture and making up the beds. This task was soon accomplished and all of the animals fed before we tumbled into bed.

The cottage had a small kitchen, a medium sized lounge, bathroom and three other rooms previously used as bedrooms. An accommodating loft ran the full length of the house. Entering the back door there was a cupboard or small room straight ahead, one wall of which contained a window overlooking the farmyard, the wall opposite backing on to the fireplace in the lounge. Noting that this was the warmest room in the house, young Geoff quickly commandeered it as his bedroom.

The week which followed was spent polishing, cleaning and unpacking the bric-a-brac. I was determined that come Christmas Day everything would be ship-shape and hearty. It was, but unfortunately, apart from cooking dinner I slept through most of the festive season.

Tarka, our mare, arrived at Tweedhopefoot in time for Christmas. By then the farm road had become impassable to vehicles and she had to be led down it. In order to reassure her I called out a welcome; at last our family was complete. After sniffing warily in the doorway of her new stable she daintily stepped inside, glad of the shelter it provided from the bitter north-east wind.

Thankfully, none of our animals suffered any ill-effects after their long journey. The ducks, as soon as they were released, quacked contentedly about the yard. The cats – Jemima, Silver, Tabby, Sooty, Sweep, Young Rambo and my beloved long-haired rascal Greystoke - after spending a couple of days shut in the old cottage eventually found their way to the back door, where they settled as though they had lived there all of their nine lives. Surprisingly, I cannot call myself a lover of cats - the reason being that they decimate the bird population. I do however, admire their independence and affection towards each other. Felines seem to attach themselves to me more than they used to. Can the reason be, that, with the passing of time, my lap has become more ample?

From the very moment their paws touched on Tweed Valley soil, the dogs, like me, were completely at home. Observing them explore every nook and cranny, their tails waving excitedly, I experienced more than a hint of sadness due to the absence of my husband's old faithfuls, the retired trials brace pair, litter sisters Jed and Trim. If only they could have been among the happy throng, my happiness would have been complete.

Before leaving Bowmont we had the agonising decision of deciding the fate of the devoted pair, then in their sixteenth year. They had followed unquestioning at their master's heels to at least twelve hill lambings, never disputing a command no matter how tedious. Both bitches were fading fast. Trimmy had become so frail that a puff of wind would have blown her over. She had to be lifted in and out of her kennel, her sight and hearing practically non-existent. Jed, always the more robust and determined of the pair, was infinitely more alert. However, when parted from her sister for any length of time, she began to fret. We had evidence of this when Trim, suffering a bout of arthritis, spent a few days in the kitchen at Swindon. Jed, on discovering her whereabouts, went delirious with delight.

After living and working as one all of their lives, their fate was the most difficult decision we have ever been called upon to make. Jed would have possibly gone on a while longer, but after a deal of deliberation, we decided that it was kinder by far to have them put to sleep together.

They lie at Swindon in the shrubbery beside Pip, Tweed and Jan, other never-to-be-forgotten friends, assured always of a place in our hearts.

Prior to our move into Tweedhope, a squatter had taken up residence, leaving his calling card everywhere. We named him 'Supermouse' for no other reason than, on the few occasions we had spotted him, we noted that he was the largest and sleekest rodent of his kind. We were to discover how he had managed to become so gross when young Geoff came to open his Christmas presents. Half of a large bar of chocolate had been completely devoured. 'Supermouse' was to put in several more appearances, one of which almost proved fatal.

It happened when Harry Thomson and his wife, Ute, who farm in Sweden, were paying us a visit. We were watching television when suddenly Harry bounded to his feet and with three enormous strides landed in the hall doorway, shouting excitedly: 'There's a mouse!' Everything happened so quickly that we were completely taken by surprise and sat there transfixed. Harry immediately brought down his large foot with a sickening thud. Young Geoff grimaced in horror, fully expecting poor 'Supermouse' to be splattered all over the newly whitened walls. 'I've got 'im by the tail.' Yelled Harry jubilantly. My heart sank into my boots. Then, 'Lost 'im,' roared Harry disappointedly. My eyes met with young Geoff's as a feeling of relief flooded through both of us.

Sadly that was the last we saw of 'Supermouse', our squatter-cum-lodger. His near demise proved too much of a close shave and he returned from whence he came.

On the property, approximately 200 yards away beside the road, stood a tiny school, reputed to be the smallest in Scotland. It is built of corrugated sheets, with a wooden interior. On the roof there is a chimney, but unfortunately the old stove that was installed to provide heating for the children had long since been removed. When we first saw the school, although in a state of disrepair, it was not without character.

The building had once provided the gift of education to shepherds' children and although on our land, it belonged to the local education authority, who had placed it under a preservation order. Built a year or two before the turn of the century the school ceased to be in use by the late 1930s. However, it did serve for a while as a Sunday school and latterly, as a camp for boys. Because the building was obsolete, I wrote to the authorities about renovating it. They were, I'm glad to say, happy to hand over the property to us.

Young Geoff would have given anything to be taught there. His schooling involved a round trip to Peebles of fifty miles. He was collected every morning by mini-bus. On reaching Tweedsmuir his journey then deviated along a winding road to scenic Talla, before connecting with a larger coach at Broughton.

22
From Shepherdess
to Businesswoman

Roads whiles may seem lanesom and braes unco' steep
For wi' fate's dire decision we're forced to compete
But the lot of the shepherd who wanders alone
Is whiles to be envied by kings on the throne.

John Dixon

Following 'the starving' I received in the waggon en route from our former abode, I developed what can only be compared to kennel cough. The illness wracked my entire frame throughout the following five months until a welcome breath of fresh spring air finally banished it completely. The memory of the hardship we experienced during our first year will remain with me always. I survived on optimism alone, learning more in those early months about the pitfalls of starting a business than I had absorbed in a multitude of previous casual deals.

Without a doubt, sheer physical effort is to be preferred to that of mental strain. The constant pressure of bombarding one's brain with a barrage of facts and figures - never mind the associated problems, is not for the faint-hearted. I believe it was my sense of humour, though on occasions somewhat diminished, that carried me through.

It is stated that money is the root of all evil. One thing that I learned early on was that instant success in business, unless one possesses a magical wand, depends solely on this commodity. No matter how impressive an idea appears on the drawing board – and I believe my idea at its worst to be original – no matter how much effort one is prepared to expend or the fact that the participants have enjoyed a great deal of publicity: at the end of the day success depends on hard cash alone.

After religiously exploring every avenue and pursuing each available opportunity, we finally arrived at the realisation that without capital we were not necessarily on to a loser, rather that our rate of development would be impaired to the extent that we would be in our dotage before we could begin to enjoy the fruits of our labour.

In the past I have often been accused of looking at life through rose-coloured spectacles. At best, I emerge from my experiences, a positive thinker. Perhaps because of my northern upbringing, I like to call a spade a spade, and prefer to adopt a direct line of approach. Some abhor this kind of frankness, I believe life is too short to observe preliminary etiquette. However, much to my advantage, I quickly discovered that in business, it is necessary to exercise extreme caution. How else can one shed the sheep from among the goats?

Big businessmen have the reputation of living on their wits and being ruthless, of riding roughshod over their contemporaries. This is not a way of life I care to be part of. I like to compare running a business to handling a sheep dog on a trial course, one must be at least ten jumps ahead. (I get much more satisfaction battling against sheep, the terrain and the elements.)

We quickly realised that the purchase of a property is nowhere near the final goal. Locations designated for tourism must be developed in order to provide the necessary facilities – amenities such as ample parking space, toilets, a craft-area and tearoom among others.

If capital is limited it is vital to arrange one's priorities in order of merit. Initially, planning permission must be obtained and plans drawn up by a qualified draughtsman. One hears stories of difficulties in some areas. I cannot speak highly enough about the understanding shown in respect of the urgency of our project by Borders Regional Council.

Except when visitors were elderly or infirm, we planned to start our programme at the farm entrance, where a coach parking area would be constructed. From this point, visitors could proceed to the school where a photograph collection would portray shepherds and their dogs both past and present.

Below the school, the ground was to be landscaped. Waterfalls, footpaths and bridges would eventually be created. When I close my eyes and allowed my imagination to run riot, I could visualise what it would look like in years to come – the loch surrounded by graceful willows, their leafy fronds trailing its glassy surface, velvet bullrushes intermingling with tall iris, lilies bobbing as the wind rippled the water and a tiny island, planted with flowering shrubs, presenting a mass of colour. To the left of the farm lane a round sheep stell built from stone was planned, where ewes and lambs of popular hill breeds would be displayed. Beside the steading a Dutch barn would provide a spacious shearing area.

The old cottage and buildings, when renovated were to provide an olde worlde tearoom and craft area. Fortunately the original cooking range was still intact, complete with swee. The upstairs would be used as B & B accommodation.

The sheep dog handling demonstrations were to be held in a natural amphitheatre, stretching down the valley, sandwiched between the river Tweed and the A701 Moffat to Edinburgh road. To keep the spectators dry in inclement weather a grandstand would eventually be erected.

New kennelling for the dogs was a must, as well as a nursery area where children could play with the puppies.

I believe that true professionalism, like an eye for stock, is a gift one is born with. It is essential that 'the goods' be produced in both a practical and professional manner, in order that business comes to you and not the other way around.

It is very tempting to advertise in every publication on offer. Here, as in other areas, caution had to be exercised.

We found word of mouth to be one of the best forms of advertising.

In business one is weighed down by monumental responsibilities, not only to oneself but also to others. As shepherds we were anchored by our duty to the sheep entrusted in our care, fully in sympathy with the hardship and deprivation of the life.

The responsibilities to others I refer to are, beside one's immediate family, an ever growing group of dependants. These include other business ventures which rely totally on the success of the 'mother' business. From day one there was no shortage of consultants – or business advisers, knocking at the door. They arrived one after another in quick succession – most of them failed business men.

Apart from the fact that we could not afford to pay them, after coming this far we relished the chance of managing the centre ourselves. All that we really required was someone who could set things out in a professional manner and was good with figures.

It was vital that our venture did not lose its character by becoming too commercial. We had to be careful not to break away from the original idea. Profit, when available, had to be ploughed back into the land in order to create a model farm.

If I could be granted a wish it would be that every family be given a plot of ground - no matter how small - whether they desired to plant roses, keep pigs, or merely grow weeds. The ownership of land creates a feeling of security and a sense of responsibility sadly lacking in today's generation. All children should experience the wonderment of viewing the miracle of nature firsthand.

At Tweedhopefoot our predecessors, Mr and Mrs Sharpe, planted no fewer than seventy different species of cultivated shrubs and flowers along the driveway, all of which flourished consecutively, providing a mass of colour all summer long. Quite an accomplishment at 1100ft. The surrounding meadows had never experienced the scourge of herbicides or the ravages of the plough. As a result, from the turn of the year until the latter part of October, gentle snowdrop, primrose, bluebell, harebell, marsh marigold, shy violet, orchid, purple and yellow pansy, cuckoo flower, ragged-robin, wild mountain thyme and purple heather, to name but a few, gladdened the eye.

Surely, there can be no sweeter prospect, than to awaken with the season's perfume and gaze on such a vast expanse of loveliness, framed by an arbour of sweet-scented honeysuckle that was growing in profusion on the front of the house?

Owning a farm with no livestock can only be compared with owning a pub with no beer. In the spring of the year Biggar mart kindly credited us with a lively flock of blackfaced hoggs - the balance to be paid when they were sold.

We spent many hours designing a sign for the roadside. Eventually it was finished. Geoff painted a collie dog on either side and the wording read 'Border Collie and Shepherd Centre'.

One morning the telephone rang. A lady inquired, 'Are they German Shepherds?' 'No,' I replied, 'we are British.' It was not until I replaced the receiver that I realised that she was referring to the canine variety.

Bearing in mind that some overseas visitors had never heard of a Border collie, never mind seen one in action, I decided to alter the name of the establishment to 'Tweedhope Sheep Dogs' thus incorporating the prefix I use for my own collies.

A leaflet was designed and several thousand copies distributed throughout the area. Newspapers, magazines, radio and television networks were informed. Friends all over the globe were told of our intention to open our gates to the public.

In what seemed like no time, planning permission was agreed and a grant to improve the existing facilities was applied for through the Scottish Tourist Board. My head buzzed with business plans, cashflow forecasts and estimates from plant-hire contractors, builders and plumbers. 'Grant applications should carry a health warning,' I moaned. Time was of the essence. Ready or not, we had to open in April. The interest on the money we had already borrowed had to be found. I realised how a diminutive wren felt nurturing a giant cuckoo.

At last all of the paperwork was completed and the Tourist Board appeared not only satisfied but, more important, enthusiastic. The bombshell fell when our bank was invited to match their grant. Head office considered that a further loan at this time might prove too onerous. To say that we felt devastated by the news following all our efforts, is putting it mildly. The decision meant that we would lose a large investment in our property.

There were two options left open to us. We could either sit and feel sorry for ourselves, or we could open regardless. Naturally we chose the latter, relying solely on the pull of our four-legged friends.

We took stock of our assets. In our opinion the scenery was unbeatable. Two litters of puppies were due, and the 'wee school' would make an ideal craft shop for the time being. I at once got busy with a paint brush and decorated the building dark green with a cheerful red roof. I obtained several old desks,

complete with graffiti, from Peebles High School and an easel was purchased from a nearby antiques dealer. I mounted and labelled hundreds of photographs on to large sheets of card. These we riveted to the wooden walls of the newly-whitened classroom.

A celebrity corner boasted autographed documentation of young Geoff's heroes - the A Team, my idol, the film star Randolph Scott, and television broadcasters Barry Norman and the late Ray Moore.

A welcome recruit arrived, in the shape of Carol, from nearby Stobo - along with her spinning wheel. She filled the little school with masses of pretty flowers and various home-made crafts. We had met the previous spring when she purchased a puppy with which to shepherd her small flock of Shetland ewes.

A dear friend of many years standing who paid us an early visit was Bobby Mitchell. Bobby possessed a gentle charm immediately obvious to all who made his acquaintance, plus an inveterate appetite for knowledge. He had dedicated his entire life to both the Clydesdale horse and the Border collie. His first recollection of the former was around the year 1920, when his father and grandfather owned a coach hire business in the Peeblesshire village of Romanno Bridge. His pride and joy is a unique collection of photographs depicting 'these great animals' – Bobby's description of them – going back to the beginning of the Clydesdale stud books. Among them are some early likenesses sketched before cameras were invented. The whole collection covers a period of almost seventy years.

Regarding sheep dogs, Bobby has in his possession a store of data covering a period of at least two hundred years. His Border collie pedigrees spanning five generations, drawn in a large circle with the names and registration numbers of the first generation appearing in the centre, are prepared with obvious artistic skill and neatness. A helpful feature is that the particulars of the male line are written in blue, while the female line is in pink.

Bobby's other hobbies are stick dressing and carpentry. One of the nicest house-warming gifts we received was a wooden bird table with a carving of a white-faced ewe and a collie dog. It was made by Bobby after Tarka our horse tried to remove a crust of bread from the previous table, demolishing it completely.

Bobby admitted that he was more than delighted to visit 'Up Tweed'. His connection with the area was through his grandfather who in his younger days was manager at nearby Stanhope, where the shepherd poet John Dixon herded. (Sadly, Bobby Mitchell is no longer with us).

23
Our First Visitors

Remembering my own ambitions as a young child living in a town - my longing to be able to hold a baby lamb, to sit astride a pony, or simply to spend time playing with a litter of cuddly puppies – all of these we hoped to be able to provide for the enjoyment of visiting youngsters.

When first we opened our gate to the public I admit to experiencing some feelings of trepidation about the interests of today's children. For example, the entertainment on offer through the media of television, exhibited a distinct scientific flavour.

As it happened my doubts were unfounded. The enraptured gazes accompanied by childish giggles, heard when they observed the antics of lambs, puppies, kittens and even the odd duckling that chose to appear, quickly dispelled any misgivings. One instance in particular stands out in my mind. The father of a small, fair-haired Dutch boy actually got into his car and drove out of the yard leaving him behind because the child refused to be parted from a litter of puppies. On reaching the main road he stopped and was treated to the sight of his young son, a pup tucked under one arm, waving goodbye to him. Added to that, the look of rapture on the face of a blind, physically handicapped girl, when I placed a new-born pup in her outstretched hands, will stay with me always. It was everyday experiences such as these that made the hard work worthwhile.

From the point of view of adult visitors, I decided that in order of priority a warm welcome would come high on the list, followed by value-for-money entertainment in beautiful surroundings and finally, that they should be able to discuss what they had heard and seen over a cup of tea before choosing a tasteful memento to remind them of their day. Goods in the craft shop include my husband's crooks, prints, stationery, my books, knitwear and numerous other items manufactured by country folk.

It was not until the following season, when the place began to take on a more business-like air that salesmen selling various trinkets began to call. It would have been easy at this time to break away from the original shepherding theme had I not been determined to sustain it. Besides the sheep dog handling demonstrations which were given seven days a week during the first season, morning coffee and afternoon teas were provided on the lawn in front of the house. Bed and breakfast accommodation was also on offer.

Young sheep dogs belonging to farmers, providing they were fully vaccinated, were taken in for training. Six weeks was needed to get them useful close at hand.

Throughout the summer, representatives from the Borders Regional Council Community Programme, the Countryside Commission for Scotland and the Scottish Tourist Board made regular visits to Tweedhopefoot in order to see how we were progressing.

In all, around 2,000 visitors passed through our gates that first season, among them John Roberts, the American vice-president of the Busch Entertainment Corporation and his family, who were holidaying in Scotland. John's company provides entertainment annually for six million holidaymakers. He kindly wrote glowing testimonials on our behalf, to all the aforementioned.

A second business plan and forecast was painstakingly prepared for the bank's head office. Estimates were again obtained, all to no avail. Surety in the shape of £12,000 was requested before further financial help was forthcoming.

Because the provision of surety was the only option, we accepted, against our principles, a much appreciated offer from a private source.

Out of the profit we made during our first season we were given permission by the bank to purchase a flock of ewes. We chose blackfaced drafts, some of which had seen better days. At £25 a head they were a gift, especially as we discovered a number of young sheep among them. When we left Bowmont we brought along with us four south country Cheviot sheep. These included a couple of wethers, named Tweedledee and Tweedledum, a gimmer called Charlotte and a ram lamb, who answered when he felt inclined, to the name of Charlie. The quartet had lived in our garden, acting as lawnmowers. Charlie had been kept originally for breeding but unfortunately he had turned out slightly 'shuttle-gobbed' or 'sow-mouthed', as the affliction is sometimes described.

After a few months 'Up Tweed', to our relief Charlie's lower jaw quickly grew to match his upper - perhaps because he was no longer required to act as a lawnmower on a steep brae. Unfortunately he never would make 'a good un', being short and round in stature, instead of the stipulated long and square but through being handled regularly in the demonstrations he developed into quite a character. In fact he could be described as our main asset. There came an occasion when a small child was lifted on to his back. Charlie took the event in his stride; splaying his short sturdy legs for added support he regurgitated extravagantly and continued chewing with what can only be described as a contented expression on his knobbly face. These 'rides' became a regular feature with the smaller visitors and Charlie became the most photographed Cheviot in Britain.

Englebert and Humperdink

Lustrous red berries clothed in a white hoar frost, accompanied by early morning mist, followed by a lazy warm sun: it was a belated Indian summer that missed by a whisker an all too brief opportunity to enhance the fiery bent, the falling leaves and the changing spruce. All had died to mellow gold. November had arrived, the beginning of the sheep year as far as upland flockmasters are concerned. That day we took delivery of Humperdink, an enormous blue-headed Leicester shearling ram who arrived complete with an understudy who we named Englebert. The latter was on loan to 'chase-up' once the rush was over and most of our blackies had been put in-lamb by his superior partner. On arrival, 'the boys' were gently persuaded into the hilly field at the far-side of the property, where Charlie the demonstration ram speedily introduced himself, by delivering a smart broadside into poor Englebert's ribs. We were quick to separate them. Small sturdy rams such as Charlie have an unpleasant habit of breaking the necks of larger ones with a powerful butt to the nose end.

We bought Humperdink in early October, his owner kindly offering to keep him until the time was ripe.

Geoff was judging Manor Sheep Dog Trial, one of the more scenic events on our calendar. My young bitch, Holly, at this her second trial, had pleased me greatly by her efforts but unfortunately failed to pen.

Once the prizegiving was over we made the acquaintance of a curly-haired young man who introduced himself as Iain Campbell of Glenrath. After talking for only a few moments it became obvious that here was someone totally dedicated to his extensive rugged domain and the sheep stock which grazed there.

Geoff and I were at this time seeking a ram of the blue-headed variety to cross with our ewes, in the hope of producing a quantity of female mule lambs, much favoured by lowland farmers for the production of fat lambs.

All flockmasters say the ram is half the flock. Our flock consisted of 114 fairly fit ewes and at that time we could not afford a ram of show proportions. However, no matter how modest our purse it was important to invest in one, preferably from high ground, physically fit and one of twins.

Iain had rams to sell - twin shearlings. 'They were triplets, but one died at birth,' he explained. 'Both are proven breeders, we used them last year as lambs.' Would we care to follow him and take a look?

Together with the dogs we hurriedly piled into the car and after driving a short distance along the haugh, overshadowed by steep autumn tinted hills, we finally ground to a halt at the burnside. The far bank was sown down to a succulent crop of rape, itself an enterprising achievement in such testing terrain. An even flock of that year's lambs nibbled greedily at the luscious leaves, standing belly deep in the dew soaked foliage, the stench of their steamy breaths cutting the evening air like a knife. They bleated suspiciously to one another as we splashed across the water, and after craning their necks in order to snatch a last bite, turned lazily away at the sight of my dog.

The two rams were standing snootily by themselves and were therefore easily shed in our direction. Geoff passed an experienced eye over their qualifications. One was slightly better in his conformation than his rangier brother. However, their owner informed us that the latter was the better breeder regarding type, having more crimp in his fleece, an important attribute that he passed on to his daughters. He was also more blue about the face and ears, as well as being finer boned, essential for milkiness in the resulting progeny. Theoretically the more blue or black the sire, the better the chance of producing the more popular dark-faced ewe. Believe me, sheep fashion is equally comparable to human whims.

Finally, after a serious debate on crimp in wool, during which I asked our host how his own hair became so curly, it was time to go home. We re-crossed the burn, this time through deep water and while I paused to empty my soaking wellies, Geoff suggested to Iain that we sleep on it and let him have our decision regarding which ram, the following day. However, before we had gone a couple of miles along the road we had made our choice. The ram with the crimped hairstyle would do nicely. His name would be Humperdink, which was perhaps wishful thinking on our part.

If only winter days could be fashioned from elastic –
Rather that they should stretch instead of shrink.
If only we could be born old and grow young … If only

I wished, as a wintry sun rode high in a near cloudless blue sky and startled sheep scattered down the valley. Slender translucent fingers of ice adorned the ragged edges of the Tweed, winter flattened reeds crackled underfoot as the dogs, happy to be alive, posed, crept, flanked and raced ahead of me in play.

In the distance, Tweedhopefoot chimney reeked grey woodsmoke, spiralling vertically, assuring fine weather.

On this chill Thursday, almost twelve months to the day following our arrival, we were given the go-ahead from the bank to begin developing the business known as 'Tweedhope Sheep Dogs,' as a centre for tourism.

As soon as the festive season was over, transformation was begun in earnest with the help of grant assistance from the Countryside Commission. Fortunately, the weather was as dry as a bone when the heavy plant moved in and due to the extremely low temperatures, the ground was iron-hard ensuring no scarring whatsoever.

An extremely efficient team of three men, headed by Jimmy Dalgliesh, using a crane, a bulldozer and a dump truck quickly transformed the uneven bog beside the old cottage into a spacious parking area. The road leading into the farm was raised and widened in order to make it more accessible and a small loch was excavated below the school. Weeping willows, iris and bulrush were donated by Strathclyde Regional Council. Twelve hundred broad-leaved trees were purchased and planted in and around the entrance to the farm by boys on a Youth Training Scheme. Steps were made leading to the school and new fences were erected. A stone wall which separated the demonstration area was demolished and transported to where we planned to build a stell.

An extremely generous grant from the Scottish Tourist Board made possible the renovation of the old cottage plus fixtures and fittings, by Moffat builder Jimmy Long and his men. Toilet facilities were provided with help from the Countryside Commission. Jim Bane, a stockman turned artist - nicknamed by me 'Precious Bane' – painted several imposing road signs depicting a crouching collie. At a later date, his sons decorated the entire establishment both inside and out in black and white – true sheep dog colours.

In January, 1988, I rose up in the world with the purchase of a word processor at a little over the cost of a new typewriter. This buy helped make the task of writing and the preparation of business documents less time-consuming.

We had made provision to have the entrance to the driveway widened to admit coaches from both directions. The previous summer, vehicles pausing at the roadside to observe the dogs had been causing a road hazard. So much so that the council decided that, in the interest of road safety, they would provide a lay-by with the help of a 60% grant from the Countryside Commission.

Work began in March when we experienced some of the coldest winter weather. Watching from the warmth of the

Holly the collie

kitchen, I felt a great deal of sympathy for the council workers who were having to labour in such an exposed area. As the work progressed we were treated daily to the exciting roar and rumble of accelerating bulldozers, the cautionary high pitched bleep of reversing trucks, the toot of horns and the whoosh of air-brakes. Orange warning lights flashed on and off as workmen toiled relentlessly in the bitter north-east wind. Never was so much accomplished by so few in such a short space of time.

The month of March also saw the arrival of 18 tons of pebbles to be spread in the yard, and our very first lamb, born on the banks of the Tweed out of Charlotte, sired by Cheviot Charlie.

Our visitor season began in April in the midst of lambing time. During the six months that followed several thousand people flocked through our gates to attend demonstrations and sheep dog trials. Life was hectic to say the least. Nevertheless, we decided to take Saturdays off in order to keep our hand in at local trials.

In July we rushed to Edinburgh Airport to catch a flight to Canada, leaving the dogs, sheep and young Geoff in the capable hands of GWB's sister, Anne, her husband, Dick, and their children. Nine hours later, we touched down in Calgary, Alberta, land of cracked windscreens, pirahna mosquitoes and

genuine cowboys. We had been invited by Richard and Mary Lynne Tipton to judge three sheep dog trials and give a training seminar. The Tiptons and their artistically talented son live in an authentic log cabin they built themselves overlooking a beaver lodge. The fun and hospitality experienced there has yet to be equalled by us. At the end of eleven informative days and nights we returned to Tweedhopefoot in time to meet Lord Sanderson of Bowden, the Scottish Minister of Agriculture, who paid us a visit in order to examine our methods of farm diversification.

Throughout the summer I was assisted by Hilary who contributed enormously in making our efforts a success and Ross Ferguson, a young man from Peebles, built a magnificent sheep stell. Jean, Sandy and Jenny followed in their wake, providing immeasurable assistance and friendship.

HOLLY the Collie

Trim's great granddaughter, my beautiful bitch Holly exhibits a disposition as sweet as an angel. Her gentle brown eyes constantly seek mine for approval. Her markings are hand-painted and her gleaming coat mirrored like a seal's. Her slender agile limbs scarcely touched the ground as she effortlessly skimmed the dyke backs.

Born at Holly Bush Farm at Christmas, 1985, in the vicinity of Abbotsford, home of Sir Walter Scott, Holly's sire is Simon Clarke's big bare-skinned Roy. She was part of a litter of six lively puppies whose ever watchful dam Nan was the daughter of an earlier Holly that we bred out of Trim several years ago.

It was a clear, crisp, starlit evening when we set forth by car to view Nan's puppies. What I remember most about the outing was my feet flying from under me on a patch of ice in Simon's yard and finding myself lying flat on my back in a most undignified pose. Worse than that, I had been the one entrusted with Nan's supper.

Simon's charges were all 'well done' as we say, meaning, in good fettle. Even in these so-called enlightened times one witnessed litters of undernourished, worm infested puppies. These were lively, bright of eye and cleanly bedded which said a lot for a young shepherd living in a bachelor pad, caring for hundreds of sheep.

Holly caught my attention from the moment I entered the building. She was very like Jan, nick-named 'the Bionic Bitch' because of her speed and ability to 'turn on a sixpence', that my husband had owned a few years previously. A shepherd once wrote 'pick a pup that speaks to you'. So I did, and was delighted to learn that just as soon as she was weaned from her mother Simon would bring her over. She had been overlooked by other buyers due to her greyhound appearance.

Until I made the acquaintance of Holly, I must admit to not being over-enamoured by the 'slape-haired' variety, as they are sometimes described south of Northumberland. Holly very quickly became the exception to the rule completely winning me over with her streamlined appearance, super intelligence, walking stick tail, character and classical method of working. Other major advantages being that smooth-coated dogs are much easier to keep clean and do not ball up with snow in wintry conditions.

I used to like to see all livestock, whether it be male or female, strongly made and thick set, with heavy bone. Now I realise that there are 'horses for courses'. A fine-boned female like a dairy cow is often prolific and 'milky' whereas a heavy boned one is not. The breeding of a powerful masculine type of male from a feminine type female, as any good blackface or Cheviot breeder will tell you, is to be recommended.

Holly proved to be an extrovert right from the word go. Her particular kind of mannerisms as yet undetected in any of our other dogs. For instance, after consuming her evening meal she will expertly tilt her dish on to its side holding it in position with her paw, whilst she licks the outer rim. When it comes to escapology she knows no equal. I nick-named her Houdini and have yet to discover a door she cannot open either by sheer force or ingenuity. When she was left alone for a few minutes in the kitchen. I was surprised to find three sliding doors, plus the refrigerator, standing agape.

In early June, 1987, Holly was heavy in pup to my husband's dog Cap; a prick-eared, bare-skinned dog, out of a sister of Jan, going back to Les Morrison of Cleugh Brae's Sweep and Midge, Johnny Rogerson's Laddie and the late John Gilchrist's Spot.

Young Geoff was Cap's greatest fan. He named him 'Bruno' after his favourite British heavyweight boxer. Of Cap he said 'He's a lean, mean, fighting machine.'

Without a doubt, young Geoff's loyalty lay with his dad's dogs. He called them The A Team, whilst mine went under the unflattering title of The Gay Team.

At the same time as Holly's pregnancy, Lucy, her kennel mate was also carrying a litter. On the second day of June, before we had barely finished lunch, Lucy went into labour, quickly producing two large dog puppies without any fuss or bother. She pupped in comfort on a redundant couch in the byre. Her sons were resplendent in black satin waistcoats with snowy white collars and cuffs. By evening poor Holly's envy knew no bounds. She decided on a spot of pup-napping while Lucy was taking a walk, surreptitiously removing the puppies to her own bed in the far corner where she immediately began suckling them wearing what can only be described as a smug expression. On her return, Lucy flopped down completely unconcerned and proceeded to top and tail her shared offspring.

By June 5th Holly had given birth to her own family of six healthy puppies – three dogs and three bitches. Because of a shortage of room both litters were housed in the same building. Holly insisted that all the puppies shared the same nest, namely her own, and resisted any effort to part them. Lucy quickly tired of motherhood while Holly revelled in it.

She reminded me of a little girl at school we all looked on as 'mother' because of her caring attitude. Her strong maternal instinct is very much in evidence in her work. When she gathers our sheep together it is done without hassle or disturbance to her charges. She quietly floats around on the distant horizon tidying the young dogs' mistakes, fetching the sheep that they leave and flushing out any hidden stragglers.

Like all 'guid beasts, I cannot recall giving her any training, she just sort of happened, everything slipping into place on its own – a most natural animal. Her example only convinces me further that good dogs, like good people, are born, not made.

At Tweedhopefoot throughout the summer months, from a tender age, she performed tirelessly alongside my other two dogs, learning both sets of commands as well as amusing the visitors with her total independence.

Neal Fadler, a sheep dog handler, trainer and Gary Cooper lookalike – 'only taller', he hastened to add – travelled from Washington State, across America and over the Atlantic Ocean to take delivery of Jill, alias Miss America, one of Holly's off-spring. She, Miss A, was the runt of the litter and by the time of her departure had completely won my heart. I would have given anything to keep her because she exhibited many of her mother's amusing traits.

Until Jill had finished eating none of the rest of the litter dared to as much as sniff at their food. They would all sit patiently in a row until she became replete. Whenever I entered their living quarters the wee moron drove her companions smartly away, jealously nipping their flanks before returning to reap all the attention.

On his return to America Neal wrote of her: 'She was a real little trooper all the way home, never flagging or complaining on the long flight'. Then came an almost poetic description which not only gladdened my heart but also made me feel justifiably proud of both man and dog. 'I am constantly amazed,' Neal wrote, 'by the instinct that little Jill shows on sheep. She has an authority that is pure pleasure to see in action. She still doesn't have any working commands on her but I put her to sheep twice a week to just let her work things out and develop her sheep sense. She is growing at a good rate and is sound in every way. I can shush her out and around and by positioning myself rightly get her to fetch evenly. She runs naturally to the left but she is now beginning to go right with just a little urging and is widening out in the process. Her manner doesn't upset sheep, yet when she moves in sheep move for her in an even positive way. She shows a good amount of eye and has a smooth soft touch unless somebody challenges her. She can be as soft as velvet or as hard as stone depending upon the situation facing her. Even one old Suffolk ewe that sometimes likes to fight with some of the other dogs doesn't put up much resistance before she turns back in with the rest of the sheep and moves on. Besides all of her great intensity and desire to work she shows a wonderful personality which is always a source of fun for us. She is of course very curious and observant about anything that goes on around her. So we never tire of her antics.'

All of Holly's litter were found good, working homes. Only Glen, a strongly made perfectly marked black and white dog pup remained. He pleased me immensely and proved to be as classy as his mother, in a 'doggy' sort of way. Apart from his low slung tail he reminded me of a pointer with a dash, and only a dash mind you, of greyhound and mastiff blood.

When he was only seven weeks old he greatly impressed me by cocking his leg at a fence post. Admittedly he lost his balance and almost tumbled over but at least he made the attempt, which must put him in with a chance.

He eventually developed into a strapping replica of his mother. When off duty he exhibited a pointer's continually flaying stern. When working, although likened to quick-silver, he is a good stopper, dropping like a stone on hearing my whistle.

When caught in sunlight his smooth coat gleamed like jet; there are, believe it or not, varying shades of black. His powerful chest, graceful neck and strong limbs were white as the driven snow. Physically he was a perfect specimen with high shoulder blades and the shadow of well sprung ribs, portraying an athlete's fitness.

Character-wise, I would describe Glen as a clown, exhibiting a wealth of humour. His countenance was ugly-beautiful, his expression dominated by enormous ears – the right pointing skyward the left, was undecided. Unfortunately he sometimes had what I call 'an attitude problem'. If a sheep looked at him in a certain way he would home in like a missile. Only time would tell whether or not he would make a genuine dog.

At Tweedhopefoot some of my dogs were smooth-coated. I underwent a complete reversal in my previous dislike of the 'skin-head' variety, as young Geoff amusingly described them.

I lay the blame for this turnabout squarely at Holly's paws who has produced forty puppies – all replicas of herself – she has developed into an extremely beautiful bitch whose quiet purposeful method of working reminds me more of Old Meg, Garry's grandmother, as each day passes.

Throughout the summer her leisure time is spent welcoming individual cars as they pull into the parking area, then acting as officiator and guide, encouraging the occupants, willing or not, in the direction of the demonstration area in order to show off her prowess.

Her children and grandchildren can truly be termed international jet-setters with four of them gracing the sheep walks of America and Canada. Dee a daughter from Holly's first marriage follows in the pawprints of the dogs of James Hogg, the

The author with Charlie the ram and Holly

famed 19th century Ettrick Shepherd, at Mountbenger.

In between working and canvassing Holly is at her happiest when exercising her strong maternal instinct. I've watched in amazement while she washed the face of a baby lamb and have observed her top and tail new-born kittens as gently as though they were her own.

I have found that puppies from Holly and Cap, my husband's dog, have an above average pack instinct with a strong urge to quarter the ground; in fact, they are true hunters and huntresses. I have witnessed Holly's whelps gather a full-grown hind from the forest and bring it unharmed to my feet. They possess an extremely keen attitude to work and are much faster and more precise than their hairy equivalents. Most of them come ready-made requiring little or no training, which suits my present life-style perfectly.

Although greyhound and pointer blood is obvious in their make-up, the mastiff's loyalty predominates. Glen's lavish show of affection warmed me through and through. He was constantly checking on my whereabouts during our numerous forays and was a ferocious guard should a strange dog approach. He shows endearment by leaning heavily against my legs like a cat, gazing up at me with affectionate dark eyes.

Besides being presented to Her Majesty the Queen along with Garry and Laddie when she visited the Scottish Borders in 1989, both Holly and her offspring have been featured in a number of TV productions. These include the BBC children's programme *Caterpillar Trail*, BBC 2's farming programme *Landward*, ITV's Landmark, BBC 2's *The Animals Road Show*, where she was filmed suckling her latest litter of six puppies as well as five of her grandchildren, and with son Glen on ITV's *Blind Date*, hosted by Cilla Black, when a young couple were sent to Tweedhopefoot to learn how to handle a sheep dog.

24
Omega

A Tribute to Garry

True friends are hard to find and keep,
When the ground is rough, and the hill is steep,
On the Cheviot Braes we herded sheep
Me and my old friend, Garry.
The bonny pup that first I saw,
Became a dog abune them a',
His back like jet, his briest like sna'
My handsome, faithful Garry.

My lifetime partner he has been,
And many's the gatherin' we hae seen,

There's no' a dog wha worked sae keen,
As my trusty old friend Garry.
Oer hills and glens we strode the heather,
Worked as a team in any weather,
We faced the trials o' life thegither,
Me and my old friend Garry.

My every thought is his command,
'Away tae me', 'come-bye', and 'stand'
The finest collie in the land,
That's my trusty Garry.
But his soft brown eyes have lost their glow,
His flying legs are getting slow,
And the time will come when he must go,
My trusty old friend, Garry.

Dogs like my Garry are so few,
And when his time on earth is through,
I'll whisper one last 'that'll do',
To my trusty old friend, Garry.
But his memory will never dim,
My thoughts will always be with him,
And he'll lie at peace wi' Jed an' Trim,
Farewell, my faithful Garry!

S. Gray

The saddest occasion of my life occurred in April 1990 when, according to the poem dedicated to him I whispered one last 'That'll do', to my trusty old friend Garry who died one month short of his fourteenth birthday.

During Garry's last summer, so as not to be outdone, he insisted on joining in the sheep dog demonstrations, endeavouring to steal the limelight. Unfortunately the younger dogs worked in a higher gear, and things didn't always happen as planned. Garry insisted on doing things his way. He caused great amusement to onlookers by only running halfway up the field on his outrun, leaving the other dogs to do the leg work so that he would have enough energy for the grand finale which would consist of him preventing the sheep from being penned (his little joke).

The time came when he began to cut corners. He thought I failed to notice when he slipped through a forest instead of

'Garry, gazing with sightless eyes in the direction I had gone'

round about it, and when the day was wet and stormy I would notice a shadow of reluctance flicker across his face when I asked him to accompany me. Who was I to criticise him for his unwillingness when there were occasions I felt exactly the same?

My faithful dog was grey around the muzzle, he was growing old and I could not help but despair at the thought of such a fine and intelligent mind trapped within the body of a dog whose lifespan compared to ours, is so tragically short. In his fourteenth year he was a dear old gentleman with a luxurious curling coat. He still managed the occasional stint around the sheep, often putting the younger dogs to shame with his clever workmanlike approach and steady intelligent method. His soft brown eyes though glazed by cataracts, showed great enthusiasm though he knew his limitations.

When I went shopping he would wander to the end of the farm road, where whatever the weather he would wait patiently, gazing with sightless eyes in the direction I had gone.

During the past thirty years I have had scores of dogs through my hands, only one worthy of the title 'Great Dog'. Garry was most worthy of this description. He patiently shepherded me through life's difficulties with unwavering loyalty and devotion. Just like friends, it is those who can be depended on that become special. Garry was a gentleman.

I count myself privileged to have known him.

Unhappily, after soldiering on at Tweedhopefoot for six arduous years with me working all hours to make ends meet, GWB and I began to grow apart. Eventually our problems became insurmountable and we decided to go our separate ways. Young Geoff was by then grown and left home to work in the woollen industry. Eventually Tweedhopefoot had to be sold and I moved six miles down the road to live in Moffat in the county of Dumfriesshire.

Leaving the farm, described as 'Heaven' by myself and many of our visitors, was a difficult time. Over the years we had welcomed over thirty thousand people and had witnessed tears in the eyes of many, who had never before experienced the remarkable understanding between shepherd and collie dog.

I moved to Moffat in 1993 to a rented cottage beside St Mary's Church and with my share of the small amount of money that was left from the sale of the farm I took a field on the outskirts of the town and another up the Crooked Road four miles away. I was grateful to have this out-bye ground because rough terrain encourages my young dogs to think, to pace themselves and to give the sheep room.

As well as my four dogs I had brought with me two horses, Tarka and her Shetland companion Sweet-Pea and a dozen black Welsh mountain ewe lambs, all that remained of our flock of a hundred breeding ewes. I found this breed to be exceptional mothers, good foragers and easy due to their size, for a woman to handle.

Moffat is an extremely attractive and friendly country town sometimes called 'The Gateway to Scotland' surrounded by rolling hills. Its name is said to come from the Celtic 'magh ubh at' meaning a deep mountain hollow. The area is steeped in history and during the summer months is smothered in beautiful blooms. On the road to Selkirk there is a spectacular waterfall called the Greymare's Tail and a little further on a statue of the famous Ettrick shepherd, poet and author James ('*have taught the wandering winds to sing*'), Hogg with his collie Hector, over-looking St Mary's loch.

In 1994 I was offered a small stone-built cottage surrounded by fields, at Hammerlands on the outskirts of the town eminently more suitable for the dogs. There I give sheep dog handling demonstrations, tuition and train dogs for farmers. I also sell sheepdog orientated gifts, providing similar facilities to those at Tweedhopefoot.

In February 1997, I lost another dear 'friend'. My horse Tarka by now in her twenties died after a short illness. She lies buried in the paddock next to my cottage. Her companion Sweet-Pea was devastated by the loss so I invited local children Hannah, Abby and Martin – who is also my 'Head Shepherd' to ride her. Hannah and Abby's parents owned the Balmoral Hotel (they have since gone to live in France) where on quiet evenings the children took Sweet-Pea for a beer, which she heartily enjoyed standing at the bar, and afterwards walked home on plaited legs.

A Tribute to Tarka

Next to the automatic washing machine, Tarka proved to be my most useful acquisition.

From the moment I saw her, I fell in love with her. At the time, she cost all my savings, but I have never begrudged a penny.

She stood 16 hands in her bare feet with skin like silk and a wonderful disposition. In winter her colour was dark chocolate brown, come summer, when she'd cast her 'winter woollies', her coat took on a hue of burnished mahogany. Her head was small and neat, her eye kindly and there was a smidgen of white on her velvet nose.

We were dining with friends at Jedburgh when I first laid eyes on her. She trotted over to greet me, followed by another mare. I liked the way Tarka moved, the proud arch of her neck and the way she chased off her companion when she vied for my attention.

Later on over drinks, we discussed her and I learned that she was to go to a sale the following day. I arranged to buy her privately, there and then.

Tarka was delivered to Swindon the following week and as she stepped from the horsebox I noticed her length of leg and nearly fainted. She had been running in a field below the level of the road the first time I saw her. I had ridden horses since the age of eight but never been on anything taller than 15 hands. I wondered if I would need a ladder to climb on board. I need not have worried for I lived in hill country with rocks, mounds and dry-stone dykes in abundance.

Buying a horse is a risky business, no matter how knowledgeable you are. Soundness, temperament, intelligence and sure-footedness all have to be considered, especially on the hill where Tarka would spend most of her time. Fortunately I found she had all of these attributes and more.

I have never had a riding lesson in my life. My first experience on a horse was a bad one, but it certainly taught me the most important rule of all - to stick on at all costs!

We were living in Wales at the time, close to where wild ponies roamed. Every evening after school, my friend and I would feed and pat them. One afternoon, for a dare, I climbed up on to one of the smaller ponies. To my horror it promptly bolted downhill and on to the road with me clinging on for dear life, its long mane grasped tightly in my fingers. Straight into town we went. Fortunately it was Sunday and there wasn't much traffic or goodness knows what the outcome would have been.

I remember quite clearly, a lady anxiously calling out as we whizzed by, 'Get off, you silly girl, before you break your neck.'

Get off!? Did she really believe that I could dismount a pony travelling at that speed and not break my neck?

After a while, to my relief, the pony began to tire. Eventually he pulled up, trembling like a leaf outside a public convenience and as I ran inside my knees were trembling too!

Mornings with Tarka

When we were shepherding at Swindon during the cold winter months, Tarka was stabled inside, sharing her quarters with the dogs, whom she teased the life out of trying to reach their suppers.

In the morning when I opened the stable door, it would often be pitch dark, all chinks of light blocked out by snow. I would walk inside speaking quietly to her. The air was always warm and smelt deliciously of horse.

Gradually, my eyes would become accustomed to the gloom and I could see her dim presence in the far corner. I would approach her, holding out my hand and stroke her silky neck. She would obligingly lower her head so that I could fasten on her head collar.

After leading her outside she would pause to stretch luxuriously, always in a different place so as to take me by surprise. Usually, I would lose my balance and topple backwards into a deep snowdrift. At the sight of this she would wrinkle up her nose and I would swear she was laughing at my predicament as I struggled to right myself.

At the gate I would turn her loose and for a moment she would pause to savour the air before kicking up her heels, snow and straw from the inside of her hooves flying everywhere. Then suddenly she would be gone, galloping quickly downhill towards the burn to drink her fill of the icy, fast-flowing water.

Within minutes she would be back again trotting to her 'special place', beside the boundary fence for a roll. Over and over she would roll, with me breathing a sigh of relief that it was snow, not mud, she was rolling in.

On the hill Tarka was much more adept at travelling through deep snow than I was, her long legs much more practicable than my shorter ones and she could keep going long after the dogs wearied.

During the lambing season she was indispensible, ferrying bags of feed across her saddle, carrying me at full speed to ewes that required calcium and would surely die without its prompt administration. When the hills were covered in deep snow drifts, she would insist on pausing at regular intervals in order to scent the depth and should she consider the way too dangerous, despite my urgings she would wheel around and seek a safer place.

There is no doubt in my mind that on many occasions Tarka was responsible for saving my life.

A Ride on Tarka From the Diary of a Shepherdess

This morning, Tarka desperately needs 'spring cleaning'. She has been wallowing in the mire to keep out the cold, and is plastered from head to foot in mud.

Thank goodness her colouring is dark brown and camouflages grime. Years ago I owned a cob that was predominantly white (or should have been!). It was then that I learned my lesson and vowed never again to keep a light-coloured horse.

When grooming 'T' in her present state it is wise to dress accordingly. I don a smock of smooth material and a headscarf tied turban style to keep the dust at bay. Thus suitably attired I proceed to the stable, ready to do battle. First of all I tether her with nearside to the light, then vigorously go to work with curry comb and dandy brush until the worst's removed.

Thankfully, she adores the attention and readily accepts grooming as a form of caress. She leans my way with what can only be described as an expression of adoration in her eyes, so that I can attend to her mane, face and forelock with the softer body brush. Last of all I groom her long black tail until it's free of tangles, allowing a little of it at a time to fall, running my fingers quickly through it, teasing out the tangles.

Suddenly, the cloud of dust dies down and I can stand back to admire my handiwork. I am justly rewarded. Tarka looks a picture with the light's reflection shining on her coat. Outside, a robin sings a shrill and warbling tune, Tarka pricks her ears, 'Where's the hoof-pick, lost as usual?' She's becoming impatient.

I reach up on tip-toe, running my fingers along the dusty shelf high up behind the stable door. At last I discover it, wrapped in cob-webs. Jubilant, I tap Tarka on her knee cap and she obligingly raises her foot for me to pick it free of straw.

Her saddle needs a quick rub over. The leather has grown damp and is covered in fine green mould after only three days of not being used. My bridle is clean, soft and supple to the touch; the steel bit and brass brow band gleam, for it hangs inside the house behind the kitchen door.

I slip the cold bit between Tarka's teeth (momentarily gritting mine!) then pulling her ears through and arranging her forelock, do up the throat lash. On with the saddle, tightening the girth and at the same time dodging the playful nip.

I clamber on board from the stone wall that gives shelter to our yard, then off we trot at speed, in an easterly direction on the black tarmac road, Tarka's dainty 4" x 4" iron shoes striking a muffled ring as we splodge among wet slush.

The homestead at Moffat

She steps out gaily with head held high, glancing sharply left and right, bright eyes missing nothing, nostrils flared wide, ears twitching back and forth. Seeing, scenting, listening, searching expectantly for the company of another of her kind to fool and flirt with, pass the time of day and show her paces to.

In the far-off distance she espies the blue-grey cows. Their company will suffice. She eagerly lengthens her stride, stretches her long graceful neck and raises her tail high above her back where it streams like a banner in the fresh breeze, gleaming like silk in the morning sun.

I slacken the reins giving her her head. Immediately she gathers speed and away we go on to hill ground with me standing straight up in the stirrups for the sake of comfort and then after a couple of playful bucks she's away, galloping like the wind. 'My kingdom for a horse!'

In December of 1988 Tarka survived the horror of the Lockerbie air crash disaster. She was in a field near the town on the night Pan Am flight 103 exploded, scattering debris over a wide area.

Terrified, the poor mare jumped out of the field, cutting her foreleg in the process, and galloped off into the darkness. Amazingly, she wasn't hurt too badly and soon recovered after her ordeal.

A few hours earlier I had said a tearful goodbye as she was driven up the winding road from Tweedhopefoot, and out of my life, I thought, forever. As the box pulled out on to the main road, what made it even worse was that Tarka swung her head in my direction and whinnied fearfully.

When we set up the Border Collie Visitor Centre at Tweedhopefoot all our efforts and finances were put into the running of the venture so reluctantly I gave my mare to an acquaintance who faithfully promised her 'a kind home for the rest of her days'.

It certainly wasn't a decision I undertook lightly and the way things turned out proved to be a grave mistake, but we are all wiser AFTER the event...

The 'acquaintance' bred a lovely foal from Tarka and then sent both mother and son down to Sussex, where the foal was to be retained by a new owner and Tarka eventually sold. I found all of this out just in the nick of time and was able to insist that Tarka be sent home.

She was reunited with me after an absence of two years. I will never forget the reunion. When the horse-box arrived in the yard, I immediately called out her name. She gave an ear-splitting whinney of joy and bolted down the ramp in my direction where she stood nuzzling my shoulder, and nodding her lovely head whilst I gave her the biggest hug I could manage.

EPILOGUE

Until recently, springtime was my favourite season of the year, with summer running a close second. Early spring wears a special fragrance all her own, a warm balmy aroma which drives out the harsh rigidity of winter, leaving one with a relaxed glad-to-be-alive feeling. I still go dewy-eyed with wonder at the sweet sound of the dawn chorus and the sight of the season's first lamb. Golden primroses, bathed in sunlight, growing wild on a mossy bank will always leave me enthralled. The feel of warm spring rain refreshes my skin and the breeze carries the delicious scent of damp earth to my nostrils. At dawn the perfume of lush young grasses and vigorous spruce intermingle deliciously. Flimsy cobwebs, soaked in dew, shimmer and sparkle to my delight.

Perhaps, like everything else, our preference for the seasons alters with time for now I find myself sighing with relief as autumn puts in an appearance. It's a time to meditate, a time to relax, a time of fleeting Indian summers and cosy evenings by a log fire. It's a time of new beginnings when ewes yearn no more for their departed offspring, as they graze contentedly on the smooth, close-cropped terrain. It's a time when swallows bid farewell. There's no rushing away at the crack of dawn, with bleary eyes to distant sheepdog trials. No anxiety about the creatures left at home. I wonder at the sight of bright rowan berries and vivid hips and haws.

On the hills nearby, sleek cattle with glossy, lick-marked coats follow the dogs and me inquisitively, through rustling fronds of dying bracken, while in-bye bare stubble patiently awaits the plough. I listen expectantly for the music of clanking stones on metal, the sound of sighing earth as it is deftly turned dark and inviting, exposed to the ever circling birds.

Half bred lambs graze the emerald fogs, pausing only to bleat a muffled welcome, their mouths filled with luscious grasses, their dams long since forgotten. The trees are gracefully adorned in mantles of gold, bronze, yellow and faded greens. There's a sharpness in the air which invigorates, and a reassurance in the knowledge that all is safely gathered in.

I bid you welcome, peaceful lovely autumn.